From Passive to Passion

A Chinese Immigrant's Journey to American Activism

Hope Grace

PUBLISHING

Alexandria, Virginia, USA

By **Hope Grace**

Published by Hope Grace Publishing
HopeGracePublishing.com
Alexandria, Virginia, USA

This book is a work of nonfiction. While the author has made every effort to ensure accuracy and clarity, some names, details, and events have been changed to protect the privacy of individuals. Any resemblance to actual persons, living or dead, is purely coincidental.

ISBN: 978-1-966423-26-3 **(Paperback)**
ISBN: 978-1-966423-28-7 **(Hardback)**
ISBN: 978-1-966423-27-0 **(eBook)**

Library of Congress Control Number: 2024927081

First Edition: 2025

Acknowledgements

Writing this book has been a journey of reflection, growth, and discovery, and I could not have completed it without the support and encouragement of many individuals who have played significant roles in my life.

First and foremost, I thank God for guiding me through every step of this journey. Without faith, this story would not have been possible, and it is my deepest belief in God's grace that has carried me through moments of doubt and challenge.

To my husband, Paul, I owe endless gratitude. You have been my rock, my sounding board, and my greatest source of strength. Your unwavering support, not only in our shared journey but also in my personal endeavors, has been invaluable. I could not have written this book without your patience, encouragement, and partnership.

To my son, David, you are the future that motivates me to fight for a better tomorrow. I want you to know that this book is as much for you as it is for the wider community. I hope it inspires you to stand firm in your values and never be afraid to speak up for what is right.

To John, whose tireless activism and devotion to our faith serves as an inspiration, thank you for being a guiding light in my life. Your courage in speaking out, both in the public square and within the church, encourages me to find my voice and stand firm in my beliefs.

A special thank you to Grace, a beloved sister in Christ, whose unwavering dedication to our shared cause continues to inspire us all. Though you are no longer with us, your legacy lives on in the work we do and in the lives you touched. Your memory reminds us that each of us has the power to make a difference, no matter how quietly we contribute.

To Dwight and Rebecca, your unwavering presence and dedication at Freedom Corner have shown me the true power of consistent, peaceful protest and compassion in action. Your commitment to standing up for justice and freedom, day after day, is a testament to what determined individuals can accomplish. Thank you for inspiring me and countless others.

To Xi Van Fleet, thank you for your tireless dedication to the cause of freedom and for sharing your insights with such clarity and courage. Our conversations and your journey have deeply impacted me, and your strength in the face of adversity is a continual reminder of why we must stay vigilant.

I also extend my thanks to the entire Chinese American community, especially those who have stood by me and contributed to the efforts we've made together in activism and advocacy. Your voices have been powerful and crucial in our collective fight for freedom, and I am proud to stand with you.

A heartfelt thank you to all the individuals who supported the political causes detailed in this book, whether through activism, conversations, or simply standing up for truth and justice in everyday life. It has been a privilege to work alongside you.

Finally, to my readers, thank you for taking the time to read this story. I hope it resonates with you and sparks a desire to be part of the positive changes we wish to see in the world.

This book is not just the story of my journey but the reflection of a larger movement. It is with gratitude, humility, and hope that I dedicate this work to the ongoing struggle for faith, freedom, and justice.

Contents

Preface

As I look back on my journey, both as an immigrant and as a political activist, I find it difficult to believe just how far my life has traveled — from the isolated deserts of Xinjiang, China, to the bustling political landscapes of Washington, D.C. The story of my life is not mine alone; it is a reflection of the broader journey that so many Chinese immigrants have experienced: moving from political repression and personal struggles to discovering a voice capable of effecting real change in a land of opportunity.

This book is an attempt to document that journey — one that transformed me from someone living in the shadows of a politically restrictive regime into an advocate for freedom, faith, and political activism in the United States. I did not begin this journey as an activist. Like many others, I remained on the sidelines for years, content to build a life for my family while avoiding the turbulent waters of political engagement. However, as my understanding of America's political landscape deepened, and as I witnessed the very freedoms I had come to cherish come under threat, I realized that remaining passive was no longer an option.

Through the pages of this book, I explore not only my personal story but also the collective awakening of a generation of Chinese Americans who have found themselves at the heart of America's ongoing political debates. From the fight for election integrity to the preservation of religious freedoms, the themes of this book resonate far beyond my own experiences. They reflect the growing involvement of Chinese immigrants in shaping the future of this great country.

I hope that by sharing my story, I can inspire others to find their own voice — to move from the quiet sidelines to the forefront of advocacy and action. For it is only when we stand up for the values that matter most — freedom, faith, and family — that we can leave behind a legacy for future generations.

This is my story, but it is also a call to action.

Disclaimer: While this book is based on true events and personal experiences, some names, dates, and details have been altered to respect privacy or for narrative clarity. The essence and message of the story remain faithful to the experiences I've lived and the lessons I've learned.

Part 1: China's Winds of Change (1970s–1995)

Chapter 1: Childhood in Xinjiang

The mornings in Xinjiang were crisp, the air biting as it swept down from the desert plains. The wind tugged at my clothes, carrying with it the scent of distant hearths and the dry, earthy fragrance of the desert. Beneath the mountains' silver peaks, our home, like many others in the community, was modest and connected to its neighbors, forming a network of lives bound together. Despite the closeness of the houses, there was still a sense of isolation as the vastness of the desert landscape loomed beyond. I would often stare at the rugged landscape, its endless horizon reflecting the uncertainty of our lives. The dry wind often carried the faint, metallic clatter of bicycle bells, the distant hum of conversation from the market, or the soft cries of a hawker selling his wares from a cart. Beneath it all, there was an eerie silence, as though the land itself was holding its breath. This was my home, a place of beauty and isolation, where the vastness of the land mirrored the uncertainty of times.

I was born in 1968, at the height of the **Cultural Revolution,** a time when China was being reshaped by the hands of the Party. I didn't fully understand the significance of what was happening around me as a child, but I could feel its weight pressing down on everything. Life in Xinjiang was distant enough from the political center of Beijing to offer a degree of safety, yet the Revolution's influence still reached us, like a long arm stretching out to grasp every corner of the country.

My father had come to Xinjiang from Zhejiang Province, answering the government's call for young people to "support Xinjiang" and help develop its economy. It wasn't just a patriotic move; it was a decision driven by survival. My father's family had been the poorest in their village, and in the volatile political climate following the Communist victory, poverty offered a kind of protection. His family's lack of wealth or status made them invisible to the Party's sweeping gaze — a luxury that many others could not afford.

It was in Zhejiang, at a local high school, that my father met my mother. My mother's father had been a lawyer and a captain during the war against the Japanese, but after the Communist Party came to power, his career was reduced to that of a humble teacher. It was in his classroom that my parents met, their relationship born from the pragmatism of the times rather than romance. My parents' marriage, like many arranged unions during that era, was based on survival. Aligning oneself with the poorest was often a safeguard against persecution.

After their marriage, my parents moved to Xinjiang, seeking refuge in its remoteness. My father found work as a clerk in a wholesale drug company, while my mother became an elementary school teacher. Life was hard, but it was distant enough from the political heart of China to provide a sense of stability. Yet, even in this far corner of the country, we could not escape the long reach of the Revolution.

Our house was modest, with cracked walls and simple furniture, but it was filled with quiet resilience. My mother was the heart of our household. She was small in stature, but her presence filled the room. Her sharp eyes seemed to see everything, and although she rarely had time to rest, she often found time to read to us before bed. She believed fiercely in the power of education. "The only mission for a student is to learn," she would tell us, her voice firm but not unkind. "No matter what happens in the world, knowledge is something they can never take from you."

Despite the long days at work, my mother's dedication to our education never wavered. At night, after we had finished our dinner, she would sit us down and read us stories — tales from her own childhood, traditional Chinese fables, and stories from her treasured books. She would tuck us in, and her voice, though tired, carried the warmth and strength of her belief in us. These bedtime stories were moments of solace in a world where little was certain. They were more than just stories; they were lessons in resilience, in perseverance.

My mother's small, wiry frame belied the strength that held our family together. As her voice carried through our tiny home, recounting stories or guiding us through lessons, I could feel her resilience — the kind born not out of desire but of necessity. It was this unspoken sacrifice that I felt most acutely. Each wrinkle around her eyes, each pause in her voice as she read, spoke of dreams deferred, of a quiet resignation to the life that was given, not chosen.

My father was a man of few words. He was of middle height, with an unassuming presence that allowed him to move through life unnoticed, which was perhaps a blessing in those uncertain times. His quiet strength, though not often shown in gestures or words, was the foundation of our family. He provided for us in the only way he knew how — by working hard and staying out of sight. He rarely spoke of his own childhood or his time in Zhejiang, but I could tell that, like my mother, he had been shaped by the hardships they had both endured.

We were a family of contrasts — my brother, Tony, although the oldest, was not the most responsible. He was shorter than average, and though bright, his focus often wandered. He had a lightheartedness that often made him the favorite among our playmates, but it was my older sister who truly carried the responsibility of the eldest child. She was calm, collected, and mature beyond her years. She took on the role of guiding us younger siblings, often helping with our studies, making sure we followed the rules set by our mother.

For me, I was different from my siblings in one important way — I could concentrate on anything, no matter what was happening around me. The world outside might have been filled with uncertainty, with the shouts of slogans and the marches of the Red Guards, but I could block it all out. I had a sharp focus, a determination that has stayed with me all my life. Whether I was reading a book or working through a math problem, nothing could break my concentration.

Tony's carefree attitude sometimes irritated me. While I was busy perfecting my assignments, he would be outside, laughing with his friends, oblivious to the pressures we all felt. I admired my sister's calm, her quiet maturity, but at times, I wished I could be as carefree as Tony, just for a moment.

In spite of the political tension that hovered over our lives, we found time for moments of joy. After school, we would play outside with the other children from the neighborhood. The dusty streets of our small town became our playground. We played for hours before dinner, chasing each other through the alleys, our laughter echoing off the walls. For a few hours each day, we could forget about the revolution, the Party slogans painted on the walls, and the ever-present Red Guards.

But the Revolution was never far away. The Red Guards — young zealots of the Party — would march through the streets, their chants echoing through the town as they waved their **Little Red Books**. They tore down anything that reminded them of the "Four Olds" — old customs, old culture, old habits, old ideas.

Teachers were humiliated, books were burned, and traditions were erased in the name of revolution. My mother, though a teacher herself, was careful. She taught only what the Party allowed, keeping her head down and avoiding the attention of the Red Guards.

I still remember the day the Red Guards came to our school, the air thickened with tension. Whispers spread like wildfire among the students, our eyes darting nervously to our teachers, who stood stiff and silent. I remember how my mother gripped the edge of her desk, her knuckles white, as if bracing for an impact that would tear through the fragile calm of our lives. They arrived suddenly, their voices booming through the halls as they pulled the teachers into the courtyard. There, in front of all the students, they forced the teachers to confess their "crimes" of teaching old ideas. As the Red Guards dragged the teachers into the courtyard, I felt my heart hammering in my chest. I couldn't move, couldn't breathe. My hands clenched into fists at my sides, nails digging into my palms. What if they took my mother? My chest tightened as I watched her standing by the edge of the crowd, silent but unmoving. My mind raced — should I run? Should I say something? The world felt fragile, as if the wrong word could crack it wide open. I watched in silence, not fully understanding why this was happening, but sensing the fear that hung in the air. As the teachers were forced to kneel in the courtyard, the air thickened with a collective silence. We remained silent, but the shock on our faces was impossible to hide. Some students cast fearful glances toward their parents in the crowd, while others clutched their Little Red Books tighter, as though the words inside could somehow shield them from what was happening. As I watched the scene unfold, a strange stillness settled over me. I wanted to shout, to do something, but my body was frozen, my mind racing with a thousand questions. Why wasn't anyone stopping them? Why did my mother stay so calm? The world suddenly felt fragile, as if it could shatter with one wrong move. My mother had seen it before, and I could see the weight of that fear in her eyes, though she never let it show to us.

Our neighbor, a section chief at my father's company, often mocked my mother for her dedication to our education. "Why do your children even bother with school?" he would sneer. "It won't get them anywhere." His words were sharp, but my mother never let them affect her. She would smile politely and continue with her lessons. She knew something he didn't — education was our way out, our key to a better life. No matter what the Party said, no matter how much they tried to control us, our minds were our own. "Knowledge is something they can never take from you," she would say, her voice steady despite the cracks in her hands from the long day of work. In a time when the Party sought to dictate what we could learn, what we could think, my mother's insistence on education became its own form of resistance. She knew that while the Party could control our environment, our thoughts, and our lives, they could not take away the knowledge we earned. It was the one freedom we could claim for ourselves.

As a child, I didn't fully understand the significance of the Party's influence, but as I grew, I began to see how the Revolution shaped not just the landscape, but the very people within it. Even at a young age, I sensed a quiet rebellion simmering beneath my mother's careful words. I knew my mother's words held more weight than they seemed. Her lessons on resilience and knowledge felt like seeds being planted deep within me — seeds that I wouldn't fully understand until much later in life. Even when teaching Party-approved lessons, I noticed how my mother would pause on certain words, her tone hinting at something deeper — something unsaid but understood. At home, her choice of bedtime stories often carried lessons of quiet resistance, of finding strength in knowledge when everything else was taken away. She kept her head down, but in our home, she taught us to question the world, to seek knowledge, to carve out our own thoughts in a time when the Party sought to control every mind. Even then, as I devoured every book my mother gave me, I knew I had to push harder. Success was more than a dream — it was a way out, a path that would lead me far beyond the walls of our home, away from the shadows of the past. The land, vast and unyielding, mirrored the lives of those who lived here — endless, harsh, but beautiful in its perseverance. In a world where survival was the only constant, freedom was a word too fragile to utter, yet it lingered on the edge of my consciousness, waiting to be grasped. As I grew older, I began to question the slogans we were taught at school. The Party's words promised unity and progress, but the silence in our home told a different story. I could sense that beneath my mother's lessons on resilience, there was an unspoken warning: that survival in this world meant knowing when to speak, and when to remain silent. "Resilience," she would say, "isn't about standing tall — it's about bending when the storm comes, so you don't break." I didn't understand those words fully as a child, but they became a mantra, echoing in my mind through every challenge that followed.

By 1976, when I was eight years old, the **Cultural Revolution** officially came to an end. This marked a significant turning point for China. In the quiet moments of the night, I could hear my parents whispering about the future, wondering if things might change. In September, when Chairman Mao passed away, it felt as though the air itself shifted... The whispers in our home became more frequent. In the weeks after Chairman Mao's death, there was a cautious hope — a word rarely spoken in the years before -- in the air, but also a lingering uncertainty. We whispered about change but feared speaking it aloud. The political landscape was in a state of flux, and people were uncertain about the future. But in the midst of this uncertainty, a new era was beginning to take shape. In 1978, **Deng Xiaoping** emerged as the leader of China, and his reformist policies set the country on a path toward economic and social transformation.

One of the most significant milestones of this period was the reinstatement of the **national college entrance exams** in 1978. This was a momentous occasion for the country and for families like mine. My mother's relentless belief in education was vindicated as key high schools began sprouting across the country, providing top students with a path toward higher learning and, ultimately, a better life. It was a time when the intellectual class, suppressed during the Cultural Revolution, began to reemerge. Education was once again seen as a vehicle for social mobility, and academic achievement became a way to rebuild a country that had been torn apart by ideological warfare.

The stories my mother shared, the resilience she embodied, and the perseverance she instilled in us became the bedrock of my determination. As China opened its doors to new possibilities in the 1980s, I held onto those early lessons, knowing that education was not just a means to survive but a path to a future beyond the shadows of our past.

Our mother's hard work and dedication paid off. Both Tony and I were admitted to the number one high school in our town — Tony as a senior high school student and I as a junior high schooler. Those years were formative, and the competition among students was fierce, as we all understood the stakes. Excelling in academics became a way to ensure a future beyond the limitations of our past. My mother's emphasis on our studies became the foundation of our lives, and I pushed myself harder, knowing that success was our only way forward.

As the country underwent **economic reforms** in the early 1980s, the winds of change began to sweep across Xinjiang. The markets, once bare, now buzzed with the excitement of opportunity as factories opened and trade expanded. The fear that had once hung over us like a shadow began to lift, replaced by cautious optimism. But even then, there was an unspoken understanding that the Party's influence had not disappeared, only softened. The once-closed markets began to open, and China took its first steps toward modernizing its economy. Factories were privatized, and people began to experience a newfound sense of personal freedom and opportunity. It was an exciting time to be a student, as new ideas and global perspectives began to flow into the country. For the first time, we had a sense that our future could be different from our parents' generation — a future filled with possibilities beyond survival.

In 1980, my brother achieved a major milestone — he was admitted to **Zhejiang University**, one of the most prestigious universities in China. It was a source of immense pride for our family, a testament to the sacrifices my parents had made and my mother's unyielding focus on education. Five years later, in 1985, I too found my path — when I was accepted into **Peking University**, the top university in the country. This achievement felt surreal, as if the years of hard work and perseverance had finally culminated in something truly significant.

As I grew older, I began to understand the depth of the sacrifices my parents had made. They had come to Xinjiang to protect us, to keep us safe from the political scrutiny that had claimed so many lives. They had given up their dreams, their ambitions, for the sake of survival. My mother, who had once dreamed of a different life, now found herself teaching in a remote province. My father, who had grown up in poverty, had found stability in Xinjiang, though it was not the life he had imagined.

At night, after the lights were turned off and the house grew quiet, I would lie awake, thinking about the stories my mother had told us. They were more than bedtime tales — they were lessons in perseverance, in resilience, in holding onto hope even when the world seemed to be crumbling around us. My parents' sacrifices, their quiet strength, and their unwavering belief in the power of education became the foundation of my life. Those quiet lessons, taught in the stillness of our home, would guide me through challenges that stretched far beyond the dusty streets of our small town, into a future I had yet to imagine.

Chapter 2: Family Life Under Political Repression

The Cultural Revolution, much like the great wars that sweep across history, was not simply a political upheaval. It was a force vast and unrelenting, leaving no life untouched. It did not merely sweep through the highest offices of government but penetrated deeply into the everyday lives of families. Like a mighty river carving its way through stone, this force reshaped not just the nation's politics but the quiet sanctuaries of home, eroding familial bonds and cutting new paths of survival. In our home, beneath the heavy hand of political repression, the quiet dignity of my parents, especially my mother, created a refuge — a sanctuary from the chaotic world outside.

In schools, the very purpose of education had been distorted. Teachers, gripped by fear of being labeled counter-revolutionary, abandoned real teaching. Lessons were reduced to mere recitations of Maoist slogans, the rhythm of rote repetition replacing the lively exchange of ideas. Education no longer served to enlighten; it had become a charade. Teachers maintained order, not knowledge. Students, sensing that political loyalty mattered more than learning, grew disengaged. The thirst for knowledge dried up, replaced by a sense that the future lay in submission rather than understanding.

But my mother stood apart from this erosion. As an elementary school teacher, she refused to allow her students to fall into apathy. Despite the omnipresent fear, despite the pressure to conform, she insisted on teaching a full curriculum, presenting her students with the subjects that had been all but forgotten in the tide of political indoctrination. While others bowed to the demands of the Party, my mother believed in something greater. She believed that education was not merely a tool for producing obedient citizens but a means of awakening the mind, of giving children the tools to better their lives, to think critically, and to dream beyond the confines of their present circumstances.

Her sense of responsibility went beyond the classroom. Often, after returning home, she would speak of the children whose teachers had forsaken them, her voice low with sadness. "They deserve better," she would say, the sorrow in her eyes betraying her own frustration with a system that had abandoned its duty to educate. In her view, teaching was not a job; it was a calling, a mission that transcended the shifting political landscape. Her dedication to that mission was unshakable, even as the world around us became ever more uncertain.

At home, we understood that our mother was different from the other teachers. While most children took their teachers' words as gospel, we brought our questions to her. "Is what the teacher said true?" we would ask, and my mother would either quietly affirm or gently correct what we had been taught. Her authority, though never imposed through fear or anger, was absolute. We trusted her implicitly, far more than any outside authority, because her wisdom came not from fear but from a place of deep love and conviction.

I still marvel at how she commanded such respect without ever raising her voice or resorting to harsh discipline. She was firm but always gentle. We were never afraid to tell her when we made mistakes. If we failed at school or found ourselves in trouble, she would guide us through it, never scolding, never punishing. Instead, she showed us how to learn from our failures. That unbreakable trust remains one of the defining aspects of my relationship with her, and it has stayed with me throughout my life.

In many families, political repression seeped into the very fabric of relationships, turning trust into suspicion. The Party had made it clear that loyalty to the state was to come before all else, even family. Children were encouraged to report any signs of dissent, even in their own homes. We often heard stories of children innocently repeating conversations they had overheard, only for their parents to be reported and punished. The fear of betrayal hung heavy in many households.

I remember how, on a quiet evening, we learned that one of our neighbors — a well-respected teacher — had been reported by his own son for speaking too freely at home. That night, as we sat in uneasy silence, my mother said quietly, "Fear is not enough reason to stop thinking." Her words lingered in the stillness of the room, a reminder that in our home, the Party did not hold sway — she did. Her strength, though wrapped in gentleness, was an iron will that guided us through those years.

This pressure to conform wasn't limited to political loyalty; it also extended into personal expression, which was considered a sign of bourgeois sentiment. Any hint of romance, elegance, or personal beauty was labeled as bourgeois and counter revolutionary. For women, makeup was strictly prohibited. There was no lipstick, no rouge to brighten cheeks, and no powder to smooth the complexion. Women were expected to embody the ideal of a humble, self-sacrificing revolutionary, devoid of any hint of personal vanity.

Yet my mother held onto a small relic of the past — an old lipstick that had once belonged to her mother. Deep red, hidden away in a drawer, it was her secret, a symbol of a life that had been taken from her. She never wore it herself, but on rare occasions, when we performed in school plays, she would carefully apply it to our cheeks. I still remember the thrill of that small act of defiance, standing on stage with that touch of color on my face. It was as if, for a moment, the old world had returned, reminding us that there was beauty still, even in such dark times.

Beyond personal appearance, clothing was another battleground for conformity. Fashion had been stripped of color and personality. Men and women alike wore only black, blue, grey, or white — the colors of the revolutionary ideal. Anything beyond these muted shades was seen as indulgent, unnecessary, and dangerous. When clothes became torn or worn, there were no new clothes readily available, and the culture of amending and reusing clothes became the norm. There was a popular saying: three years as new, three years as old, and three more years as amended. When our clothes tore, my mother would stitch them with colorful threads, turning the mended patches into flowers or animals, as though the repairs were decorative rather than out of necessity. Her skillful hands made these amendments seem intentional, a quiet way of adding beauty in a world that was otherwise stripped of it. Even as the Party dictated what we could wear, how we could speak, and what we were allowed to think, my mother found ways to slip through the cracks. She saved what little we had, mending torn clothes with threads that she embroidered into flowers and birds, adding color to the otherwise drab fabric of our lives. It was a small thing, but it was a reminder that beauty still existed, that even in the darkest times, there was room for art, for creativity, for joy.

Popular songs, movies, and plays were banned unless they served as propaganda tools for the Party. Literature, too, was restricted. Only works that praised Mao and the revolution were allowed, while novels, poems, and art that once represented the richness of Chinese culture were branded as counter-revolutionary and destroyed.

Even basic resources like food were rationed through government-issued coupons. These coupons were necessary to purchase staple goods such as rice, flour, oil, and meat. At first glance, this seemed like a simple response to resource scarcity. China was recovering from the disastrous economic policies of the Great Leap Forward, and food shortages were widespread. But these coupons were also a tool of political control. By regulating access to food and other essentials, the government ensured that citizens remained dependent on the state. Families, including ours, carefully saved their ration coupons, calculating how much we could afford to eat each month.

One of the highlights of our week was the meal we had on Sundays, when we could finally afford to buy meat. We could only buy meat once a week, and the anticipation of that meal was almost as delicious as the food itself. I still remember standing by the stove, watching my mother as she cooked, the savory smell filling our small home. The joy we felt as we sat down to eat was unmatched. The meat was so tender and flavorful, and we savored every bite. I can still recall the happiness I felt then, a kind of pure, uncomplicated joy that I find hard to replicate now. That simple meal with my family, made possible by the ration coupons, remains one of my most cherished memories, though it is tinged with a sense of loss. I've never felt that level of happiness or tasted meat that delicious again.

This rationing system added another layer of control over people's lives. The state not only controlled what you thought and said, but it also controlled how much you ate, what clothes you wore, and how you lived. In this sense, the food shortages were not only a reflection of economic hardship but also a way for the Party to assert its power over every aspect of daily life.

In the broader context of society, this eradication of personal expression was aimed at controlling every aspect of life. Arts, entertainment, and literature were seen as potential threats to the Party's control. Anything that could inspire individual thought or allow people to connect to a world beyond revolutionary ideals was deemed dangerous. The Party wanted people to see themselves as mere cogs in the larger machine of socialism, not as individuals with personal desires, talents, or dreams.

In many ways, this attempt to destroy creativity was just as damaging as the political repression. It flattened human experience, removing joy and beauty from everyday life. In a world where songs, fashion, and art had been taken away, people lost not only their freedom of expression but also their ability to find moments of happiness and connection in small, personal ways. It was this cultural oppression that hung heavily over families, further disconnecting them from the values that had once defined Chinese life.

Yet in our home, my mother protected us from this erasure. Though we conformed outwardly, inside our walls, she preserved the values of our heritage, teaching us the stories and traditions that had been passed down through generations. Through her, we remained connected to our ancestors, to the beauty of the past, even as the present seemed determined to erase it.

The Party also worked to dismantle the traditional bonds that had long held Chinese families together, particularly through the elimination of ancestor worship. For generations, Chinese families had honored their ancestors through rituals and ceremonies, often gathering in ancestral halls that served as both spiritual and social centers. These rituals weren't just about honoring the dead — they reinforced the bonds between living family members and maintained the continuity of tradition. But during the Cultural Revolution, these traditions were labeled as "old customs" and targeted for destruction. Ancestral halls were torn down, and families were forbidden from practicing the rituals that had once been integral to Chinese culture.

Though we no longer practiced these rituals openly, my mother made sure we understood their significance. She told us stories of our grandparents and great-grandparents, ensuring that we remained connected to our family's past. In her own way, she resisted the Party's attempt to erase these traditions by keeping the spirit of them alive in our home.

Another critical aspect of traditional family life that the Party sought to undermine was the hierarchical respect for elders. In Chinese society, respect for one's elders had always been a core value. Elders were revered, their wisdom sought out, and their role in the family unquestioned. But during the Cultural Revolution, this hierarchy was challenged. Children were taught to question their parents and grandparents, and to report on them if they expressed "counter-revolutionary" ideas. This led to a breakdown in trust between generations, as loyalty to the Party took precedence over loyalty to one's family.

In our home, however, this respect for elders never wavered. My parents ensured that we upheld the traditional values of honoring and listening to our elders. My mother made sure we understood the importance of respecting family over the pressures of the outside world. We were taught to value our grandparents' wisdom, and though we lived in a time where that respect was challenged, it remained central to our family life.

Despite the constant pressure to conform, our family remained a refuge of sorts. We understood the rules of the outside world — what to say, how to behave — but within our home, we lived by a different code, one built on trust, respect, and a shared sense of responsibility for one another. The Party may have encouraged people to turn on each other, but in our family, that bond was unbreakable.

My mother was the pillar of this stability. Her influence went beyond discipline or guidance; it was as if she was the moral compass that kept us grounded, even as the world around us seemed to spin out of control. I often wondered how she managed to create such a strong sense of security in such an unstable time. There was never any fear in our relationship with her, only deep trust and love that guided us through those difficult years.

My father, too, played his part in maintaining this delicate balance. Though not as outspoken as my mother, he quietly supported her efforts. He understood the dangers of saying the wrong thing, but he never allowed fear to dictate his actions. Together, my parents managed to shield us from the worst of the political turmoil while instilling in us the values they believed in — values that were often at odds with the propaganda of the time.

Even though the government's reach extended into every aspect of life, my parents found ways to preserve their dignity and protect us. They knew what to say and what not to say. They understood the necessity of navigating the political landscape with care, but they never allowed that caution to overshadow their core values. In the end, it was their love for us, and their unwavering commitment to our well-being, that defined our family life under political repression.

Though the government sought to define us, it was the values my parents instilled — dignity, respect, resilience — that carried us through those difficult years. In the end, it was not the Party that shaped who we were, but the quiet strength of our family.

Chapter 3: Entering Peking University

I was 17 when I left home for the first time, just like most of the other freshmen. It took three nights and four days by train to finally arrive in Beijing. The journey was long, but it felt as though I was crossing a threshold into a new world — one filled with the promise of intellectual freedom and personal growth.

A Journey Toward Independence

As the train pulled out of the station, the faces of my family grew smaller, their outlines blurring into the crowd. My mother waved, but her eyes, usually so steady, held something unspoken — perhaps a hope that I would find my way, or perhaps the realization that this goodbye was different from all the others.

As the train sped across the vast country, the landscapes blurred, and with every passing mile, the familiar threads of my past unraveled, releasing me into a future filled with excitement and uncertainty. I couldn't help but wonder if they, too, longed to leave behind their pasts, to embark on a journey that promised something greater. The rhythmic clatter of the train's wheels on the tracks seemed to echo the steady beat of my heart, one that carried equal parts excitement and trepidation. As the train sped through vast stretches of land, the scenery changed, but a part of me still clung to the familiar. Every mile seemed to pull me farther from the life I had known — the world of my mother's quiet reassurances, the structured simplicity of home. Yet with every passing moment, the excitement of an unknown future grew stronger. My thoughts oscillated between yearning for the security of the past and the exhilarating pull of a future I couldn't yet see. The hum of the train at night lulled me to sleep, though my mind raced with thoughts of what lay ahead.

As the train pulled away from the station, my classmates likely thought about returning home after graduation. Many of them assumed they would go back to their hometowns, find work, and live near their families. But for me, something was different. I distinctly remember thinking that I would never return. And indeed, I didn't, except for a few visits over the years. Life took a different turn.

Later, my father passed away, and my family gradually dispersed. My mother and brother immigrated to Canada, and my sister's family returned to Zhejiang, where all our relatives still live. Leaving home that day wasn't just about starting university; it was the beginning of a lifelong journey that would take me far beyond the boundaries of my hometown.

First Day on Campus

Life back home had scattered in ways I hadn't anticipated. Yet here, at Peking University, everything seemed to converge — the hopes, the knowledge, the unspoken dreams. As I crossed through the West Gate on my first day, I knew this place would mark the beginning of a new chapter.

The first day I stepped onto the campus of Peking University, I was overwhelmed. The campus was the most beautiful place I had ever seen — immersive, grand, and serene all at once. As I stood before the West Gate, its towering presence seemed to whisper promises of wisdom, of intellects past and future. This wasn't just a campus; it was a crucible for transformation. Every brick, every tree, felt infused with the energy of those who had walked here before me — scholars, thinkers, revolutionaries. For the first time, I saw myself as part of something much larger, a continuum of knowledge stretching far beyond my lifetime. Standing at the entrance, I felt a mix of anticipation and awe. The grand architecture, the serene stillness of the lotus pond — everything whispered of a knowledge yet to be discovered, of a life that would forever alter the course of my existence. Standing at the entrance, the magnitude of what lay ahead struck me. For the first time, I felt small — not in a belittling way, but in the sense that the university, with all its history, wisdom, and grandeur, was larger than me, larger than any one person. And yet, I felt drawn in, like a drop of water merging into a vast, boundless ocean of knowledge. Walking through the famous West Gate, I was struck by its magnificence. The classical palace-style gate stood tall, its vermilion hue glowing under the sunlight. As the main entrance to the university, it wasn't just a way in; it was a symbol of everything Peking University represented — history, wisdom, and a gateway to intellectual enlightenment.

Stepping through the grand West Gate, I was enveloped by the scent of lotus blossoms mingling with the crisp autumn air. The sun was warm on my face, but there was a breeze that made the leaves rustle gently. The murmurs of students drifted through the air, a soft hum of voices filled with curiosity and energy, as if the campus itself was alive, inviting us to join in its legacy.

Beyond the West Gate, the lotus pond stretched out before me, its still waters reflecting vibrant pink blooms and the lush greenery surrounding it. The tranquility was captivating, a peaceful contrast to the bustling energy of the city outside. The soft rustle of leaves and the gentle ripple of water made me feel as though I had entered a sacred space of learning and contemplation.

Further inside, I came upon the Unnamed Lake, an iconic landmark that mirrored the sky and the towering Boya Tower on its surface. The Boya Tower, with its elegant pagoda-style architecture, stood tall on the lake's edge, serving as the symbol of Peking University. It wasn't just a tower — it was a beacon, a reminder of the university's towering legacy and the generations of scholars who had passed through its doors.

Surrounded by such beauty, it was easy to get lost, both physically and emotionally. And in fact, I did — several times. Finding my classrooms in the maze of the university's sprawling grounds was no small feat. One particularly cold morning, I found myself lost on campus, unable to find my classroom. It was the first time I felt the weight of solitude — there was no one to ask, no familiar face to guide me. I stood still for a moment, fighting the rising panic, and then something shifted. I realized that if I didn't act, no one else would. So, I took a deep breath, retraced my steps. I wandered through the paths, past buildings with ornate facades and ancient trees, trying to orient myself, and eventually found my way. It was a small triumph, but it stayed with me, a reminder that in this new world, I was more capable than I believed. Navigating both the campus and my sense of self would take time, but each day brought a new discovery. It took me almost a week to navigate the campus without getting lost, but each day, the charm of the place drew me deeper into its spell.

Along the lawns and benches scattered across the campus, students engaged in various activities. Some sat on the grass with books spread open, absorbed in reading or discussing academic topics. Others strolled leisurely along the tree-lined pathways, deep in conversation or lost in thought. There were groups practicing tai chi in the mornings, their slow and graceful movements harmonizing with the serene environment. On the jogging paths circling the lake, students ran in the early hours or just before sunset, seeking moments of solitude or clarity. The vibrant energy of student life was everywhere, and I couldn't help but feel excited to be a part of it all.

Dorm Life in Building 31

Life in the dormitory was another adventure. I was assigned to Building 31, a dorm specifically for undergraduate female students. It had four stories, with two wings at each end. The path outside the building was lined with Ginkgo trees, their golden leaves creating a beautiful canopy overhead, especially in the autumn months. Walking through that path was almost meditative, a brief escape from the hustle of university life.

Our room, 312, was located on the third floor and housed six students. The room was modest, with three double-deck beds, a small cabinet for each of us, and a large steel bookshelf where we stored our textbooks and personal belongings. It wasn't much, but it was enough to make the space our own.

Each floor had public washing rooms and toilets, but there were no shower rooms in the dorm itself. For showers, we were given two tickets per week to use the facilities in a separate building on campus. It was a bit of a walk, but I didn't mind.

Unlike most other mothers, mine wasn't worried about me leaving home. Some of her friends criticized her, questioning how she could send her child off to university without knowing how to do laundry or cook. But my mom, always calm and confident, simply smiled and replied, "If my child can excel at school, she'll figure out how to do laundry on her own." And she was right.

When I arrived at Peking University, it quickly became clear that the transition to university life involved more than just academic challenges. We didn't have washing machines in China back then. The first time I washed my clothes, I felt utterly lost. I hadn't even considered the fact that clothes needed to be wrung out properly before hanging them up. I remember my hands aching after twisting the fabric. My roommate saw the still twisted pants hanging there and couldn't help laughing out loud. Gently, she showed me how to straighten the pants properly before hanging them. When I saw the crooked mess I'd made of my laundry, I couldn't help but laugh at myself along with her. But soon, these tasks that once seemed insurmountable became routine. Each time I hung my clothes to dry, I felt a quiet pride in my ability to adapt and thrive in this new world. The path outside the dorm became my sanctuary, the golden leaves of the Ginkgo trees guiding me back to a growing sense of independence. The laughter of my roommates became a constant in the first few months, a thread that wove together our shared experiences of homesickness and discovery. Late at night, when the day's lessons had been absorbed, we would huddle together in our small dorm room, exchanging stories of home and laughing over our missteps. At first, our dorm was a space filled with awkward silences, each of us strangers navigating our new lives. But as the weeks passed, those silences gave way to late-night conversations — about our families, our dreams, and the challenges we faced. We bonded over the little things, like laughing about the washing disasters or sharing our frustrations over a particularly challenging philosophy text. In those moments, I realized that it wasn't just the university that was shaping me — it was these friendships, forged in the crucible of discovery. Late-night debates with my friends weren't just about academic theories — they were conversations that pushed us to question our own beliefs and assumptions. Nietzsche's critique of society didn't just challenge our worldviews — it challenged our sense of who we were becoming.

A Time of Freedom and Exploration

From 1985 to 1989, the four years I spent at Peking University unfolded during a rare window of intellectual freedom in China. Just as the country itself was undergoing seismic economic reforms, loosening the iron grip of a state-controlled economy, so too was the university experiencing a quiet revolution of ideas. For the first time in decades, books once deemed dangerous by the authorities — works by Nietzsche, Sartre, Schopenhauer — found their way into the hands of students, like contraband promising liberation. The writings of Freud, too, stirred controversy, not just for their psychological insight but for their subversive analysis of power, identity, and repression. Novels like *Lady Chatterley's Lover*, *The Second Sex*, and *Capitalist Ethics* also became available. This influx of new ideas fueled a wave of intellectual curiosity on campus, as students eagerly devoured these works, discussing them in small groups and clubs. I still remember the first time I held *The Second Sex* in my hands. It was like peering into a world that had been hidden from me, a world where ideas about gender, power, and independence challenged everything I had known. My friends and I would gather late into the night, huddling in our dorm rooms, passing books back and forth like contraband. We would read aloud to each other, dissecting every sentence, our minds ablaze with questions. I felt a shift within me, as though my world had widened immeasurably, and for the first time, I understood what it meant to think freely. One day, my professor asked a simple question: 'What is truth?' It was a question I had heard countless times in the abstract, but in that moment, it felt as though the ground beneath me had shifted. I realized that truth wasn't a fixed concept — it was something to be grappled with, to be questioned. For weeks, I walked around campus lost in thought, the words of these philosophers swirling in my mind, challenging everything I had believed to be certain. Late at night, we would sit on our bunk beds, whispering about everything from philosophy to the latest poetry we had read, laughing about the day's mishaps. We grew close, not because we shared the same backgrounds or interests, but because we were all learning how to navigate this new world together. The dorm became not just a place to sleep, but a space where we could wrestle with ideas and with ourselves.

During this time, student clubs flourished, providing outlets for creative and intellectual expression. Poetry clubs, literary societies, and groups devoted to art and philosophy thrived. Famous poets like Bei Dao and Gu Cheng visited the campus to meet with students. One of my roommates was a member of a literary club and often brought back journals filled with poems and short stories for us to read. These journals opened windows into new worlds, and our dorm became a space for discussions about art, literature, and society.

The freedom to engage with such diverse material was something I cherished deeply. It wasn't just about academic growth; it was about exploring new ways of thinking and seeing the world.

Dreams of Intellectual Freedom

When I finally stepped into my first class, it wasn't just the culmination of a dream — it was the beginning of an adventure. The grandeur of the campus, the intellectual energy, and the sense of freedom filled me with anticipation. I had always been curious about the world, eager to ask big questions and solve the mysteries of the universe. Peking University, with its rich history of fostering great thinkers and leaders, seemed like the perfect place to pursue these dreams.

One of the most exciting aspects of my university experience was the freedom to think and explore ideas in ways I had never done before. Gone were the rigid classroom structures and rote memorization. Instead, we were encouraged to question everything, to debate ideas, and to explore new perspectives. Professors, many of them leaders in their fields, urged us to engage with the material critically and to challenge long-held assumptions.

At the beginning, I felt deeply confused. The foundations I had grown up with were suddenly in question. I reached out to my mother for guidance, as I had always done when troubled. But, to my surprise, she refused to guide me this time. She told me she didn't want to misguide me and that she was no longer able to help with such matters.

Because of my grandfather's status as a former lawyer and captain, my mother had been barred from attending a 4-year college and was only given the opportunity to attend a two-year program to become an elementary school teacher. She had never had the chance to pursue higher education beyond that, and as a result, she didn't feel equipped to advise me on something she had not experienced herself.

At first, I was angry with my mother for not guiding me as she always had. But in the weeks that followed, I realized that this was her final lesson — the most important one she could give. By stepping back, she forced me to trust myself, to seek my own answers. It was terrifying, but it was also liberating. Her wisdom lay not in giving me direction, but in teaching me to chart my own course. She knew that this was a journey I needed to take on my own.

It was a shock to realize that I had to navigate these complex ideas on my own. For the first time in my life, I felt that no one would be there to guide me through my intellectual struggles. Only later did I understand how wise my mother had been to step back. It took courage for her to admit that she could no longer provide the answers I sought, and even greater wisdom to allow me the space to find my own path.

The Philosophy Courses That Changed My Life

Among the most impactful experiences during my time at Peking University were the two courses I took: *Philosophy History of Western Thought* and *Chinese Philosophy History*. These courses opened my eyes to a world of thought I had never been exposed to before.

The Challenge of Philosophy: A World of Contradictions

Philosophy, for me, was not just an academic pursuit; it was a mirror that reflected all the inconsistencies in my world and forced me to confront them head-on. Until that point, the only philosophy taught in China's basic education was Marxism, presented as the ultimate and unquestionable truth — the lens through which we were expected to interpret all of society and history. It was ingrained in us that Marxist thought explained everything and left no room for alternative perspectives. But once I encountered the works of Nietzsche, Sartre, Schopenhauer, and other Western philosophers, it was as if a crack had formed in the solid structure I had relied on. That crack quickly widened, and I began to see that the world was far more complicated and ambiguous than I had ever realized.

Nietzsche's writings in particular hit me with the force of a revelation. His relentless critique of morality and his assertion that "God is dead" challenged everything I had believed in. I found myself questioning not only the societal norms I had accepted but also my own values and purpose. Nietzsche asked whether we, as individuals, could transcend the limitations of tradition and create our own values. This question haunted me. I had grown up in a world where conformity was valued and where social expectations dictated much of our behavior. Now, I was being asked to question all of that — to imagine a world where I, alone, had to create meaning.

Existential Questions: Sartre and Schopenhauer

Sartre's existentialism pushed me even further. His assertion that "existence precedes essence" turned my understanding of identity on its head. According to Sartre, we are not born with predetermined purposes; rather, we create our essence through our choices and actions. This was a radical idea, especially in a society that valued collectivism and a prescribed path. Suddenly, the idea that I could define my own existence, free from external constraints, both thrilled and terrified me.

Yet, while Sartre offered freedom, Schopenhauer presented a much darker view of human existence. His concept of the "will to live" suggested that we are all driven by blind, irrational forces, constantly striving for desires that ultimately bring us more suffering. Schopenhauer's pessimism struck a chord with me during moments when the uncertainty of my future weighed heavily on my mind. Was it true that life was just a constant struggle against forces beyond my control? Was my journey through university — and through life itself — nothing more than an endless series of desires and disappointments?

These were not just abstract philosophical questions; they were deeply personal. The more I read, the more I began to feel that philosophy wasn't about finding answers — it was about learning to live with the questions. I realized that life, like philosophy, is full of contradictions, and the pursuit of truth often leads us to more complex and uncomfortable realizations. There were no easy answers, and perhaps that was the point.

A Journey of Intellectual Awakening

These philosophical explorations were not just confined to late-night study sessions. They spilled into every aspect of my life. As I walked through the campus of Peking University, I found myself thinking about Nietzsche's concept of the "will to power." Were we, as students, striving for knowledge out of a genuine desire to understand the world, or were we seeking power in the form of degrees, recognition, and social status? When I sat in a lecture hall, listening to professors explain the intricacies of history or politics, I couldn't help but question whether these interpretations of the world were just one version of truth, shaped by those in power.

The debates with my friends became an extension of this intellectual awakening. We questioned everything — from the role of the individual in society to the nature of truth itself. These conversations were not just theoretical exercises; they were a way for us to navigate our changing realities. The more we read, the more we realized that truth wasn't a fixed concept. It was something to be wrestled with, questioned, and, ultimately, lived.

Embracing Uncertainty

In the end, the most profound lesson philosophy taught me was to embrace uncertainty. I no longer sought definitive answers to life's biggest questions because I had come to understand that the search itself was what mattered. The process of questioning, of continually challenging my own beliefs and assumptions, became a way of life. Philosophy wasn't just about understanding the world; it was about understanding myself.

Nietzsche, Sartre, and Schopenhauer opened my eyes to the fact that life is filled with contradictions, and it is through engaging with those contradictions that we grow. The truth is not something to be found and held onto but something that must be continually pursued. In my years at Peking University, I came to realize that philosophy wasn't just a subject I studied — it was the lens through which I would view the rest of my life.

My Major in Religion

Although I was admitted to the Philosophy department, my major was religion, a field almost foreign to me and most Chinese people at the time. Peking University was the only institution in China offering a religion major, with just ten students accepted per year. The primary reason for creating this major was to train government officials to understand religions and communicate with people of faith.

Although I wasn't a believer, I found Christianity the most appealing of all the religions I studied. The study of religion opened new perspectives for me, and while I remained an atheist, the philosophy and history behind belief systems fascinated me.

Personal Growth and New Perspectives

In addition to academic growth, my time at Peking University shaped me in many other ways. Living away from home for the first time, I learned to take care of myself and navigate life in a new city. These challenges were overwhelming at first, but they helped me develop a sense of independence and resilience. Every task, from washing my clothes to making sure I arrived at class on time, was a reminder that I was truly on my own. At first, the loneliness was palpable — a heavy presence that filled the quiet moments. But as the weeks passed, that solitude transformed into something else: strength. Each small triumph, whether it was successfully navigating campus or mastering a complex philosophical argument, became a testament to my growing independence. I realized that this journey was not just about intellectual discovery; it was about discovering myself.

The friendships I made at university were another important part of my growth. My peers came from all over China, each bringing different perspectives and experiences. Late-night debates with friends often left me questioning my worldview, pushing me to think in new ways.

A Lifelong Pursuit of Knowledge

Entering Peking University was not just a moment of personal triumph but a turning point in my life. It deepened my love for learning and set me on a path that would continue long after I left campus. Peking University wasn't just a place to earn a degree; it was where I began to understand who I was and what I wanted from life. Knowledge, I learned, is not just something to be consumed — it is something to be pursued endlessly.

In the quiet moments after class, walking by the Unnamed Lake or sitting under the shade of the ancient trees, I often found myself thinking not just about knowledge. Life, like philosophy, was full of contradictions, questions without clear answers. But it was here that I learned to live with that uncertainty, to embrace it even, as the true path to growth.

Looking back at my time at Peking University, it is not just the knowledge I gained that lingers, but the lessons of resilience and curiosity. The loneliness of the first train ride, the philosophical debates that left me questioning the world — these were the moments that shaped me. Life, I learned, is constant questioning, a journey without clear answers. Peking University was not just the place where I gained knowledge; it was where I learned to think, to question, and to face the unknown with curiosity rather than fear. The lessons I learned there, both inside and outside the classroom, would guide me through the rest of my life, far beyond the gates of that hallowed campus.

Years later, I would still return to the lessons learned at Peking University. It was there that I learned to embrace life's most profound questions, knowing that the answers often remain elusive. The philosopher's journey, I realized, was not about reaching a destination but about finding meaning in the search. In that search, I found myself.

Chapter 4: New Friendships and Political Discussions

Arriving at Peking University, I knew that academic growth was just one part of the university experience. What I didn't anticipate was how deeply new friendships would shape my understanding of the world. Among those friendships, none had as profound an impact as my relationship with **Li Wei**.

Meeting Li Wei

I met Li Wei during our junior year, when we were both just beginning to understand the complexities of the world we inhabited. Li Wei was a **computer major student**, and like many of her peers, she had been approached by **campus missionaries** working under the guise of various professions. These missionaries, operating discreetly, sought to spread Gospel on campus. Li Wei, along with her roommates, became Christians after being invited to several gatherings by these missionaries. She was one of those rare people whose energy seemed boundless — whether she was deep into her computer science studies or discussing faith with a quiet fervor. But beneath her curiosity and passion, I sensed something else: a tension, as though her heart was constantly balancing on the edge of something deeper. To openly embrace Christianity in a country where atheism was the official doctrine required more than belief — it demanded courage. Yet Li Wei carried it with a quiet defiance, her faith fueling her activism, pushing her to question not just political systems but the very soul of the society we lived in. Her passion was infectious, but there were moments when I found myself wondering how long that fire could burn. Idealism, I had learned from my studies, often carried a cost — and it was rarely the leaders who paid the ultimate price. Even in the safety of our intellectual debates, I couldn't help but wonder whether Li Wei's belief in a better world might eventually collide with the harsher realities of power. Her struggle, though unspoken, was constant: How could she live out her faith in a world that denied its existence?

At one event, **we were invited to a party** hosted by one of these missionaries. At one point, the host turned off the light switch and asked, "If I turn this switch back on, will the light come on?" Without hesitation, we all replied, "Of course." He smiled and said, "That's faith." We were amused by the simplicity of the analogy but didn't think much more about it at the time. Yet even then, a small doubt flickered in the back of my mind. Was faith really as simple as a light switch? Or was there more at play — unseen hands controlling the current, deciding whether the light would come on at all? I began to wonder how many of us had placed our hopes in leaders or movements, only to find the switch turned off when we needed the light most. The conversation quickly moved on, and the rest of the evening faded from memory. Looking back, though, I see how these subtle moments were part of a larger effort to frame faith as something intuitive and inevitable — just like expecting a light to come on when a switch is flipped.

The Chinese government was always wary of foreign influences, and this caution was well-founded. Yet, despite this, Christianity had made its way into the lives of students like Li Wei. The more I got to know her, the more I saw how deeply committed she was to her faith. She spoke about it with confidence and conviction, which became a central part of our friendship.

Li Wei's journey to Christianity was not immediate. As a computer science major, she approached problems with logic and analysis. Initially, the idea of faith seemed distant to her, almost irrelevant in her life of algorithms and code. However, the missionaries who had approached her and her roommates were patient, taking the time to listen to their concerns and doubts. Over weeks, they invited Li Wei and others to more gatherings, each conversation more intense than the last. It was during one such meeting, when one of the missionaries shared a personal story of faith during a time of deep crisis, that Li Wei began to see Christianity as more than just a set of beliefs. For her, faith became intertwined with the ideas of purpose, community, and action.

Interestingly, one of the students from the computer science department, who had also been approached by the missionaries, would eventually marry one of them. **She moved to Canada with him, where they now have three children.** She continues to work as a programmer, while her husband serves as a pastor. This was a powerful testament to the lasting impact these missionaries had on some students' lives.

The Student Group: Exploring Activism and Faith

Li Wei didn't just share her faith with me in passing through, she introduced me to a small circle of students who gathered regularly to discuss both politics and religion. At first, the meetings felt casual, held in dorm rooms or quiet corners of campus. We would talk about literature, philosophy, and the latest political developments in China. But it soon became clear that these discussions were not just intellectual exercises; for many in the group, including Li Wei, they were about **the future of China and how faith could play a role in shaping it**.

The group had a dynamic mix of ideas, and not everyone shared the same level of commitment to religion. Some were there purely for the political discussions, while others were more invested in the religious aspect, like Li Wei. There were often debates — sometimes heated — about whether religion should influence political activism or whether it should remain a personal matter. For Li Wei, faith and activism were deeply intertwined. She believed that **Christian values** — compassion, justice, and human dignity — were essential guiding principles for any meaningful reform.

One student in the group, who was not religious, would often challenge Li Wei's perspective. He argued that religion had no place in politics, especially in a country like China, where secularism had been the foundation of governance for so long. But Li Wei remained steadfast. She would quote passages from the Bible and speak about how **Christianity had inspired movements for social justice** in other parts of the world. For her, faith wasn't a barrier to progress; it was the foundation of it. And yet, as Li Wei's confidence grew, so did the quiet voice inside me that asked how many of those movements had stayed true to their principles. I had read enough history to know that leaders who preached justice often found themselves swept up in power — and I couldn't shake the feeling that even the purest ideals were at risk of being twisted by ambition.

The group was diverse, not just in thought but in background. Some were passionate about political reform, citing the works of philosophers and activists from around the world, while others, like Li Wei, felt that the real change had to start with the individual. In the back of my mind, I thought about the revolutions we had studied in our philosophy courses. Too often, I had seen how movements fueled by idealism had been corrupted by the same thirst for power they claimed to oppose. I began to wonder if the leaders we looked to now, those rallying students to the cause, would fare any better. Would they stand with the people when it mattered most, or would they slip away when the flames of revolution grew too hot? The discussions were often lively, with palpable energy in the room. One student, a law major, often brought up constitutional reform and how legal frameworks could drive social change. Another, an engineering student, questioned whether moral reform was even possible without addressing economic inequality first. There were heated debates, but there was also a shared understanding that something bigger than ourselves was at stake. Each meeting left us more energized, more determined to make sense of the changing world around us.

The conversations often extended late into the night. There was an urgency in our discussions, fueled by the rapidly changing social and political landscape. Each of us brought our own perspectives and passions, but Li Wei's religious convictions gave her a unique lens through which to view the challenges of our time. For her, activism wasn't just about policy change — it was about a deeper moral obligation to live out one's faith in the service of others. Yet as her resolve deepened, so did my uncertainty. I admired her unwavering commitment, but the world outside our discussions was changing faster than any of us could anticipate. It was in May 1989. Troops were moving closer to the city, the rhetoric from the government growing harsher. I couldn't shake the feeling that soon, we would have to make a choice: stay and fight for ideals that might never be realized, or leave before it was too late.

Outside of our group meetings, Li Wei and I shared many conversations that had nothing to do with politics or religion, at least on the surface. Li Wei and I often walked through the campus, our conversations meandering from our studies to our families, touching on the fragile hopes we carried for the future. One afternoon, as the warmth of late spring settled into the air, we found ourselves sitting by the Unnamed Lake. The sun dipped low on the horizon, casting long shadows over the water, its surface a glassy reflection of the towering Boya Tower. Li Wei sat beside me, quiet for once, her gaze fixed on the shifting colors of the sky. "Do you think we'll ever make a difference?" she asked, her voice barely louder than the breeze rustling through the nearby trees. The question hung between us like the descending twilight, heavy with uncertainty. I looked at her, seeing not just my friend but someone grappling with forces far larger than herself — the pull of faith, the push of activism, and the overwhelming weight of living in a world resistant to change. Li Wei spoke about her dreams of helping people, not just through activism but through small, everyday actions. 'Change starts with how you treat the people around you,' she said softly. 'It's easy to talk about justice in the abstract, but it's much harder to practice kindness in the moment.' Her words carried a deeper resolve that began to unsettle me. She was ready to take action — real action — and while I admired her courage, I couldn't help but feel the creeping fear that such idealism was a luxury. The protests were growing, the rhetoric more charged. I began to see that standing on the sidelines, as I so often had, might not be an option for much longer. But the idea of stepping fully into that world filled me with a quiet dread. Her words stayed with me long after that evening. It was in those quiet moments that I began to understand the depth of her belief — not just in God, but in the power of individual actions to shape the world.

For Christians like Li Wei, the challenge of integrating faith into activism was more than a personal struggle — it was about redefining the role of faith in public life. The misconception that Christians should remain detached from politics, or that faith should be confined to private life, overlooks a fundamental truth: faith without action is inert. Li Wei embodied the belief that being a Christian meant being a force for good, not just within the walls of a church, but in the wider world.

The political climate at the time was one of cautious reforms, where any movement toward social change had to navigate the government's strict control over ideological expression. In China, where secularism was deeply ingrained in governance, Christianity was seen as potentially destabilizing — an external influence that could challenge the state's authority. Despite this, Li Wei and others like her saw political engagement as not only a right but a responsibility, a calling rooted in their faith.

Li Wei often spoke passionately about how Christian values were inherently tied to justice, compassion, and dignity for all people. She believed that politics, with all its complexities and compromises, was a necessary arena for Christians to bring those values to life. She would often cite the Bible, particularly the verse from James 2:26, "Faith without works is dead," as a rallying cry for political involvement. For her, being the "light of the world," as Jesus called his followers to be, required stepping into the public sphere, even into politics, to be a voice for the marginalized and oppressed.

This belief was not without its challenges. Many people, both within the group and outside it, argued that religion and politics should be kept separate. Some believed that faith was a personal matter, while others felt that politics was too corrupt or secular for Christians to engage with meaningfully. But Li Wei remained firm in her conviction. She saw politics not as a dirty game to avoid, but as a necessary platform for promoting justice, equality, and compassion. She would often say, "If Christians do not engage with the world, including politics, we leave it to others to shape our future — and we are called to do more than that. We are called to be the light."

Li Wei's involvement in political discussions wasn't just about intellectual debates. She viewed political engagement as a practical way to live out her Christian values. In our discussions, she frequently talked about how Christian principles could shape policies that upheld human dignity and justice, and how faith could provide a moral compass in navigating political complexities. The group itself, diverse in thought, often debated whether religion had a place in politics, but Li Wei consistently reminded us that ignoring politics only meant forfeiting our right to influence the future.

In fact, Li Wei's perspective echoed broader Christian thought. Throughout history, many Christian leaders — from Martin Luther King Jr. to Desmond Tutu — understood that their faith called them not only to prayer but to political action. These figures, much like Li Wei, saw that being the light of the world meant engaging directly in the struggles of the day, particularly in the political arena where decisions affecting millions of lives are made. For Li Wei, and for many Christians, avoiding politics was not an option; it was an abdication of responsibility.

The misconception that Christians should avoid politics is rooted in the fear that faith and public life cannot coexist without one corrupting the other. But as Li Wei often said, "How can we be the light of the world if we refuse to step into the darkness?" For her, politics was not a secular activity to be avoided, but a realm where faith could make a transformative impact. Christians are called not to shy away from the world but to engage with it — to bring hope, justice, and love where they are most needed.

As Li Wei's story demonstrates, faith can be a powerful motivator for political involvement, especially when that involvement is driven by the desire to serve others and make the world a more just place. In her view, Christians — or anyone, for that matter — who chose not to engage in politics were relinquishing their right to speak and influence the direction of society. Her legacy, in this way, was not just one of personal faith but of active engagement, showing that faith and politics are not mutually exclusive but can, and should, work together to shape a better future.

Professor Lee and the Challenge of Belief

One memory stands out vividly in my mind. Before revealing her Christian faith to me, Li Wei had invited me to a small discussion group with a few other students. To my surprise, **Professor Lee**, a middle-aged woman and a respected scholar, joined us. During the meeting, she spoke passionately about her faith and tried to convince us that God was real. I had never encountered such direct evangelism before, especially from someone as educated and successful as Professor Lee.

Although I knew many brilliant scientists throughout history had been Christians, the ingrained belief that **only weak people believe in God** was still deeply rooted in my thinking. I was shocked to see someone like Professor Lee, who was highly accomplished and clearly intelligent, express such deep belief in God. This was the first time someone who genuinely believed in God had told me, in person, that God was real. The experience left a profound impression on me, not because I was immediately convinced, but because it challenged my assumptions about faith, intelligence, and belief.

Professor Lee was a woman who commanded respect both in the classroom and outside of it. She often shared stories of how her faith had guided her through difficult decisions in her career. Her personal journey was one of intellectual rigor paired with a deep sense of spiritual conviction. As she spoke, I realized that faith, for her, was not a refuge for the weak but a source of strength and clarity.

Professor Lee wasn't just an academic — she was a force to be reckoned with. As a scholar, she had earned the respect of her peers, and her influence extended well beyond the classroom. What I didn't know, until that meeting, was that she was also a devout Christian. Her passion for faith was as strong as her passion for her research. As she spoke, I could see the tension in the room rise. Some students listened intently, nodding their heads in agreement, while others seemed visibly uncomfortable. One student, sitting across from me, leaned back with his arms crossed, his expression unreadable. Professor Lee, though, was unfazed. She spoke with conviction, her voice unwavering as she described how faith had been the foundation of her success, both professionally and personally.

Li Wei's Enduring Legacy

In the years after our time at Peking University, I often found myself thinking back to Li Wei's unwavering courage. While others were quick to separate faith from activism, Li Wei saw them as one and the same. In time, I would come to see that not all who stood on the front lines of the protest were as steadfast as Li Wei. Many of the leaders we once followed abandoned their ideals the moment they found safety abroad. But Li Wei's legacy stayed with me, a reminder that true change requires more than words — it requires a willingness to sacrifice for something greater than oneself. Her willingness to stand up for others, even at great personal risk, left a lasting imprint on me. I realized that real change — whether political or social — requires more than intellectual arguments or theoretical frameworks. It requires action, driven by a deep sense of empathy and moral conviction. In my own journey after university, I began to see how her principles could apply to my own life. Every time I faced a decision that called for courage, I would think back to Li Wei's example, and it would push me forward, reminding me that love for others is the most powerful motivator for change.

Li Wei's views on faith and activism weren't just limited to our small group. She had a larger vision for how these principles could be applied, and her commitment went far beyond words. **Her courage and love for others were evident in her actions**, and she made personal sacrifices that would have a lasting effect on all of us who knew her.

In fact, her views remain relevant to this day. Looking at the social and political landscape in **America**, I see how Li Wei's perspective — grounded in Christian values — still holds true. Her belief in using faith as a tool for justice, equality, and reform resonates with the ongoing debates about religion's role in public life. But what has stayed with me most is the way she lived her beliefs. Li Wei didn't just talk about change; she embodied it, often at great personal cost.

Li Wei's dedication to others ultimately **led her to sacrifice much of her personal freedom**. She took bold stands, and her willingness to risk her own safety for the sake of others left an indelible impression on me. Even today, her example continues to inspire me to take action — not just as an intellectual exercise, but as a moral imperative. Whenever I think about moments of courage and love for others, I am reminded of Li Wei, and her story pushes me to act when I see injustice.

Chapter 5: Conversations on Freedom with Professor Zhang

Freedom is a word often taken for granted, but through my conversations with Professor Zhang at Peking University, I learned that it is a concept as complex as it is vital. In Professor Zhang's office, I would come to question not only what it meant to be free, but also how freedom shaped the way we navigate our lives and societies.

Throughout my time at Peking University, I had the privilege of engaging with many brilliant minds, but none left as deep an impression on me as **Professor Zhang**. A renowned scholar, Professor Zhang was not only admired for his extensive knowledge of **philosophy** but also for his unique ability to challenge his students' preconceptions. He had a reputation for being demanding, and his debates were often as intense as they were illuminating. For me, the conversations I had with him would come to shape my understanding of one of the most elusive and contested concepts: **freedom.**

The First Debate: What Is Freedom?

I first met Professor Zhang after a lecture on existentialism. As we left the classroom, I worked up the courage to ask him about something that had been on my mind: "What does it really mean to be free?" Professor Zhang stopped in his tracks and looked at me with piercing eyes.

"Freedom," he began, "is one of those concepts that seems simple, but once you dig into it, you'll find it's more complex than it appears." He then asked me, "Do you believe that freedom means being able to do whatever you want, whenever you want?"

I hesitated, unsure of how to respond. "I suppose that's part of it," I replied, "but isn't it more about having the ability to make choices without external constraints?"

Professor Zhang nodded but smiled slightly, as if anticipating the next question. "Yes, that's a common way to define freedom. But tell me this: Are we truly free if we are constantly ruled by our desires, by societal expectations, or by the consequences of our actions?"

His question lingered in the air. Before meeting Professor Zhang, I thought of freedom as a straightforward right: the ability to do as one pleased, as long as no one was directly harmed. But as our conversations deepened, I began to see that it wasn't just about external limits — it was about mastering the internal, understanding consequences, and living within a complex web of social expectations. But how could I reconcile this complex understanding with reality outside his office, where the demands for freedom were more immediate, and the risks all too real?

As I walked away from Professor Zhang's office that day, a strange mix of unease and exhilaration settled in my chest. I had come seeking answers, but instead, I left with more questions. The world, once so neatly defined, had become an ocean of uncertainties. My mind raced, trying to reconcile these new complexities with the simplicity I had once known. The weight of our discussion pressed down on me. Freedom, something I had always taken for granted as a simple right, now felt like an impossible puzzle. I found myself wandering the campus in a daze, my thoughts spinning, unsure of how to reconcile the theoretical with the personal.

Does the Source of Constraints Matter?

In one of our later conversations, I asked Professor Zhang a question that had been bothering me: **"Does the source of the constraints matter?"**

He raised an eyebrow, intrigued. "What do you mean?" he asked.

"Well," I began, "if freedom is about navigating constraints, does it matter whether those constraints come from a higher authority, like a government, or something more abstract, like moral or social norms? Were **Adam and Eve free in Eden** even though they were told not to eat from the tree? Are **Americans truly free** in a system that promises liberty but imposes laws? Are the **Chinese free** under their government's rules? And what about the future — will humans still be free if **AI guides us** in our decisions?"

The room seemed to be quiet as Professor Zhang pondered the questions. "Ah, you're touching on one of the oldest debates in philosophy: the tension between authority and autonomy."

He leaned forward in his chair. "Adam and Eve, Americans, Chinese citizens — everyone is free within the framework of their circumstances, but the nature of that freedom depends on the relationship between the individual and the source of the constraint. Adam and Eve were given a choice, but with consequences. Some might argue that freedom is meaningless without such consequences. As for political systems, whether in the United States, China, or anywhere else, the constraints imposed by the state are always at odds with personal freedom. However, how much freedom people feel they have often depended on how legitimate or fair they perceive those constraints to be." At Peking University, we spoke often about freedom, but it wasn't until I felt the sting of censorship — when an essay I had written was quietly suppressed because of some unconventional ideas — that I truly began to understand the limits imposed on us. These were not abstract concepts for me anymore; they were boundaries I encountered in my everyday life, silently reminding me that freedom, even in the academic world, had its limits. In China, the idea of freedom was complicated by the ever-present weight of the state. Our desire for more personal liberty felt like walking a tightrope, constantly balancing between the promise of reform and the fear of reprisal. The discussions in our classrooms, while intellectually stimulating, were a sharp contrast to the cautious reality outside.

Then he continued, "Now, your question about **AI** is particularly interesting because it touches on the future of human autonomy. If AI becomes advanced enough to guide or even make decisions for humans, are we still free? Some might argue that if AI provides more efficient or 'correct' choices, we are simply being aided in our freedom. Others might see it as a profound loss of human autonomy. The answer will depend on whether we view AI as a tool we control — or as a force that controls us."

Professor Zhang's musings on AI stirred a lingering question in my mind: If humans delegate more and more decision-making to machines, will our sense of freedom diminish? Would the efficiency of AI strip away the richness of human choice? The thought of a future where algorithms know us better than we know ourselves — making our decisions before we even realize we're making them — haunted me. In such a future, would freedom become a relic of the past, or could we find new ways to assert autonomy?

As I contemplated a future shaped by AI, I wondered how we would redefine freedom in a world where decisions are increasingly automated. Would we lose touch with the essential human experience of making choices, even flawed ones? Would efficiency come at the cost of our sense of individuality, or would AI free us to pursue higher aspirations beyond mundane decision-making? The potential for both liberation and control in this AI-driven future left me unsettled, yet intrigued.

The more I thought about AI, the more I realized it was not a distant future, but a present reality. In our everyday lives, algorithms already shaped our decisions — from what news we read to how we formed our opinions. As I scrolled through algorithm-curated newsfeeds, I realized that my decisions were already being subtly influenced. What stories had I missed? What narratives had I absorbed without question? I began to wonder whether AI-guided decisions would ultimately replace our own. Already, algorithms shaped the news I read and the choices I made. Was I choosing, or was the data choosing for me? These questions haunted me as I reflected on Professor Zhang's words about autonomy and control.

After grappling with AI's implications on autonomy, it became clear that the erosion of freedom wasn't just technological. This erosion was embedded deeply in every political and societal structure, a quiet force shaping the choices we believed were our own.

As Professor Zhang spoke, his words were heavy with intellectual rigor, but my mind wandered to more personal dilemmas. Did my own choices reflect true freedom, or was I, too, shackled by unseen constraints?

The Relativity of Freedom

In one of our later conversations, I proposed to Professor Zhang that **freedom is a relative term**. "It's impossible to speak about freedom without context," I said. "Everyone has a level of freedom, and without specifying the boundaries, freedom becomes too vague to be meaningful."

He listened intently, prompting me to continue.

"For example," I added, "even **prisoners have freedom** — they are free to pace within their cells, to sing, to shout. Their level of freedom is constrained by the walls, but within those walls, they still have choices. **Adam and Eve were free** to do anything they wanted except eat from the Tree of Knowledge. **We are all free,** but only within the boundaries of our circumstances."

Professor Zhang smiled thoughtfully. "That's a very important insight," he said. "Freedom is not an absolute. It exists in degrees, and those degrees depend on the constraints placed upon us — whether by physical limitations, laws, or moral obligations. But this raises an interesting question: If freedom is relative, how do we define when we are 'free enough'? Is it simply a matter of expanding the boundaries of what we are allowed to do?"

The conversation deepened, and I realized that understanding **the relativity of freedom** was crucial for making sense of social and political struggles. Many of us had protested for greater freedom, but what exactly did we mean? Did we know the boundaries we were asking to break or expand?

I thought about the student protests happening around us, and how the demand for more freedom in China meant something very different than the protests I had read about in the United States. In China, we were asking for a voice in a system built on collective harmony, while in the U.S., protests often sought to expand personal liberty in a system already built on individual rights.

In China, the emphasis on collective harmony often means personal freedoms are balanced with societal well-being. This is in stark contrast to the U.S., where the focus on individual rights sometimes leads to clashes between personal liberty and public order. For example, while protests in the U.S. are seen as an expression of personal freedom, in China, they are often viewed through the lens of social stability and national unity. Professor Zhang's insights helped me understand that freedom means different things depending on the cultural context in which it is exercised.

Freedom, as Professor Zhang often reminded me, exists within boundaries. Whether in a prison cell or a bustling city, we are all confined by constraints — but true freedom lies in how we navigate them. The challenge is in recognizing those limits and making authentic choices despite them.

Freedom with Specification: What Do We Mean by "Freedom"?

Professor Zhang then asked me a question that caught me off guard: "When students protest for freedom, do you think they know what they really mean by it? Have you ever thought about what they are asking for in specific terms?"

His question made me pause. I had participated in many discussions and debates with **Li Wei** and other students about freedom — freedom from censorship, freedom to express our ideas, freedom to choose our future. But now, I realized we had rarely specified what we meant by freedom beyond these abstract ideals.

"Most students, including me, often speak about freedom in general terms," I admitted. "We know we want more freedom, but we don't always define what that freedom would look like in practice. We want freedom to protest, but are we ready for the responsibilities that come with it? We want freedom to challenge authority, but what happens when that freedom is used recklessly?"

Professor Zhang leaned back and said, "Exactly. **Freedom without specification** is like a blank slate — it means different things to different people. For some, it's about personal liberty; for others, it's about societal change. But unless you define the parameters of freedom, you risk it becoming an empty word, one that's easy to shout but hard to implement."

Freedom and Responsibility

We often think of freedom in its most tangible forms — the ability to make choices like where to live, what career to pursue, or whom to love. But as I would soon learn, these choices, while important, were only surface-level freedoms. Beneath them lay far deeper layers of constraint and responsibility. Our discussions often circled back to the idea of **freedom and responsibility**. Professor Zhang emphasized that true freedom was not just about the power to choose but also about understanding the responsibility that came with those choices.

"Freedom without responsibility," he once said, "is chaos. When you make a choice, you must accept the consequences that follow. That is the burden of freedom."

This idea struck a chord with me. It reminded me of the political discussions I had with **Li Wei** and our group. So many of us were focused on fighting for greater social and political freedom, but Professor Zhang made me realize that freedom also carried the weight of accountability. It wasn't enough to fight for freedom to act; we had to be prepared to bear the consequences of those actions, no matter how difficult they might be.

This notion of responsibility was new to me. It made me question the choices I had made — not just the large ones, like protesting for more freedom, but also the smaller decisions: how I treated my peers, the career paths I was considering. Suddenly, freedom wasn't just a matter of fighting against external forces, but of understanding my own role in the consequences that followed my actions. I thought back to the protests, where students chanted for freedom without fully grasping the responsibilities those freedoms entailed. Would we have been ready to handle the complexities of political freedom, to bear the weight of our choices in shaping the nation's future?

The protests unfolding outside our campus felt like a living embodiment of the freedom we debated in class. My participation, though limited, was marked by a mix of hope and fear. I marched alongside my peers, chanting for change, yet I couldn't shake the feeling that true freedom might require more sacrifice than I was ready to give.

Political unrest swirled around us, growing louder with every passing day. Outside, the air was tense. But within Professor Zhang's office, everything felt suspended. The quiet walls seemed to breathe with the weight of our debates.

Leaving his office, I was not the same person who had entered. My thoughts churned, creating a storm within me, challenging everything I thought I knew about freedom and control. The clarity I once held seemed to dissolve, leaving behind an unsettling new world of uncertainties.

The Paradox of Freedom

One of our most memorable debates revolved around the paradox of freedom. "Can one be truly free in a world that is governed by rules, laws, and limitations?" I asked during one of our conversations.

Professor Zhang leaned back in his chair and thought for a moment. "Ah, the paradox," he mused. "Many people believe that freedom is the absence of constraints, but true freedom often exists within boundaries."

He explained further. "Consider a musician. Without mastering the rules of music theory or the limits of their instrument, they cannot be free to create beautiful music. It is through discipline and mastery that they attain true creative freedom. In life, we often think of freedom as breaking away from restrictions, but in reality, it is often about finding our own way to thrive within them."

His words stayed with me long after that conversation. It became clear to me that freedom wasn't just about breaking chains, but about knowing how to live meaningfully within the inevitable constraints of life. This was a perspective I had not encountered before — one that redefined my understanding of liberty. I began to see the limits not as barriers to freedom but as the very structures that enabled meaningful choices. As I moved into my career and personal life, this more nuanced understanding of freedom remained a guiding force, helping me navigate both the visible and invisible constraints that defined my choices.

I realized that every act of liberation carried with it an inherent constraint, whether imposed by society or self-discipline. This paradox became especially clear to me as I navigated university life. Even in an academic setting that prided itself on intellectual freedom, there were unspoken rules — whether political, social, or cultural — that quietly shaped the boundaries of our expression. In breaking some chains, we inevitably forged others.

Freedom and Society

As our discussions evolved, we began to delve into the idea of **freedom within society**. Professor Zhang challenged me to think about how individuals relate to the collective and whether personal freedom can truly exist in a society governed by rules and norms.

"In any society," he argued, "there is always a tension between the individual and the collective. While societies create structures to maintain order and harmony, these same structures often limit personal freedom. So, the question becomes: How do we balance the need for social order with the need for personal liberty?"

Professor Zhang often brought up the complexities of governance, pointing out that every society must balance personal liberty with the need for social order. He challenged me to think beyond theory — how would this balance play out in real life? How do governments like those of the United States and China differ in defining where personal liberty begins and ends? And how do individuals within these systems negotiate the tension between their desires and societal rules?

I struggled with this question. It seemed that in any society, compromises must be made. But Professor Zhang insisted that it was not about eliminating this tension but about learning to navigate it. "Freedom is not the absence of society's influence," he said, "but the ability to act authentically within it."

In comparing the systems of China and the United States, I saw two different approaches to balancing individual liberty with societal needs. China, with its emphasis on collective harmony, often restricted personal freedoms for the sake of social order. In contrast, the United States prided itself on individual rights, though this sometimes led to chaotic expressions of personal liberty. Professor Zhang's teachings helped me see that no society offers pure freedom — every system requires compromise, but how we navigate those compromises defines the essence of freedom within that society.

I began to realize that the choices we make in everyday life — whether in relationships, career paths, or moral decisions — were also bound by the same principles. We might claim freedom of choice, but every decision comes with responsibilities, some of which we cannot foresee. Professor Zhang's insights made me more conscious of the long-term effects of my actions, not just in academic or political spheres, but also in my personal life.

When it came to time to decide on my career path, the weight of freedom and responsibility was more apparent than ever. I realized that choosing a career was not just about personal fulfillment — it was about the long-term impact on those around me and the broader society. Every option carried with it unseen consequences, and Professor Zhang's words echoed in my mind: freedom without responsibility is chaos. This understanding helped me navigate these decisions with more awareness of the responsibilities they entailed.

As we debated the meaning of freedom, the growing unrest outside the university gates cast a long shadow over our conversations. It was one thing to talk about liberty within the confines of the classroom; it was another to witness students risking their lives for the very freedom we discussed. I found myself questioning whether we truly understood what we were asking for — and whether we were ready for the price it might demand.

As the protests intensified, the debates about freedom felt less academic and more urgent. The chants for democracy reverberated outside the lecture halls, challenging me to reconcile the abstract ideals we discussed with the physical risks students were willing to take.

I had always considered myself an advocate for freedom, yet as I stood at the edge of the protest, watching my fellow students raise their voices, I hesitated. Was I truly prepared for the consequences of pushing against the boundaries? Professor Zhang's words about responsibility echoed in my mind, reminding me that freedom came not without cost.

The city outside continued its rhythm, indifferent to our deep discussions. In the office, the hum of fluorescent lights seemed to emphasize the silence that followed each weighty question. Meanwhile, outside the university, the tensions of political unrest echoed faintly, like distant thunder before a storm.

Each conversation with Professor Zhang was not just intellectually stimulating but emotionally unsettling. I often left his office feeling as though the foundations of my beliefs had been shaken. It was difficult to reconcile the simplicity with which I had viewed freedom with the complexity he revealed. The debates challenged not only my mind but my sense of self.

Redefining My Understanding of Freedom

Through these debates with Professor Zhang, my understanding of freedom shifted. Whether under societal norms, governmental rules, or even future AI guidance, freedom at every level seemed to be about navigating constraints — not eliminating them. Whether these constraints came from society, our desires, or advancing technologies, Professor Zhang helped me see that the essence of freedom lay in how we understood and responded to these limitations.

Each conversation left me feeling simultaneously enlightened and unsettled. The simplicity with which I had once viewed the world now seemed naive. Professor Zhang had not just broadened my intellectual horizon; he had challenged the very foundations of how I understood myself and my role in society. There were moments after our debates when I would sit by the Unnamed Lake, grappling with these new complexities, feeling both exhilarated and unmoored.

In the end, I learned that freedom isn't a singular concept to be grasped once and held forever. It's a continuous negotiation between desires, responsibilities, and the boundaries that shape our lives. And it is in this tension where the true essence of freedom lies.

I realized that our pursuit of freedom is not just a battle against external restrictions, but a profound exploration of what it means to be human — always navigating between desire and restraint, between the individual and the collective. And perhaps it is in this constant struggle, rather than its resolution, where our humanity truly resides.

I wondered then, and still do now — is true freedom ever fully attainable, or is it forever entwined with the constraints we choose to navigate? As I left the university, I knew one thing for certain: the pursuit of freedom is not about breaking free from all constraints but learning how to navigate them in a way that defines our humanity.

Chapter 6: Growing Tensions on Campus

By April 1989, the tension that had been building for months at Peking University was no longer subtle. What had started as quiet murmurs of discontent had transformed into something far more volatile. The atmosphere on campus, once a haven for intellectual debate, had shifted dramatically. It was no longer a place where ideas flowed with the carefree spirit of academic curiosity; instead, an unspoken urgency weighed heavily on every conversation, as though the very air had thickened.

Conversations that had once been light-hearted now carried a weight none of us could ignore. The rules of engagement had changed, and even those who had never been particularly interested in politics found themselves drawn into discussions about China's future. There was no longer room for silence — neutrality had become a statement in itself. It felt as though we were collectively holding our breath, waiting for something to happen, though none of us knew exactly what.

What had once been theoretical discussions about freedom, the state, and reform had taken on an intensity that was impossible to ignore. Every word seemed to linger in the air, as though the weight of its meaning hadn't fully sunk in. We were no longer simply debating abstract concepts; we were preparing for something real — something that could change everything.

This shift in tone was evident not just in our conversations, but in the very fabric of campus life. The Triangle Area, once a lively hub for socializing and exchanging ideas, had become the heart of a growing movement. Tension was visible everywhere: in the haphazardly strewn bicycles, the posters plastered on every available surface, and the crowds that gathered daily to discuss, debate, and plan.

Beyond the Triangle, the rest of the campus buzzed with the same charged energy. The dormitories to the right housed thousands of students, many of whom had become caught up in the fever of political reform. On the left, the familiar shops — the general store, the bookstore, the food stalls — now felt irrelevant, as if the routine of daily life had been overshadowed by the movement. Even the bicycles, usually lined up neatly along the pavement, leaned precariously against one another or lay abandoned on the ground, their wheels spinning aimlessly. It was as if the campus itself was beginning to unravel, its once-orderly routines giving way to a chaotic and unpredictable force.

Further down the road, the university's departments and the large auditorium stood like silent witnesses to the unfolding drama. These buildings, once symbols of academic pursuit, now seemed secondary to the movement that had overtaken the campus. Students still moved in and out of classrooms, but their focus had shifted. The latest declarations, the growing debates about freedom, corruption, and China's future, held their attention.

In those early days of April, the campus felt alive with a sense of possibility, yet there was an underlying current of foreboding. It was as if we all knew that something monumental was approaching, something from which there would be no easy return. And yet, even as excitement crackled through the air, doubt tugged me. I felt torn between wanting to be part of this moment in history and feeling unprepared for what lay ahead.

I wasn't a natural revolutionary. Even as I debated with my peers, there was a part of me that wanted to retreat, to return to the safety of my dorm room, where the world still felt familiar and manageable. But the momentum was too strong to resist. Each time I stood on the edge of the crowd, watching the fervor around me, I felt a pang of guilt. Was I truly committed to this cause, or was I simply swept up by the current, too afraid to pull away?

The speeches and debates stirred something deep within me — a yearning for change, for justice — but they also filled me with fear. What if we were wrong? What if our idealism led us not to liberation, but to disaster? Yet when I looked around at the faces of my fellow students, I saw only conviction. Their certainty drew me deeper into the movement, even as doubt gnawed at me during quieter moments. I wanted to believe we were on the verge of something great, something lasting. But a voice in the back of my mind whispered doubts: What if this unstoppable energy was leading us down a path from which we could not return?

The weight of responsibility pressed down on me, but I had no answers — only questions. And yet, the determination in the faces of my friends made it impossible to turn back. Even when fear crept in, there was no escaping the pull of history being made.

Each day, I teetered between exhilaration and dread, as though I stood on the edge of a precipice, unsure whether to leap or retreat.

The excitement in the air was undeniable, but so was the fear — a low hum in the background that grew louder with each passing day. The passion for change was real, but so was the danger. The realization that my own future might be at risk gnawed at me in those quiet moments, yet I couldn't stay away. The pull was too strong.

The Death of Hu Yaobang: A Catalyst

On April 15, 1989, news of Hu Yaobang's sudden death sent shockwaves through the campus, intensifying the already charged atmosphere. Hu, a former Communist Party leader, had been a symbol of hope for many of us. He was one of the few within the system who had dared to push for political reform, and his willingness to listen to the frustrations of students like us had made him a beacon for change. His death felt like the final extinguishing of a fragile hope.

When the news broke, the campus felt as though it had been hit by a wave. Hu's death was not just an event; it was a rupture. Conversations shifted from grief to anger. His absence was a stark reminder of how easily those who pushed for reform could be silenced. For many of us, Hu had represented the last flicker of hope for change within the system. Without him, the future felt uncertain, as if the ground beneath us had given way.

Hu's death did more than trigger mourning — it opened a space for rebellion. It felt as if the last tether to a world where compromise was still possible had snapped. With Hu gone, there was no longer anyone within the system who represented the potential for peaceful reform. His death wasn't just the loss of a leader; it was the death of the belief that change could come from within the system. In that moment, we knew: if change was to happen, it would have to come from us.

Within hours, students began organizing impromptu memorials to honor Hu, but the focus of these gatherings quickly shifted. What had started as tributes to Hu Yaobang soon became platforms for students to voice their frustrations with the government. Eulogies pinned to the billboard were joined by others, and soon the calls for broader reform spread across campus. The demands were no longer just about Hu — they had grown to encompass the issues that had been simmering for years: corruption, the suppression of free speech, and the widening divide between the people and the ruling elite.

I remember standing in front of the billboard, reading one of the first handwritten tributes to Hu: "He was the one voice of reason," it read, "the one leader who spoke for us, who understood the future we were fighting for." But as more posters appeared, the message began to shift.

It was at this moment that the air began to change again. The once-bustling campus, with its disordered bicycles and makeshift gatherings, now brimmed with palpable energy. Students crowded the Triangle Area, their conversations blending with the screeching of bicycle brakes and the shuffle of feet. Street vendors, who had once been part of the mundane backdrop, now seemed out of place against the growing intensity of political dissent. The heat rising from the concrete seemed to mirror the mounting tension.

With Hu Yaobang's death, the spark had been ignited. The protests, no longer simmering beneath the surface, were now a full-fledged movement.

The Triangle: A Nexus of Revolution

The Triangle Area quickly became the epicenter of this newfound activism. Facing the billboard, students gathered in clusters, their conversations blending into the ambient noise of bicycles clattering, vendors calling out their prices, and the constant hum of movement. The familiar stores and cafés that lined the streets had become mere backdrops to the impassioned debates filling the air. Bicycles, once neatly parked, now formed obstacles in our path, as though even the physical space of the campus could no longer contain the energy of the movement.

Leaning against the stone walls of the dorms or standing on the pavement, students debated long into the night. The Triangle, once a bustling crossroads of campus life, had transformed into something far more significant. Each day, the crowd grew larger, the discussions more heated. It felt as though the entire campus had gathered at the Triangle, their collective will pushing against the boundaries that had once held us in check.

Even bicycles, once a symbol of the ordered routines of student life, now seemed to reflect the growing chaos. Some lay on their sides, tires deflating slowly, while others leaned precariously against walls or poles. It was as if the physical environment itself was mirroring the inner turmoil we all felt. Nothing was neat or tidy anymore — not the roads, not the buildings, and certainly not the movement. Like the scattered bikes, our cause sprawled out in every direction, lacking a clear path but gaining momentum all the same.

Each day brought new voices to the Triangle. Alongside the dormitories, students emerged from their rooms to join the cause, while others retreated, unsure of how far things would go. On the road that led toward the classrooms and the auditorium, professors and intellectuals occasionally passed by. Some stopped to listen, while others quietly observed the growing fervor, as if uncertain about where the movement might lead.

A Rising Movement, a Growing Risk

But even as the movement grew, a sense of uncertainty lingered. The more daring our demands became, the more ominous the consequences seemed. We all knew the risks we were taking. Speaking out against the government in such a public way was no small act. Many of us were acutely aware of China's long history of repression, and yet it felt as though we had no other choice. Hu Yaobang's death had crystallized something that had been growing for years, and now that it had been released, there was no way to turn back.

I found myself returning to the Triangle each day, not just to observe but to participate. I lingered at the edges of the groups, sometimes engaging in the debates, sometimes simply watching. There was an undeniable exhilaration in being part of something that felt so much bigger than myself. But that feeling was always tinged with fear. We all knew that the government wouldn't sit idly by forever.

Rumors began to spread with increasing frequency. Whispers of plainclothes officers mingling with the crowds, of students being quietly questioned and reported. Every glance from a stranger carried a new layer of suspicion. Was that person leaning against the wall an informant? Was the student who had just joined our conversation taking notes to report back to the authorities?

Paranoia began to spread like a contagion, infecting even the most well-meaning of us. The solidarity we had once felt so strongly began to fray as trust became a dangerous thing. Conversations that had once flowed freely now felt stilted, measured. I found myself hesitating before speaking, wondering if my words would come back to haunt me. Even the laughter we used to share felt out of place now, as though it belonged to another time.

We started to look over our shoulders, wondering if the person standing next to us was a fellow protester or an informant. Paranoia cast a shadow over the camaraderie we had once taken for granted. Trust, once implicit, became fragile and elusive. We avoided eye contact with even those we had once considered friends, afraid that a misplaced glance or a careless word could be enough to draw suspicion.

A Voice of Caution: Conversations with Professor Zhang

In the midst of all this, one voice stood out in my mind — a voice of caution. Professor Zhang, who had always been a guiding presence, remained steadfast in his belief that change was necessary, but he had his reservations about the path we were taking.

"The winds of change are blowing," he had said to me during one of our final conversations before the protests escalated. "But remember, wind can be destructive. What you and your fellow students are asking for will come at a price — a price that may be higher than you realize."

His words haunted me as I moved through the throngs of students each day. He was right, of course. What we were doing was dangerous, and none of us fully understood the consequences we might face. But the momentum felt unstoppable. We were no longer just students; we were revolutionaries, even if most of us had no idea what that truly meant.

The Triangle Area, once a place of daily routine, had transformed into a stage for history. The tension, like the scattered bicycles across the campus, lay in disarray, yet it was alive with possibility. But as the days wore on, I couldn't shake the feeling that we were heading toward something far more complex — and far more dangerous — than we had ever imagined.

A Nation on Edge

By late April, the protests had grown beyond anything we could have anticipated. The city was alive with demonstrations, marches, and sit-ins. And yet, the government remained silent. But still, the movement pressed on. There was a collective sense that we had reached a point of no return.

The death of Hu Yaobang had lit a spark, but what followed was an inferno. We were no longer simply mourning a leader; we were fighting for the future of our country. The tension on campus was palpable, but so was the hope. The choices we made felt monumental, as though each step we took was shaping history in real-time.

But as the days passed, it became clear that the government's patience was wearing thin. The growing unrest had turned into a full-scale movement — one that would not be easily quelled. What none of us knew was how close we were to the point of no return.

Chapter 7: The Beginning of the Tiananmen Protests

By late April, the sense of urgency and anticipation that had enveloped Peking University spilled over into the heart of Beijing — Tiananmen Square. What had started as a localized student movement was rapidly growing into something far larger, drawing attention from across the country. Tiananmen Square buzzed with life; the once tranquil space now flooded with bodies pressed shoulder to shoulder. The scent of sweat, the rhythmic clapping of hands, and the fluttering of protest banners in the hot breeze created a tapestry of urgency and hope. It was no longer just about student grievances; it was about the future of China itself.

As the sun dipped lower behind the horizon, the temperature in the square dropped. I shivered, not just from the chill, but from the strange quiet that had settled over the crowd as the day wore on. The clapping and chants had faded, replaced by murmurs and occasional bursts of anxious laughter. The air, thick with the smells of sweat and incense, felt heavy — as if the square itself was holding its breath.

For many of us, the move to Tiananmen felt monumental. The square held deep symbolic significance — a place where China's history had been forged, a place where the people's voices could not be ignored. As more and more students gathered in the square, the mood was infectious. There was a surge of hope, a feeling that we were on the cusp of something transformative. It was impossible not to be caught up in the fervor. We marched, we chanted, we held up banners calling for reform. In those early days, the energy in the air was electric, crackling with possibility.

But beneath the surface of that enthusiasm, quiet uncertainty began to take hold. As more people poured into the square, the movement's goals seemed to blur. What had started as a call for political reform and an end to corruption now felt diffuse, as different factions within the protest voiced different demands. Some wanted greater freedom of speech and democratic reforms, while others simply wanted an end to the economic hardship that had plagued the country for years. In the midst of it all, I found myself wondering: what were we really fighting for?

The sheer scale of the protests added to the uncertainty. Each day, the crowds grew larger, swelling with workers, intellectuals, and ordinary citizens who had been drawn to the square by the promise of change. The diversity of voices was both a strength and a weakness. On the one hand, it was clear that the desire for reform extended far beyond the student body. On the other hand, the lack of a unified message made it difficult to see how we could achieve our goals. What did we truly want? And how could we expect to get it without a clear plan?

As the square filled with faces I didn't recognize — factory workers with rough hands, families with children in tow, professors carrying signs — the clarity of our purpose began to blur. We were united, but what were we united for? A thousand voices, a thousand visions for China's future, but no single path forward.

In the midst of the sea of banners and chanting voices, I couldn't help but feel a gnawing sense of doubt. Was this movement driven by idealism, or were we simply being swept along by the tide? What once felt like unshakable hope now clung to me like a brittle shell, cracking under the pressure of the mounting tension. I could feel the weight of uncertainty gnawing at me with every passing day, as though it could be shattered at any moment by the harsh realities of the political system we were challenging.

And yet, the sense of hope was undeniable. For the first time in our lives, it felt as though change was within reach. We had taken our demands from the campus to the very heart of the nation, and the government could no longer ignore us. There were moments when it felt as though anything was possible — that the system, long resistant to reform, might finally bend to the will of the people.

But with that hope came an undercurrent of fear. The deeper we ventured into the protest, the more I realized that none of us truly knew what we were asking for, or what the consequences of our actions might be. Our chants for freedom echoed against the cold, unyielding face of the regime we were challenging. With each step, I felt the ground beneath us crack, as if we were marching on a fault line — one side driven by the rush of idealism, the other, by the dark void of the unknown. In the back of my mind, I wondered if we were naïve to think that we could bring about real change without facing severe consequences.

Each day in the square was a mix of exhilaration and anxiety. As I marched with my fellow students, I felt the weight of the moment pressing down on me. We were making history, but at what cost? Were we prepared for what might come next? Could we sustain this movement, or would it collapse under the weight of its own contradictions?

For every step I took, propelled by the electric hope coursing through the crowd, there was another moment of hesitation. One minute, I believed we could rewrite history, that our voices were finally being heard. The next, I would catch a glimpse of a soldier patrolling the edge of the square, and fear would crash over me like a wave, washing away my confidence. We were fighting for change, but what if change brought something worse?

I thought of my father, his wrinkled hands gripping the morning newspaper, always afraid to speak his mind at the dinner table in case a neighbor might overhear. For years, he'd told me to stay away from politics, to keep my head down. Now, I wondered if he had been right all along. I thought of my father's voice, worn thin by years of silence, warning me of the dangers of speaking too loudly, too boldly. 'They don't forgive,' he would say, eyes clouded with memories he never shared. His fear, passed down like a relic from another generation, felt heavier now. Maybe he was right. Maybe we were only tempting fate, daring to believe that we could change what had always been.

Despite the questions swirling in my mind, I couldn't bring myself to walk away. The pull of the movement was too strong. There was a sense that if we didn't seize this moment, we might never have another chance. And so, I stayed, torn between hope and fear, caught in the tension between idealism and pragmatism, unsure of where this path would lead.

As the protests in Tiananmen Square gained momentum, that tension only grew.

But as the days wore on, the movement began to lose its steam. It wasn't just exhaustion that slowed us down; the lack of clear leadership and unified goals began to take a toll. The call for a class boycott during the height of the protests seemed to be short-lived, though I hadn't been fully aware of it at the time. Now, students have begun drifting back to their classrooms, as if retreating into familiar routines could offer some kind of clarity. The once-large crowds in the square started to thin, and with that thinning came a sense that our purpose was beginning to fracture. The energy that had once surged through the movement was faltering, replaced by uncertainty.

Behind the scenes, however, things were more chaotic than we realized. Student leaders were struggling to keep the movement cohesive, but they weren't the only ones grappling with internal discord. Within the government itself, officials were divided on how to respond to our growing presence in Tiananmen Square. Some, like Zhao Ziyang, called for dialogue and reform, while others pushed for a harsher crackdown. The government's hesitation reflected a deepening rift, and that indecision trickled down to us, feeding our uncertainty.

Meanwhile, new forces were getting involved. The workers' unions, once hesitant, began to lend their support to our cause, sensing that the movement could serve as a platform for their own grievances against the regime. Their involvement complicated things, adding new voices and demands to an already fractured protest.

And then there was Gorbachev.

Word spread that Mikhail Gorbachev, the Soviet leader, was scheduled to visit China in just a few days. His arrival was highly anticipated — a symbol of openness and reform that many of us admired. We knew that his visit put the Chinese government in a difficult position. The international spotlight would be on Beijing, and we believed this could be our chance to force the government's hand.

Some of the student leaders, including Wang Dan and Wu'erkaixi, saw Gorbachev's visit as a potential bargaining chip. The eyes of the world would be on China, and the government wouldn't want a public relations disaster during such a high-profile visit. The leaders planned to escalate the protests ahead of Gorbachev's arrival, convinced that the government would be forced to negotiate.

But the government had other plans. Rather than risking a confrontation in front of the world, they decided to move the welcoming ceremony. The grand event, which had been planned for Tiananmen Square, would no longer take place there. The students' hope to leverage the visit faded as the government sought to avoid the square altogether.

Amidst all this, behind closed doors, the student leaders debated their next move. Internal discord had fractured the movement, and some leaders, like Wang Dan and Wu'erkaixi, were growing impatient. They had little faith in the government's offers of dialogue, dismissing them as stalling tactics. They wanted to escalate — and they settled on a hunger strike.

The strike was set to begin on May 13th, just two days before Gorbachev's visit. At first, the idea of a hunger strike drew mixed reactions. Some feared it would be too extreme, while others saw it as the only way to push the movement forward. Early attempts to mobilize students for the strike met with only modest success. Many were exhausted, unsure of what lay ahead.

That was when Cai Ling stepped forward.

I had been walking near the Triangle Area when the familiar crackle of a loudspeaker caught my attention. The sound was coming from the campus broadcast room, where Cai Ling's voice, clear and full of conviction, echoed across the square. She was addressing us from the very heart of the campus, the Triangle Area, where so many of our debates and gatherings had taken place.

"We cannot let our voices grow quiet now," Cai Ling declared, her words cutting through the stillness. "This is not the time to back down. We are standing on the edge of something great, something that could change the future of China forever. But we must show them that we are serious, that we will not be ignored."

The crowd around me began to stir, students pausing in their tracks, drawn to the urgency in her voice. I stopped as well, listening intently as Cai Ling continued.

"We need to act, and we need to act now," she said. "That is why I am calling for a hunger strike. We will refuse to eat until our demands are met. We will show the government, and the world, that we are willing to sacrifice everything for the future of our country."

The words hung in the air, heavy and electric. A hunger strike? It was a bold and dangerous step, one that would take our protests to a level none of us had anticipated. The students around me exchanged glances, their faces a mixture of shock and determination. The casual conversations that had filled the

Triangle just moments before were replaced by murmurs of urgency.

Cai Ling's emotional appeal was exactly what the movement needed. Her speech, broadcast across the square, reignited something within us. The hunger strike was not just a symbolic gesture — it was a challenge, a statement of our commitment. Her words resonated through the crowd, carried by the loudspeaker, amplifying the intensity of the moment. It was clear that this wasn't just a protest anymore. We were stepping into uncharted territory, and the risks were growing.

As I stood there, listening to the last echoes of Cai Ling's speech fade away, I felt a renewed sense of purpose, but also a deepening sense of unease. The hunger strike had raised the stakes in ways I hadn't fully considered. It wasn't just about demanding change anymore — it was about survival, about how far we were willing to push ourselves to make our voices heard.

The tension was palpable. The excitement that had once filled the square was now laced with fear and uncertainty. We were no longer just protesting — we were challenging the very fabric of the system. And as the crowd dispersed, there was a sense that we were moving toward something far bigger than any of us could predict.

Cai Ling's call for a hunger strike had reignited the passion of the movement, but with it came new dangers. We had crossed a line, and now, there was no turning back.

Chapter 8: A Million in the Streets

By mid-May, the protests in Beijing had reached a scale none of us could have imagined. What had started with a few thousand students on our campus had grown into something far larger, with over a million people flooding the streets of the capital. But this was no longer just about Beijing. The movement had spread to over 400 cities, with protests erupting across the country. Students from distant provinces were now traveling to Beijing, arriving by train and bus, determined to add their voices to the growing call for reform.

Tiananmen Square was overflowing with people, and the streets surrounding it were packed with those who had come to join us. Banners waved in the air, some hastily scrawled on bedsheets, others meticulously painted with slogans calling for freedom and reform. The sound of chanting voices echoed through the city, and for a moment, it felt as though we were on the verge of something monumental. The energy was electric, pulsing with the thrill of possibility.

Among the crowd, I spotted Li Wei, whose familiar face brought both a sense of comfort and concern. Li Wei had always approached political and social issues with a unique blend of passion and spiritual conviction. Her faith, deeply rooted in Christianity, drove her activism in a way that was unlike anyone else I knew. She had been at the heart of our small group discussions on campus, always willing to connect her beliefs with political reform and the growing call for justice. Now, standing in Tiananmen Square, I could see the weight of this moment bearing down on her.

But there was something different about Li Wei that day. As the tension in the square grew, with rumors swirling about the government's response, I noticed that Li Wei seemed unusually calm. While other students debated nervously about what might come next, Li Wei moved through the crowd with quiet confidence, speaking to small groups of students. I soon realized she was evangelizing, sharing her faith with those who seemed uncertain, offering her beliefs as a source of strength and hope.

At one point, I overheard her talking to a small group, her voice steady and reassuring. "I'm not scared," she said, her words piercing through the uncertainty that hung in the air. "Because I know that no matter what happens, I have something greater to believe in." The students around her nodded, but I could see the difference in their eyes. While many of us were driven by a mixture of hope and fear, Li Wei's faith set her apart. She wasn't just here for political reform; for her, this was something deeper, a spiritual mission.

Her calm demeanor and unwavering belief in something beyond the physical world offered comfort to those around her, but it also filled me with a sense of unease. I admired her conviction, but I couldn't shake the feeling that her fearlessness came from a place I couldn't reach. As much as I wanted to believe in the cause, the looming threat of violence and repression weighed heavily on me. But for Li Wei, fear seemed almost irrelevant. Her faith in God had made her immune to the fear that gnawed at the rest of us.

As more students arrived from other cities, the excitement grew. It reminded me of the stories I had heard about the Cultural Revolution, when students from all over China had similarly traveled to Beijing, full of idealism and fervor. There was a kind of madness in the air, as if we were swept up in something much larger than ourselves, a force we couldn't fully control or understand. I couldn't shake the feeling that this was history repeating itself, but in a way that left me unsettled. Was this the same kind of energy that had fueled the Cultural Revolution? And if so, what was the outcome we were really seeking?

The sheer size of the crowd was staggering. Over a million people had taken to the streets, swelling Tiananmen Square and stretching down Chang'an Avenue as far as the eye could see. It was exhilarating to see so many young people, from every corner of China, coming together for the same cause. They came in waves, exhausted from their journeys but full of determination, their bags slung over their shoulders and their faces lit up with hope. They joined us in the square, swelling our ranks, and for a moment, it felt as though the entire country was united behind our movement.

Li Wei was among those determined faces, and her presence was a grounding force. She had always believed that real change started with the individual, and that political reform was an extension of living out one's faith. As we watched the crowds chant and wave their banners, she turned to me and said, "This is important, but remember — change isn't just about what we demand from the government. It's about how we treat the people around us every day." Her words stayed with me, a reminder that even in the midst of mass protests, there was a deeper moral obligation to live out the values we claimed to stand for.

Standing among the crowd, I couldn't help but feel swept up in the euphoria of the moment. We had done it. We had brought the city — and, it seemed, the nation — to a standstill. People were smiling, laughing, and chanting, their faces alight with optimism. It was hard not to feel that we were part of something historic, something that could change the course of China's future.

But even as I soaked in the energy around me, a sense of unease began to creep in. The crowd was massive, but the movement felt directionless. Everyone was here, but for different reasons. It felt as though the unity that had brought us this far was starting to unravel, stretched thin by the weight of so many competing voices.

As I wove through the crowds, I overheard conversations that reflected this growing confusion. People debated endlessly about what we were fighting for and what the next steps should be. Some talked about demanding meetings with government officials, while others insisted on continuing the hunger strike. And then there were those who believed that simply being here, in such vast numbers, was enough to force change. I found myself wondering: What were we really fighting for now? And who was leading us?

The hunger strike, which had begun a few days earlier, was still ongoing, but it was clear that it wasn't having the immediate impact we had hoped for. The government hadn't moved to meet our demands, and the strikers were growing weaker by the hour. I saw some of them lying on the ground, pale and exhausted, their resolve still strong but their bodies beginning to fail them. The sight of them filled me with admiration, but also with fear. How far were we willing to go? How long could we sustain this?

Li Wei joined me later that day, and we stood together at the edge of the square, watching the crowds. "We need more than just numbers," she said quietly. "We need a clear vision, something that goes beyond demand for reform. Otherwise, this could all fall apart."

Her words echoed my own growing doubts. The leadership of the movement, once so vocal, now seemed hesitant and divided. Behind closed doors, they debated the next steps, unsure of how to move forward. The government, meanwhile, remained silent, watching us, waiting. The lack of response was unnerving, as if they were simply biding their time, hoping the movement would collapse under its own weight.

Despite the size of the protests, there was a growing sense of helplessness. We had mobilized millions, but to what end? Without a clear plan, without strong leadership, it felt as though we were standing on the edge of a precipice, unsure of whether to leap or retreat. The euphoria of the moment was slowly being undercut by the nagging realization that we might not know how to finish what we had started.

Li Wei turned to me and smiled, her eyes full of resolve, but there was something else too — something I couldn't quite name. In the shadow of her unwavering determination, there was a quiet sadness, like she already knew how far this could go. I wanted to ask her, to pull her back from the edge, but the words never came. Instead, I just nodded, pretending that her conviction was enough for both of us.

Amidst all this uncertainty, our graduation process had been halted. Normally, by this time of year, students would be looking ahead to receiving their diplomas in early July and stepping into their new jobs. But now, everything was in limbo. The protests had ground everything to a halt, and none of us knew when — or if — things would return to normal. The future, once so carefully planned, now seemed as uncertain as the movement itself.

By May 20th, the government had declared martial law, and everything changed. The once-celebratory atmosphere in the square gave way to fear and uncertainty. Soldiers began appearing in the streets, their presence as a stark reminder that the situation was far more serious than many of us had realized. I couldn't help but think of the Cultural Revolution again, of the chaos and violence that had gripped the country back then. Was this where we were headed?

As the reality of martial law set in, I began to hear that many local students were choosing not to return to Tiananmen Square. It made sense; they had the option to retreat, to return to the safety of their homes or dormitories. That decision, I later learned, was one of the reasons the death toll among local students remained low. But for those who had traveled from other cities, who had come to Beijing with nowhere else to go, staying in the square felt like their only choice. The weight of responsibility had shifted, and those who remained were left to face whatever was coming.

I made the difficult decision to leave Beijing. It wasn't an easy choice, but I couldn't ignore the growing sense of dread that had taken hold of me. This movement, which had once felt so full of promise, was now teetering on the edge of disaster. The protests had reached a scale we had never imagined, but the path forward was uncertain. The leadership was faltering, the goals were fragmented, and now, with martial law in place, the stakes had never been higher.

As I left the city, I couldn't shake the feeling that this would be the last time I'd see some of the faces I had marched beside. As the train pulled away, I thought of Li Wei, standing resolute in the square, and a strange weight settled in my chest — as though time itself had begun to stretch, pulling us apart. I wondered if I would ever see her again, but I pushed the thought aside, clinging to the hope that somehow, against all odds, she would find her way through this.

Chapter 9: Conversations with Professor Zhang

By late May, the sense of excitement that had once fueled the protests had begun to unravel. The crowds in Tiananmen Square were still vast, the banners still waved, and the chants still echoed through the city, but there was a palpable shift in the air. Fear had seeped into the edges of the movement, and the more time passed, the more I felt the weight of that fear pressing down on me. I could no longer ignore the growing sense that we were marching toward something far darker than we had anticipated.

In the midst of this uncertainty, I sought out Professor Zhang. His voice of reason had always been a guiding force in my academic life, and now, I needed his perspective more than ever. As the protests spiraled into something none of us could control, I found myself questioning the very movement I had once believed in so strongly.

I found him in his office on a humid afternoon. The room was a sanctuary of calm, with books lining the walls and the air thick with the scent of old paper and dust. Sitting across from him in this familiar space, I couldn't help but feel the growing dissonance between the chaos outside and the quiet wisdom of Professor Zhang's world.

"I've been expecting you," he said, his voice low and steady. "You look troubled."

"I am," I admitted, my voice betraying the inner turmoil I had been trying to suppress. "Everything feels like it's slipping out of control. We've come so far, but I don't know where we're headed anymore."

Professor Zhang leaned back in his chair; his eyes fixed on me. "That's the nature of movements like this," he said. "They begin with hope, with the belief that change is possible. But hope alone is not enough. You need a clear goal, a strategy. Without that, even the most passionate movements can lose their way."

I felt a surge of frustration. "But isn't idealism what drives change? Without it, how do we even begin to challenge the system?"

He smiled faintly, shaking his head. "Idealism is powerful, but it's also dangerous. You see, throughout Chinese history, student movements alone have never mounted to much. Students are not the real targets of the government — they're just byproducts of casualty. The government knows that the real threat comes when students are joined by workers or farmers, and when they are led by visionary intellectuals. That's when a movement becomes meaningful and impactful."

I hesitated before asking the next question that had been weighing on me for days. "Do you think it's even possible to fight against a one-party government? Not just in China, but anywhere in the world. Is it really possible to make any meaningful change unless the party is willing to change?"

Professor Zhang was silent for a moment, his expression thoughtful. He seemed to consider my question carefully before answering. "That's a very difficult question," he said finally. "One-party systems, by their nature, are designed to resist change. They are built on control, and control is something they will fight to maintain at all costs. You're not just fighting against policies or laws; you're fighting against an entire system designed to preserve itself."

He leaned forward slightly, his gaze steady. "In China, this system has been refined over decades. The government has perfected the balance of maintaining power while appearing to offer concessions when necessary. They are experts at waiting, at playing for time. That's why, unless there is a significant shift — something that forces their hand — real change is unlikely to happen from the outside."

His words settled heavily in the room. For the first time, I began to realize the enormity of what we were up against. I had always known that the Chinese government was powerful, but I hadn't fully considered just how deeply entrenched that power was, or how resistant it would be to any challenge, no matter how justified.

"So, what are we doing, then?" I asked, my voice quieter now. "What's the point of all this if it won't lead to real change?"

Professor Zhang sighed softly. "The point is that you're showing the world that people are willing to stand up for what they believe in, even when the odds are against them. You're shining a light on the issues, and that in itself is powerful. But if you're asking if this movement will bring down the one-party system — no, it won't. Not unless the party itself decides to change."

His answer was brutally honest, and it left me feeling more conflicted than ever. For weeks, I had been swept up in the energy of the protests, believing that we were on the brink of something monumental. But now, sitting here, I began to wonder if we had been naive, if our hopes had blinded us to the reality of the forces we were up against.

"And what about the Cultural Revolution?" I asked, grasping for something to compare this moment to. "Do you think this is similar?"

Professor Zhang paused again, his expression thoughtful. "There are some similarities," he said slowly. "The Cultural Revolution, much like this movement, started with idealism — a belief that the system could be torn down and rebuilt into something better. Both were led by young people, students, full of passion and a desire to change the world."

He leaned forward, his gaze sharpening. "But there's a crucial difference. The Cultural Revolution was sanctioned by those in power, even manipulated by them. Mao himself ignited that fire, using students as a tool to eliminate his rivals. It was chaos disguised as revolution, but it served a political purpose."

I listened closely, absorbing his words. The Cultural Revolution had always been a haunting presence in my mind, the stories of violence and destruction woven into the fabric of our history. But what Professor Zhang was saying made sense — that movement had been supported, even encouraged, by those at the top, while ours was fighting against the system itself.

"And this?" I asked, gesturing vaguely to the city outside. "What about now?"

Professor Zhang's expression grew somber. "This movement is different. It's not being used by the leadership to settle political scores. This is the real opposition, and that's what makes it so dangerous. The government sees it as a threat, and they're watching carefully. They won't hesitate to act if they feel their power is truly at risk."

His words struck a chord. I thought of the protests, of the students who had traveled from distant provinces, full of idealism and hope. But it was true — many of us had begun to realize that our movement, powerful as it seemed, lacked the broader support needed to create real change. Workers had begun to show interest, and there were whispers of unions forming, but without unified leadership or a clear vision, the movement was beginning to falter.

Professor Zhang continued, his voice more serious now. "The Communist Party knows better than anyone the power of aligning students with workers and farmers, under the leadership of visionary intellectuals. That's how they came to power, and they know the risks if such alliances form again. But right now, your movement is fragmented. And as long as that remains the case, the government knows they can control it."

"What are you saying, Professor?" I asked, my voice quieter now.

"I'm saying that you need to be careful," he replied, his tone gentle but firm. "I know how much you believe in this movement, and I respect that. But you also need to recognize the limits of what you can achieve. The government has remained silent for a reason. They're waiting, watching, and when they strike, it won't be with words."

His words brought an image to my mind — the soldiers who had been stationed just outside Beijing for days, watching the city from a distance. There had been rumors circulating, whispers of armed forces waiting for the government's signal. But until now, we had convinced ourselves that the soldiers wouldn't act, that the government wouldn't dare resort to violence. Sitting across from Professor Zhang, I began to question that belief.

"But what if we're too late?" I asked. "The soldiers, they're already waiting. What if the government decides to use force?"

Professor Zhang sighed, and for a moment, the weight of his years seemed to settle heavily on his shoulders. "That's always a possibility," he said softly. "You're always in danger when you challenge power, especially when that power has no intention of compromising. I'm not saying you should abandon the fight, but I am saying you need to be smart about how far you're willing to go. Idealism can only carry you so far."

I sat in silence, absorbing his words. I thought of the students still gathered in the square, their faces full of hope, but also of exhaustion. I thought of Li Wei, standing resolute in her faith, unafraid of what lay ahead. And I thought of myself, caught somewhere in the middle — torn between my desire for change and the growing realization that we might be in over our heads.

"What do you think I should do?" I asked, feeling more vulnerable than I had in weeks.

Professor Zhang looked at me for a long moment before answering. "Only you can make that decision. But know this: movements like these, they take a toll. Not just on those in power, but on the people who lead them. You need to decide if you're willing to pay that price."

His words lingered in the air, and I felt the weight of them settle deep in my chest. For weeks, I had been driven by the belief that we were fighting for something bigger than ourselves. But now, for the first time, I began to wonder if that belief was enough to justify the risks we were taking.

"I'll think about it," I said quietly, though I already knew that his words had planted the seed of doubt.

Professor Zhang nodded, his expression thoughtful. "Whatever you decide, be careful. Change doesn't happen overnight, and sometimes, the bravest thing you can do is step back and live to fight another day."

As I left his office, I couldn't shake the feeling that something fundamental had shifted within me. The idealism that had once driven me felt distant, replaced by a creeping sense of doubt. I had always believed that the movement was worth the risks, but now, with Professor Zhang's words echoing in my mind, I wasn't so sure.

The days that followed were a blur of tension and uncertainty. The soldiers remained stationed outside the city, their presence a silent threat that loomed over everything we did. The protests continued, but the energy had changed. There was fear now, a sense that we were standing on the edge of something far darker than we had anticipated.

In the end, it was Professor Zhang's words that tipped the balance. His warning had resonated with the fears I had been trying to suppress, and as the situation in Beijing grew more precarious, I made the difficult decision to leave. It wasn't an easy choice, but it felt like the right one.

As I boarded the train out of the city, I couldn't help but think of the faces I had marched alongside. I thought of Li Wei, her calm confidence, a stark contrast to the uncertainty I felt. And I thought of Professor Zhang, his quiet plea for caution still echoing in my mind. I wondered if I would ever see them again, but I pushed the thought aside, focusing instead on the road ahead.

Chapter 10: The Crackdown

By early June, the protests had reached a tipping point, though I was no longer in Beijing to witness the final, brutal crackdown firsthand. The last time I saw Li Wei was late at night on campus, just before I made the difficult decision to leave. Her calm, unwavering presence had given me a strange sense of peace, though now, in the face of the violence that was unfolding in the capital, that peace felt like a distant memory.

The reports of the crackdown began filtering through in the early hours of June 4th. At first, it was difficult to believe — the images and stories seemed so far removed from the hope that had filled Tiananmen Square just weeks earlier. But as more news trickled in, the reality of what had happened became impossible to deny. The government had made its move, and it had done so with overwhelming force.

I wasn't there to witness the tanks rolling into the square or to hear the crack of gunfire as soldiers opened fire to unarmed protesters, but I could picture it all too vividly. The last time I had stood in Tiananmen, the square had been alive with energy, filled with banners and chants of hope. Now, it had become a place of death and devastation.

The first wave of information came from the news, then from friends who had managed to flee the city. What had started as a peaceful protest had become a massacre. Soldiers had descended on the square in the dead of night, firing into the crowds without hesitation. Tear gas filled the air, and the sounds of gunfire and screams echoed through the streets. The death toll was rising, though the government was doing everything in its power to suppress the true number.

As I sat listening to the reports, my thoughts kept returning to Li Wei. The last time I had seen her, she had been on campus. Her words had stayed with me — her belief that something greater was guiding her through this moment. Now, as the stories of the crackdown unfolded, I couldn't shake the feeling that something terrible had happened to her.

It was a few days later when the news of her death finally reached me.

Li Wei had been in Tiananmen Square when the soldiers arrived. She had remained, as she always did, calm and resolute, even as the chaos erupted around her. A mutual friend who had managed to escape the square relayed the story: Li Wei had been standing near the front of the crowd, offering words of comfort to those around her, when the soldiers opened fire. She had been shot, her body crumpling to the ground as those around her scattered in panic.

I hadn't been there to see it, but the image of her lying in the square, her life cut short, haunted me. Li Wei had always been fearless, her faith giving her a sense of peace that I could never fully understand. And now, that peace had carried her through to the very end.

The grief hit me harder than I had expected. In the days leading to my departure from Beijing, I had felt conflicted about the movement, torn between my desire to believe in its potential and my growing sense of fear. Li Wei, on the other hand, had never wavered. Even as the situation grew more dangerous, her resolve had remained unshaken. Her death, so senseless and violent, felt like the final blow to whatever idealism I had left.

The crackdown in Tiananmen Square had shattered more than just the protest. It had shattered the belief that we could make a difference, that our voices could change anything. The government's response had been swift and brutal, and now, the hope that had once filled the streets of Beijing felt like a distant dream. For those of us who had believed in the possibility of reform, there was only grief and disillusionment.

As the days passed, more stories of the crackdown emerged. The death toll was uncertain — some said hundreds, others claimed thousands — but what was clear was that the government had crushed the movement with ruthless efficiency. Soldiers patrolled the streets, ensuring that any lingering resistance was quickly stamped out. Tiananmen Square, once a symbol of hope, was now a place of death and silence.

On the evening of June 3rd, the government issued an emergency announcement, broadcast across the city, urging citizens to "stay off the streets and away from Tiananmen Square." It was a clear warning, a final attempt to deter the massive crowds that had gathered in defiance. Yet, even as the government made its plea for people to retreat, broadcasts from protesters echoed across university campuses, urging students and citizens to arm themselves and assemble at intersections and the Square.

The contrast between the two broadcasts could not have been starker. On the one hand, the government's warning crackled over radios and loudspeakers, its tone dire and final, a thinly veiled threat. On the other, the calls from the protesters rang out, full of desperation and defiance. They urged students to resist, to take a stand, even as the possibility of violence loomed larger by the hour.

Most local students had heeded the government's warning. Fearful of what might come next, they chose to stay on their own campuses, sheltering themselves from the danger they knew was just beyond the gates. It was a rational decision, one that I now wished I had made sooner. But there were others, like Li Wei, who could not be swayed by fear.

While the government's announcement was enough to convince many to stay away, Li Wei had responded to the calls from the protesters with characteristic resolve. Despite the growing danger, she remained determined to stay on the course, to see the movement through to the end.

As the night wore on, the streets of Beijing grew eerily quiet, save for the occasional rumble of military vehicles making their way toward the city center. Soldiers had been stationed outside the capital for days, waiting for the order to move. Now, they were on the march.

Li Wei's roommates, along with many others, had already made the difficult decision to stay away from Tiananmen Square, retreating to the relative safety of campus. But even there, the fear was palpable. Rumors spread quickly, fueled by panic: after the crackdown at Tiananmen, Peking University would be next. The idea that soldiers might storm the campus sent students into a frenzy, scrambling to find places to hide.

Li Wei's roommates, like many others, fled, hoping to find refuge. They went to a local classmate's home, hoping the family would take them in. It was late at night when they arrived, their faces streaked with sweat and exhaustion from the tension of the previous days. The streets were unnervingly quiet as they approached the small house, its windows dark. They knocked softly, and after what felt like eternity, the door creaked open a crack.

Behind the door stood their classmate's mother, her face pale and drawn with fear. She peered out at them, her eyes darting nervously up and down the street. "What are you doing here?" she whispered, her voice barely audible, as if speaking too loudly might invite danger into the house.

Li Wei's roommates exchanged glances, their desperation clear. "We just need a place to stay," one of them said, her voice hoarse from days of shouting and fear. "Just for the night."

The mother hesitated, her hand gripping the edge of the door tightly. She glanced back into the house, where the dim glow of a single lamp illuminated the hunched figure of her husband, sitting at the kitchen table. He didn't look up, didn't say a word, but the weight of his silence was oppressive. The room felt like a sanctuary, safe from the chaos outside, but also stifling in its fear.

"I'm so sorry," the mother whispered, her voice trembling. "But it's too dangerous. We can't take that risk."

The students pleaded softly, their voices tinged with panic. "Please, we have nowhere else to go. Just for a night, we won't stay long."

The mother shook her head, her eyes filling with tears. "I wish we could help; I do. But if anyone finds out... we can't. I'm sorry."

The door closed gently, leaving Li Wei's roommates standing on the doorstep, their hearts heavy with the rejection. The night seemed darker now, the silence of the streets almost suffocating. There was no anger, only a deep understanding of the fear that had taken hold of everyone. No one could afford to take risks anymore, not even for friends.

With nowhere else to turn, the students left the city. They boarded a train to Hebei province, their faces drawn and exhausted as they huddled together in the dim light of the train car. The rhythmic clatter of the tracks was the only sound as they fled the city that had once been their home, leaving behind the chaos and uncertainty of Beijing for the relative safety of the countryside. They stayed with another classmate for a few days, hiding and waiting for the storm to pass before finally returning to campus, unsure of what they would find when they arrived.

The fear that had gripped the campus in those days was unimaginable. The rumors alone had been enough to send students fleeing, and even when they returned, the sense of safety that had once existed was gone. The crackdown had left its mark, and none of us would ever be the same.

In the aftermath, as the stories of the massacre spread, grief was overwhelming. Li Wei's death weighed heavily on me, but she wasn't the only one we lost. The faces of friends and classmates who had marched alongside us now haunted me — some of them had disappeared, never to be seen again. For those of us who survived, the world felt darker, the future more uncertain than ever.

The movement that had once been so full of hope had been crushed under the weight of the government's brutal response. The dream of reform, of change, had been shattered, leaving in its wake only fear, loss, and disillusionment. But even in the face of such devastation, Li Wei's unwavering faith and courage remained with me. Her death, though tragic, served as a reminder that even in the darkest of times, there were those who stood firm in their beliefs, who refused to be silenced.

As the weeks passed, the reality of what had happened began to settle in. The government moved quickly to erase any trace of the protests, scrubbing the streets of the blood that had been spilled and silencing any dissent. The media reported nothing of the true scale of the massacre, and those who dared to speak out were swiftly punished. Tiananmen Square, once a symbol of hope, had become a graveyard for the dreams of a generation.

In the end, it was not just the protesters who suffered, but the entire country. The crackdown sent a message that reverberated far beyond the streets of Beijing — a message that any challenge to the government's authority would be met with unrelenting force. The idealism that had once united us was gone, replaced by fear and resignation.

But even in the midst of that fear, I couldn't forget Li Wei. Her strength, her courage, and her unwavering belief in something greater than herself continued to inspire me, even in the darkest moments. And though I had left Beijing before the final crackdown, I knew that her spirit would remain with me, a reminder of the cost of standing up for what we believed in, and the sacrifices that so many had made in the name of change.

The violence of June 4th had torn through the heart of our movement, and it had also left a scar that would never fully heal. We had lost more than just a protest — we had lost our friends, our dreams, and our faith in the possibility of a better future. And yet, despite the overwhelming sense of defeat, the memory of those who had given their lives, like Li Wei, would continue to live on, a testament to the power of hope, even in the face of unimaginable loss.

Chapter 11: The Aftermath

The grief was overwhelming. As I sat in the silence of my own thoughts, I wondered if leaving had been an act of cowardice. Had I abandoned the cause too soon, leaving others to fight battles I was too afraid to face? Or had I simply accepted what the rest of us couldn't yet admit — that the fight had already been lost, and I had spared myself from witnessing the inevitable end? Now, in the cold aftermath, all that was left was silence. No words could fill the void left by the lives lost, the dreams shattered. It wasn't just the people who had died that night — it was the movement itself, the hope we had clung to, and the belief that our actions could bring about meaningful change.

Li Wei had always believed in something greater than politics, something eternal. I had envied her conviction, even as I questioned it. And now, I wondered if that faith had been her undoing. She had stayed in Tiananmen Square, not for the fleeting promises of democracy, but for something far deeper — and that was what made her stronger than any of us. I just wished strength had been enough to keep her alive.

The reports from friends who had stayed behind painted a bleak picture. The government's erasure of the Tiananmen Square protests was swift and deliberate. In the days following the crackdown, it was as though the protests had never occurred. The vast square, once packed with banners, students, and citizens calling for reform, was suddenly sterile and empty.

In the early morning hours, before most people were awake, teams of workers descended upon the streets like ghosts, wiping away every trace of the protest. The square, littered with broken banners, blood-stained clothing, and abandoned personal items, was scrubbed clean. The asphalt had been washed down, as if rinsing away the blood would also erase the memories of those who had fallen.

Workers moved with practiced efficiency, gathering anything that hinted at the chaos of the previous nights. Piles of discarded signs and leaflets were quickly swept into garbage trucks. Torn banners, once raised high with messages of hope, were stuffed into black bags and carted away. Bullet casings, broken shoes, even the remnants of burned candles used for vigils — all removed, leaving behind a pristine, undisturbed surface.

Tiananmen Square itself became a sanitized space. The stone slabs gleamed under the sun, as if untouched by the violence that had stained them just days before. The tanks, soldiers, and barricades had vanished without a trace. The lingering smell of tear gas and gunpowder had been replaced by the faint scent of disinfectant, a cleanliness that seemed to mask the truth. Government workers even repainted walls and lampposts where protest graffiti had been hastily scrawled, ensuring that no message of dissent remained.

The streets leading to the square were eerily quiet, free of the debris that had once lined them. Public transportation resumed, the buses and taxis rolling over the same streets where thousands had once marched. No scorch marks remained from the Molotov cocktails, no shattered windows or remnants of hastily erected barricades. It was as though time had rolled backward, returning the city to an unsettling normalcy.

Even the official government messaging was calculated. State media made no mention of the protests or the violence. No reports of deaths or injuries appeared in the papers or on television. Instead, the country was told to move forward, as if the events of June 4th had been nothing more than a nightmare to be forgotten.

In place of the protestors' cries for justice and reform, the government launched campaigns of unity, emphasizing the importance of stability and progress. Billboards with smiling families and workers began to fill the city, extolling the virtues of a harmonious society, erasing any mention of the chaos that had temporarily disrupted their version of reality.

To the casual observer, Beijing appeared unchanged, as if the protests had never happened. The crowds of students and workers had been replaced by everyday citizens going about their routines. But beneath the surface, a deep scar remained — invisible, but felt by everyone who had been there, by everyone who knew what had been lost.

The deliberate erasure of the movement sent a chilling message: not only had the protests failed, but even the memory of them would be denied. Tiananmen Square, once a symbol of hope, had become a graveyard of history, its truth buried under the weight of denial and fear.

The event, once the pulse of a nation's collective demand for reform, was wiped clean from the public record. The Tiananmen protests became a forbidden topic, absent from textbooks, blacklisted from the media, and whispered about only in secret. Within weeks, it was as if the movement had never existed. The government had not just silenced the protests; they had obliterated the memory of them, leaving behind a generation that would grow up with no knowledge of the sacrifices made in that square.

Those of us who had participated in the protests were left to pick up the pieces. The student leaders who had once rallied us with impassioned speeches had fled, leaving their followers behind to face the consequences. Most had escaped to the West, where they took advantage of scholarships, business opportunities, and what we in the Chinese community bitterly called "blood cards" — the green cards awarded to those whose involvement in the protests had made them political refugees. The irony was not lost on us. While their escape secured their futures abroad, it left the rest of us grappling with the aftermath of a movement that had been crushed underfoot.

Few of the prominent leaders stayed true to the ideals they had once championed. Instead, many found success in foreign lands, building careers and lives far removed from the struggles they had once rallied against. The democracy they had once demanded for China now seemed a distant memory, replaced by personal ambitions. It was a bitter pill to swallow, watching from afar as they thrived while we mourned the dead.

Their speeches had once filled us with fire, their words a beacon of hope. But now, those same voices were silent, their owners scattered across foreign lands, building new lives on the bones of our failed revolution. I had once looked up to them, seen them as the harbingers of change. But now, all I could feel was the bitterness of betrayal. They had preached sacrifice, but it was we who had been left to pay the price. They had traded our ideals for green cards — blood cards, as we bitterly called them — and left us behind to bury the dead.

Within China, the crackdown had reshaped everything. At Peking University, the campus was unrecognizable. Where once we had debated the future of our country, now silence reigned. The clubs, once filled with lively arguments and spirited conversations, were dissolved. Lectures that had once encouraged critical thinking were now carefully measured, with professors choosing their words as if walking on thin ice. It felt like the soul of the university had been ripped out, replaced by the hollow echo of fear and obedience. A mandatory year of military training was added to the curriculum for freshmen — a constant reminder of the government's power and the consequences of defiance. Professors told us that we were the luckiest class, having experienced the last years of a truly open university. From 1985 to 1989, they said, had been the golden era of Peking University, a brief window when students could think freely and question authority without fear of repercussion. That window had slammed shut, and we were left to wonder what had been gained — and what had been lost.

I often found myself asking whether the movement had accomplished anything at all. In the days after the crackdown, it seemed impossible to see any positive outcome. The government had tightened its grip on the nation, making it clear that any dissent would be met with swift and brutal retaliation. The dreams of reform, of greater political freedom, had been crushed. We had pushed for change, but instead, the walls around us grew higher. We had fought for something larger than ourselves, but the cost had been far too high.

The world had seen our struggle, but what difference had it made? Outside of China, the Tiananmen protests became a symbol of resistance and sacrifice, but within the country, the memory was erased. The government had done its job too well. Thirty-five years later, the Tiananmen Square massacre was a ghost story whispered only in the darkest corners. A generation had grown up with no knowledge of what had happened on that day. I watched them — young people with no idea of the sacrifices we had made, no memory of the banners, the cries for justice. It was as if we had never existed. The government had not just silenced us; they had erased us from history. The lessons we had tried to teach — the hope we had fought to keep alive — were forgotten.

And yet, as I reflected on those months, I couldn't help but wonder if the movement had left a deeper mark, one not visible in the immediate aftermath. Change, as Professor Zhang had warned me, rarely happens overnight. The seeds we planted in those streets, the voices that had cried out for justice, would not disappear so easily. Even if the government had succeeded in suppressing the memory of the Tiananmen event, it could not erase the desire for change that had taken root in the hearts of so many.

But still, the question lingered. Was it all in vain? Had Li Wei's death, and the deaths of so many others, been for nothing? I found myself struggling to reconcile the hope that had driven us with the grim reality of what we now faced. For every student who had fled, there were hundreds left behind, their lives forever altered by the movement's failure. Peking University was no longer the place of intellectual freedom it had once been, and China had retreated further into the tight grip of state control.

As I looked back on those final months, I couldn't help but think of the faces I had marched beside. Many of them were gone now — lost to the violence of the crackdown or scattered to the winds, their dreams of democracy and reform abandoned. And yet, even in the face of such overwhelming defeat, I still held onto a sliver of hope. The government could erase the memory of the Tiananmen event from the history books, but it couldn't erase it from my heart. And perhaps, one day, the seeds we had planted would bloom into something greater than any of us had imagined.

But for now, all that remained was grief. Grief for Li Wei, grief for the movement, and grief for the China we had dreamed of but would never see. The idealism that had once driven me was gone, replaced by the sobering understanding that real change, if it was ever to come, would take far more than we had been prepared to give. In the aftermath of the Tiananmen event, the only certainty was that nothing would ever be the same again.

I had once believed that idealism could ignite change, like a spark that would set the world aflame. Now, it felt more like a faint candle in a vast, unrelenting darkness, fragile and easily extinguished by the cold hand of reality. Professor Zhang had warned me that our movement was destined to fail — that systems built on control would always find a way to crush dissent. He had been right. Idealism alone was no match for the walls of power and fear that had been constructed over decades. And yet, without that flicker of belief, what remained to guide us through the dark?

Chapter 12: Farewell to China

By the time I left China in 1995, it wasn't a sudden decision, nor was it born purely out of the events of 1989. The Tiananmen Square protests had left an indelible mark on me, but in the years that followed, I focused on my work and life within the system. I was employed by the central government, working for the National Family Planning Committee, the very institution responsible for enforcing the one-child policy. It was the early 1990s, and in Beijing, the rules were strictly upheld. Even married couples who met the required conditions to have a child were forced to apply for a birth permit before getting pregnant.

Typically, couples would apply for the permit as soon as they became eligible, avoiding any legal complications in case of an unplanned pregnancy. But when I found myself unexpectedly pregnant, the permit had not yet been processed. In most cases, obtaining an exception for an unplanned birth permit was a simple matter of logistics, but due to delays — caused by our recent move to a new government building — my situation was more complicated. There was a risk I might not receive the permit in time for my due date. This was no small problem, especially considering that I worked for the very organization responsible for enforcing the law.

Our new government building was impressive, a far cry from the outdated hotel we had previously occupied. The view from our office window was striking, with Beijing's streets bustling below. Neon signs buzzed with life, pedestrians hurried through crosswalks, and cyclists wove between cars. Yet, from behind the glass, the scene felt more like a silent movie, distant and unreachable, as though the city's vibrancy couldn't penetrate the rigid walls of bureaucracy. The office floors were polished marble, the scent of fresh paint still lingering in the air, and the floor-to-ceiling windows let in a harsh glare of sunlight. The city stretched below, the streets alive with activity. It was a scene of energy, but from where I stood, it felt cold and impersonal, much like the institution I worked for.

I shared my new office with Li, a man in his late fifties who had once been a department head. Though nearing retirement, he still carried himself with a vitality that made him seem much younger than his years. He was of average height, with a lean and healthy build, and his face was always friendly, framed by graying hair that gave him an air of wisdom. Despite his demotion from a position of real power, he had a calmness about him, as if he had long accepted the way things worked in the system. His friendly demeanor made him approachable, and I trusted him in ways I didn't trust many others in the office.

Li had seen enough to understand how the system truly worked, and it was he who first warned me of the real stakes. One afternoon, as we sat in the office, the noise of the city far below us, Li leaned in and spoke in a low voice, his words cautious yet direct. "If you agree to consider abortion," As Li spoke, his fingers absentmindedly tapped the desk, a habit I noticed he often did when he was particularly stressed. He gave me a quick glance, perhaps checking if I truly understood what was at stake, before continuing in his usual calm, measured tone, "they won't bother getting the permit for you. They'll delay and delay until it's too late. But if you refuse to even consider it, they'll make sure you get the permit."

His words hung in the air between us, a quiet understanding of how things worked. I had known it all along, but hearing him say it so plainly made it real. Li's eyes, though tired from years of navigating the system, still held a glimmer of quiet defiance. "Show up to the office every day," he continued, glancing at the paperwork on his desk. "No matter what they tell you. Even if they suggest you can stay home, don't listen. Come in, sit at your desk. As long as you're physically here, they can't punish you. You're protected."

There was a strange comfort in Li's advice — a reassurance that despite the rigid system, there were still ways to fight back. He knew the rules well enough to understand their loopholes, and I knew then that I could trust him. His quiet presence in the office became a lifeline, a reminder that I wasn't entirely alone in navigating this delicate situation. Li was more than just a colleague — he became a trusted friend during this difficult time. His quiet wisdom and advice were invaluable, helping me navigate the bureaucratic maze and offering a sense of support that I desperately needed.

My superior, the head of my department, was different. She was known for her unyielding adherence to policy. Her office, with its dark-red wooden desk and rigid, matching chairs, reflected her strict nature. The floor-to-ceiling windows gave her a sweeping view of Beijing, but inside the office, everything felt suffocating. One day, she called me in for a conversation.

"Understand," she said, her voice devoid of any warmth, "this isn't about you. It's the policy. We all have to follow the rules." Her face was a mask of cold professionalism, her sharp features illuminated by the glare of the city skyline behind her. Her hair was pulled back in a tight bun, and she wore a gray suit that made her appear even more severe. She asked me, in the same tone one might use to discuss mundane paperwork, whether I would consider terminating the pregnancy if the permit didn't come through in time.

I didn't hesitate. "No."

Her thin lips pressed together in a line, her hands resting neatly on the desk in front of her. The sun streaming through the windows cast a harsh shadow across her face, accentuating the lines of frustration and bureaucratic indifference. She gave a small, resigned sigh but said nothing more.

The encounter left me shaken, but Li's words had already given me a way forward. I could see the system for what it was now—a machine, impersonal and indifferent. As I sat in my apartment that evening, watching the city below, the streets bathed in the neon glow of shop signs and streetlights, I knew my time in Beijing was coming to an end. The city felt both familiar and alien to me now — a place I had called home, yet one that had slowly suffocated the ideals I once held. The life bustling below me, with its chaotic mix of bicycles, cars, and pedestrians, felt disconnected from the cold, calculated decisions being made in the office I worked in.

I had no real assignments at work anymore. With nothing to occupy my time, I spent my days practicing the best Eugenics methods our committee had promoted for healthy newborns. These were practices designed by another department to foster optimal child development. I would carry a small music box to the office every day, pressing it against my stomach to play classical music, believing that these early influences would help shape my child's future. My coworkers would smile indulgently, but I didn't care. It gave me a sense of control in a situation where I often felt powerless. It was my way of making sure my child had the best start, even in the most absurd circumstances.

Despite the mounting tension with my superiors, something surprising happened — my coworkers remained friendly. I had worried they might distance themselves from me, fearing any association with a colleague caught up in such a sensitive situation. But instead, we continued with our daily routine as if nothing had changed. During lunch breaks, we still played poker around the small table in the break room, laughing and chatting, the way we always had. It was a strange juxtaposition — the warmth of their camaraderie set against the cold bureaucratic machinery I was pushing against. In those moments, the office felt less like a battlefield and more like a place where people could still connect despite the walls of rules and regulations around us.

It was right before the annual performance review, and I knew what was coming. I received a failing grade, and the department began making moves to fire me.

But they had underestimated me. I worked in the Law and Policy Division, and I knew my rights. The law was clear: no employer could fire a pregnant woman. Armed with this knowledge, I confronted them. I made it clear that if they fired me, I would take them to court, and regardless of the verdict, they had already lost. First, their own employee had gotten pregnant without a permit, and second, they had tried to fire a pregnant woman. Although they would claim it was for incompetence, nobody would believe that a Peking University graduate was unfit for a central government research position.

The tension during those weeks was unbearable. I remember sitting in the sterile waiting room, the cold air from the vents brushing against my skin as I waited for their decision. My palms were damp with anxiety, my heart pounding with both fear and defiance. They had the power to ruin me, to strip away everything I had worked for. But I also knew I had leverage — they couldn't afford the scandal, not with their reputation and control hanging in the balance.

When the final agreement came, I felt a quiet surge of victory — a rare moment where the system, for once, had not beaten me. In the end, we reached a compromise. They agreed to maintain my employment status, complete with full medical benefits and salary, until the end of my legal maternity leave of nine months, and in that time, I began to plan for a new life outside of China.

As the days passed and my departure grew closer, I found myself in moments of quiet doubt. Could I really leave behind everything I had ever known? The streets I had walked, the friends

I had fought alongside, the country I had once believed could change? Yet, every time those doubts crept in, I felt a stronger pull — toward a future free from the crushing weight of policies and permits. Singapore wasn't just a place on a map; it was a beacon of possibility. And that possibility outweighed every fear.

As I packed up my office for the last time, I couldn't shake the feeling that I was leaving behind more than just a job. I was walking away from the country that had shaped me, the place I had called home all my life. But in leaving, I was also acknowledging that the ideals I had once held — of reform, of change within the system — were no longer aligned with the reality I faced. It felt like I was severing a part of myself, yet at the same time, I understood that clinging to a sense of national identity wasn't worth the price of my freedom or my child's future. My love for China hadn't disappeared, but it had transformed — into something quieter, distant, and more complicated.

Leaving China didn't fill me with sadness; in fact, it was quite the opposite. As I walked through the airport terminal with my son in my arms, the weight of the past began to lift. The whispers of control and fear were fading with every step, replaced by the hum of possibility. Ahead of us was Singapore, a place I had never called home, but one that offered the freedom I had long craved. I didn't know what the future would hold, but for the first time in years, the uncertainty was thrilling. The day I boarded the plane with my young son, I was excited. As the plane ascended, Beijing shrank beneath us, and with it, the burdens I had carried for so long. The future was unknown, yes, but that was part of its beauty.

For the first time in years, I wasn't bound by anyone else's rules. Life ahead was mine to build, step by step, with my son by my side. And as we soared through the clouds, the weight of the past fell away, replaced by the exhilarating sense of possibility that stretched out before us. There was a palpable sense of anxiety, but also a glimmer of hope. The head of my department had been the voice of the old system, one that demanded control over the most intimate aspects of my life. But as I prepared to leave, I wasn't bitter. I was ready.

Stepping into the unknown was daunting, but it was a challenge I embraced. I wasn't leaving behind my country in defeat; I was moving forward with the belief that there was more waiting for me, and for my son, beyond its borders.

Part 2: Strangers in New Land

Chapter 13: Arriving in Singapore

I arrived in Singapore with my first husband, Wayne, in 1995, after he accepted a postdoctoral position at the National University of Singapore. Wayne had just earned his PhD in mechanical engineering from Tsinghua University, and the opportunity felt like a lifeline after the abrupt end of my own career in China. The university had arranged an apartment for us, offering a temporary sense of stability in a world that now felt entirely new.

Changi Airport was unlike any place I had ever seen. The moment we stepped off the plane, I was struck by the cool, crisp air — completely free from the usual airport bustle and staleness. It was like stepping into a sanctuary. The floors gleamed, polished to perfection, while the soft lighting created a calming, almost dreamlike atmosphere. I felt like I had entered a different world, far from the chaotic, noisy terminals I was used to in China. The ceiling stretched high above us, making the terminal feel open and airy, as though the space itself breathed.

The sheer scale and cleanliness of the airport was remarkable. Signs in English, Chinese, Malay, and Tamil guided us effortlessly, reflecting the multicultural tapestry of this small island nation. As we moved through the corridors, lush greenery greeted us at every turn — plants and flowers were artfully arranged throughout the space, giving the airport a vibrant, tropical feel. There was a sense of nature in harmony with modernity. Even the air smelled fresher, as if it had been carefully filtered to welcome travelers with a breath of comfort. Outside, I could see manicured gardens and water features that sparkled in the sunlight. Fountains bubbled gently, their soft sounds blending with the peaceful hum of the terminal, as if even they had been designed with purpose, serenity in motion.

It wasn't just an airport; it was a statement of Singapore's meticulous attention to detail. Every corner, every surface, had been polished to an extraordinary shine. I couldn't help but feel like the country itself was welcoming me with open arms, promising order and calm amidst the uncertainties of this new chapter in our lives.

As we made our way through the city toward our new apartment, **Singapore's streets** amazed me. Wide, tree-lined boulevards were bordered by impeccably maintained sidewalks, lined with towering modern buildings that gleamed in the sunlight. The sleek glass facades of skyscrapers reflected the city's dazzling lights, while flowering trees dotted the sidewalks, adding a touch of natural beauty to the urban landscape. There was a sense of balance between nature and progress here that I had never encountered before.

Unlike the chaotic streets of Beijing, where bicycles and pedestrians competed with cars in a whirlwind of noise and movement, Singapore felt ordered and calm. Traffic moved smoothly, without the constant honking of horns I had grown accustomed to. Even the busiest parts of town, like **Orchard Road**, felt more like an elegant parade than the frantic rush I had known back home. Everything moved with purpose but without haste. The air was fresh, almost unnaturally clean for a city, and the streets were litter-free. It felt surreal.

After a month of settling into life, Wayne and I made a difficult decision. In China, it was customary for grandparents to help raise young children before school age. So, after some discussion with my mother, we decided to send our son back to China to stay with her. The separation was painful, but it was what we believed was best for his care during those early years.

Once our son was back in China, Wayne and I rented a master bedroom in an HDB (Housing Development Board) flat near the university. The owner of the flat was an elderly single woman who lived in the other bedroom. The streets around our flat were as orderly as the rest of the city — tree-lined avenues, with impeccably maintained roads and wide sidewalks. The community around us felt alive but never chaotic. People moved with purpose but without the frantic pace I had known in Beijing. Even the traffic was calm. Cars glided silently down the streets, many of them luxury vehicles, given Singapore's high taxes on car ownership. The cleanliness was astonishing — no litter, no debris, just well-kept pathways and neatly trimmed shrubs lining the roads. It was clear that everything in Singapore was planned, regulated, and maintained to perfection.

At first, we did our grocery shopping and cooked at home, eager to maintain a bit of the familiar routine. But soon, we realized that the old woman never cooked. Curiosity got the better of me, and I asked her where she ate. She smiled and told us that Singaporeans didn't really cook at home because the food at the nearby food courts was both delicious and affordable.

We began to explore the local **food courts**, and they became a central part of our lives. These food courts were the heart of every neighborhood, bustling yet impeccably clean, offering an overwhelming variety of dishes. Unlike the crowded, sometimes chaotic street markets of China, Singapore's food courts were well-organized and hygienic. The stalls were filled with Chinese stir-fried noodles, fragrant Indian curries, savory Malaysian satay skewers, and even some Western dishes. The aromas of fresh spices, sizzling meats, and fried noodles filled the air, making it impossible to resist the temptation to try something new each time. Every meal was a delight, prepared fresh right in front of you, and despite the richness of the flavors, I never felt overindulgent. The portion sizes were just right, enough to leave you satisfied but never too full. Eating at the food court felt like discovering a treasure trove of flavors at an affordable price.

The **HDB flat** itself, while modest, reflected the efficiency of Singaporean life. It was simple but comfortable, with white-tiled floors and functional furniture. Our landlady was kind but quiet, keeping to herself most of the time, though her presence offered us a sense of stability in this new place.

As I began to explore more of Singapore, I became increasingly impressed with the city's public transportation. **Singapore's buses** were unlike anything I had experienced in China. The buses were clean, air-conditioned, and surprisingly spacious. I had never seen a bus completely full. It was a stark contrast to Beijing, where getting onto a bus often meant squeezing into an overcrowded space, with people standing shoulder to shoulder, jostling for room. Here in Singapore, the buses moved through the city with a quiet efficiency, connecting every corner of the island. The bus routes were easy to navigate, and the air-conditioned interiors provided a welcome respite from the tropical heat. For most people, buses were the preferred mode of transport, as cars were prohibitively expensive.

Owning a car in Singapore came with a heavy price — there was a 100% tax on all vehicles, and that wasn't the end of it. To even be eligible to buy a car, you needed a permit, and the maintenance costs were sky-high. Fuel was expensive, and cars with over 100,000 miles would fail inspection. For many, it was cheaper to take taxis or buses to work than to bear the financial burden of car ownership. Everything in Singapore was designed with efficiency and practicality in mind, from the transportation to the layout of the city itself.

We frequented **Orchard Road** often, Singapore's famous shopping district. The wide sidewalks were lined with towering shopping malls and high-end boutiques. Every time I walked down its broad sidewalks, I felt like I was wandering through the future. Towering malls stretched upwards, their glass windows reflecting the busy streets below. Neon signs advertising the latest designer brands flashed everywhere, tempting passersby with promises of luxury and exclusivity. On either side, greenery softened the city's modern edges — trees lined the streets, and small gardens were tucked into every available corner. In between the commercial glitz, I'd spot clusters of people sitting on benches, enjoying an ice cream cone or resting after hours of shopping. It was a shopper's paradise, but I quickly realized that the prices for brand-name goods were far beyond what I was willing to spend. On my first shopping trip, I bought a pair of Italian leather shoes for S$98 and a silk dress for S$150 — both seemed like bargains compared to China, where such items would have cost several thousand yuan. But I soon learned that I could find equally beautiful clothes at a fraction of the price elsewhere.

With our son now safely in my mother's care, I turned my attention to finding a job. My English skills, though strong in reading and writing, were weak in speaking and listening, which made job-hunting difficult. But I was determined to adapt. It was then that I found my first job at a **futures trading company**. One of the girls from my workplace introduced me to **Chinatown's underground shopping center**, where everything was unbelievably cheap. In those narrow, bustling shops, I found clothes for less than S$20 that fit just as well as anything I had seen on Orchard Road. The shoes I had splurged on wore out quickly, and I regretted wasting so much money on them. The silk dress, however, remained a favorite — though, for a while, I hated it because it reminded me of my foolish spending. I never cared much about brands; my standard for clothing was always how it looked on me. My friends often assumed my clothes were expensive, but when they learned where I bought them and how cheap they were, they were always amazed.

Chinatown's underground shopping center was like a hidden treasure chest, teeming with bargains that seemed too good to be true. The narrow corridors were packed with shops, their tiny displays brimming with clothes, shoes, and accessories that could rival anything sold at Orchard Road's high-end boutiques. The contrast between the glitzy storefronts of Orchard Road and the down-to-earth atmosphere of Chinatown was striking. Here, you didn't shop for prestige or luxury — you shopped for practicality. Bargaining was expected, and the thrill of getting a great deal made every shopping trip exciting. I soon became a regular, honing my skills as a savvy shopper.

Our after-work routine took us to the riverside, where our boss would treat us at a nearby bar after the trading markets closed. The **river** glistened under the city's evening lights, and as I sat with my colleagues, I began to absorb bits of Singapore's history and culture. English had been declared the official language, but many older generations, who had attended Chinese schools, struggled with the transition. The government had initially allowed Chinese schools to continue, but over time, these students found themselves at a disadvantage in the job market. Slowly, Chinese schools were phased out, and English became dominant, though most people spoke with heavy accents that were difficult for even native English speakers to understand.

Through these interactions, I learned to adapt, and though my grasp of spoken English was far from perfect, I began to navigate the language and the culture with growing confidence. Singapore was a place of contrasts, blending the old with the new, East with West. And amidst all this, I was learning to find my place.

In the months that followed, I started to find my rhythm in Singapore. The unfamiliar streets, once overwhelming with their neatness and order, now felt more welcoming as I began to understand the city's pulse. While we had sent our son back to China for the time being — a decision that weighed heavily on me — I knew it was a temporary separation, a step toward ensuring his care while I found my footing. Adjusting to a new land was not without its challenges, but each day brought small victories: learning the language, navigating the transport, and finding comfort in the local food courts. There was still much to learn and overcome, but with each passing day, the hope of building a future here seemed a little brighter. I wasn't just surviving anymore; I was beginning to adapt.

Chapter 14: Starting a New Career

After months of adjusting to life in Singapore, I found my footing when I accepted a job as a Chinese language teacher at a private kindergarten. This wasn't my first teaching job, though it felt worlds away from where I had begun. After graduating from Peking University, I was first assigned to a Communist Party School to teach Democratic Socialism in Eastern Europe. I was only 21, and my students — middle-level local officials — were nearly twice my age, around 40. It was an unusual situation, and the irony wasn't lost on me. I was teaching party ideology, yet I had never joined the Communist Party myself, a fact the school deliberately hid from my students.

The Party School where I taught was nothing like the cheerful, child-filled halls of my new workplace. It was a solemn place with dimly lit classrooms, where stern-faced officials sat with notebooks open, jotting down political theory as I lectured from a podium. The walls were adorned with portraits of Marx, Engels, Lenin, and Mao, each casting a heavy gaze over the room. The air was thick with a seriousness that permeated every interaction. My job there had been instilling ideological discipline, delivering lessons on how socialism was evolving in Eastern Europe, all while knowing that I wasn't fully part of the system myself.

For three years, I navigated that unique role, delivering lectures with a sense of detachment. My time there gave me a strong foundation in public speaking and managing a classroom, but I was always aware that I didn't quite belong. My life had felt like a balancing act — remaining professional, yet emotionally distant. That role hadn't been about nurturing or inspiring; it had been about reinforcing a system I wasn't entirely aligned with. After three years, I decided to take the national exam for a position at the National Family Planning Committee. Out of 221 candidates, I was the only one offered the job. The odds had been in my favor, and stepping into that role had felt like a leap toward something bigger.

But that life in China now seemed so far away. Here in Singapore, my new job couldn't have been more different. Teaching at the kindergarten brought me back to the basics of human connection. The classrooms were bright and filled with the sounds of children's laughter. Colorful posters of Chinese characters hung on the walls, and the smell of fresh crayons and glue sticks filled the air. My lessons were simple — songs, stories, and games designed to introduce young children to the Chinese language. It wasn't about politics or ideology. It was about helping children learn to communicate, to express themselves in a language that connected them to their cultural roots.

The kindergarten had three Chinese language teachers, including myself. One of the teachers, Anna, was an older woman who had attended Chinese schools in Singapore before they were phased out. Her face was etched with lines of experience, and she carried herself with quiet dignity. She spoke little English and often seemed isolated from the other staff, except for Joyce, another Chinese teacher who was around my age. Joyce had moved to Singapore through marriage. She was practical, almost to a fault, and had once told me that when she was searching for a husband, her two main criteria were that both of his parents were deceased and that he was an only child. It was a pragmatic approach, but it suited Joyce perfectly.

Both Anna and Joyce confided in me about the subtle condescension they felt from the English-speaking teachers. The English teachers seemed polite on the surface, but there was always an underlying sense of superiority. Anna and Joyce struggled with their daily summaries, which each teacher was required to write in English at the end of the day. Their English was limited, and the task felt daunting to them. While I sympathized with their frustration, I realized my situation was different. My English, though not perfect, was strong in writing. I had scored full marks in grammar on the TOEFL exam, and writing the daily summary was an easy task for me.

One day, an English teacher came to me, visibly surprised. "I saw your summary," she said, her voice filled with an odd mix of respect and disbelief. "It's perfect. I didn't expect that."

I could tell from her tone that they hadn't expected much from me, despite knowing I had graduated from Peking University. It was as if they assumed that because I was a Chinese teacher, I wouldn't have a strong command of English. Her reaction marked a turning point. From then on, the English teachers treated me differently, with more respect. I was no longer just another Chinese teacher; I had earned a place in their eyes as someone who could navigate both worlds. Even Anna and Joyce began to rely on me, asking for help when they needed to communicate with the English-speaking staff.

Cindy, my teaching assistant, was an essential part of my success in the classroom. She was young, probably just out of high school, with a round, chubby face and short hair that always framed her face neatly. Despite her youth, she was extremely capable and organized. The children in our class were typical toddlers — mischievous and always eager to test the boundaries of new authority figures. At the beginning, I struggled to maintain order in the classroom. The children sensed my uncertainty and were quick to take advantage of it. Cindy, however, had a natural way with them. She assisted me in maintaining control when things became chaotic, stepping in just at the right moments to settle disputes or calm a tantrum. Her help was invaluable, and I was deeply grateful for her support.

Each teacher had a teaching assistant, but I always felt Cindy went above and beyond what was expected. She could anticipate the children's moods and knew how to distract them with small tasks or games when they were about to act out. Her youthful energy, combined with a quiet authority, commanded the children's respect in the ways I struggled to in the beginning. Little by little, I gained favor from those toddlers. Their mischief became more playful than rebellious, and eventually, going to work wasn't something dreadful. The day I was able to teach the class on my own, with minimal help from Cindy, I felt an immense sense of pride. It was a small victory, but it was mine, and it marked my growth as a teacher in this new chapter of my life.

The kindergarten itself was a mix of cultures, reflecting the diversity of Singapore. The children came from a variety of backgrounds — Chinese, Malay, Indian, and Western — and the classrooms echoed with a chorus of languages. English was the dominant language of instruction, but Chinese remained an important part of the curriculum. The school's layout was spacious and well-organized. Bright murals decorated the walls, and the playground outside was a haven of laughter and activity. The air was filled with the sounds of children playing, their shoes tapping against the tiled floors, and the occasional chime of the school bell signaling the end of a lesson.

My colleagues were a varied group. Aside from the English-speaking teachers, there was one teacher with a Bachelor's degree in Divinity. Her husband was a pastor at a local Chinese-speaking church, and she often sat with me during breaks, chatting about life and inviting me to attend her husband's Sunday services. At first, I was hesitant. My years of studying religion as an atheist had shaped my views, and while I respected different beliefs, I had never considered them for myself. But her warmth and persistence wore down my resistance, and I eventually accepted her invitation.

One Sunday, I attended a service at her church. The atmosphere was welcoming, but the idea of faith was still foreign to me. That day, a guest speaker was giving the sermon. She was a remarkable woman who had earned her PhD in Buddhism from Tokyo University, yet had converted to Christianity. She was now working on her second PhD, this time in Theology. Her presence commanded the room, and though I can't recall her exact words, I remember feeling something stir within me. For the first time in my life, I felt as though I had glimpsed something beyond the material world, a sense of the supernatural that I had never believed in before. That day marked a turning point for me, a small step on the path toward faith, though I wouldn't fully embrace Christianity until much later.

As I navigated this new job, I found teaching young children to be deeply rewarding in a way I hadn't expected. The children's enthusiasm was infectious. Their eyes would light up when they successfully wrote a new character or recited a sentence in Chinese. It wasn't just about language — it was about watching them grow in confidence, knowing that I was helping shape their understanding of the world. Each day brought small victories, and those moments made the challenges of adapting to life in a new country feel more manageable.

The salary wasn't much, but it gave me a sense of independence. It allowed me to contribute financially, and the structure of my days gave me a sense of purpose. With Wayne busy at the university and our son still in China, I had often felt adrift. The job provided an anchor, a way to feel connected to the community around me. And while it was far from the political roles I had once held, it offered a kind of fulfillment that those positions had never given me.

Occasionally, I reflected on my past life in China. My role at the Party School and later at the National Family Planning Committee seemed like distant memories, part of a life I had left behind. Those experiences had shaped me, but they no longer defined me. Here in Singapore, I was building something new, something rooted in education and personal growth. The transition from political educator to kindergarten teacher had been a dramatic one, but it had also been liberating.

Outside of work, I continued to attend the Chinese-speaking church occasionally. Though I still had many questions about faith, I found myself more open to the idea of spirituality. The conversations I had with the teacher whose husband was a pastor deepened my curiosity. She never pressured me, but her quiet confidence in her beliefs was compelling. Over time, the seed that had been planted by the PhD guest speaker began to grow, and I found myself contemplating faith in a way I never had before.

Teaching at the kindergarten became more than just a job; it was a way for me to contribute to the community, to connect with others, and to find my place in this new chapter of life. While I still missed my son deeply, I found solace in the children's laughter, the relationships I built with my colleagues, and the satisfaction of teaching. Singapore, once unfamiliar, now felt like a place of opportunity — a place where I could grow, adapt, and build a future not just for myself but for my family. Though there were many challenges ahead, I approached them with a renewed sense of purpose, knowing that each day brought me closer to creating a life of my own in this city.

Chapter 15: Loneliness and Cultural Displacement

The initial excitement of arriving in a new country, while exhilarating, quickly gave way to an overwhelming sense of isolation. The busyness of adapting to a new city, the challenge of adjusting to a different job, and the excitement of exploring unfamiliar streets had masked an emotional void that I didn't recognize at first. As the days passed and life in Singapore began to take on a routine, the reality of being so far from home, from everything familiar, settled in.

I had left behind not just a country, but a way of life that had shaped me for almost thirty years. The feeling of cultural displacement hit me hardest in the quiet moments — late at night when the city finally grew still, and I found myself alone in the small bedroom of our HDB flat. It was in those moments, as the sounds of the city faded away, that the weight of my new reality would close in. I missed the crowded, noisy streets of Beijing, where every corner felt familiar. I missed the smell of home-cooked meals and the comforting buzz of family conversations that had filled my life. But most of all, I missed my son.

Sending him back to China had been a practical decision, but it left an ache that I couldn't shake. His absence was like a void in my life that no amount of teaching or exploring could fill. I wondered every day if I had made the right decision — if he was happy, if he missed me, if he would remember me. The separation from him made everything feel more distant and unfamiliar. Even though I knew he was in good hands with my mother, the emptiness lingered.

While I had made some connections at work, I struggled with the language barrier, which amplified my sense of isolation. Despite being able to write and read English fairly well, my spoken English and listening comprehension were still weak. The frustration of not being able to express myself clearly in conversation left me feeling inadequate. I was surrounded by people — on the buses, at work, in the food courts — but I felt alone. It was a strange sensation, to be in the middle of a bustling, vibrant city, yet feel like a stranger in every conversation.

The cultural differences deepened this sense of displacement. Singapore's efficiency, though admirable, made life feel somewhat mechanical. Everything was meticulously organized — too organized, almost. People were polite, but distant, and interactions felt transactional. I missed the spontaneity of life back in China, where the chaos of everyday interactions — negotiating prices at the market, running into an old friend on the street — added color to the monotony. Here, life moved smoothly, but there was a lack of warmth, of human connection, that left me feeling unmoored.

Even the simple things — like food — reminded me of my displacement. Although Singapore was known for its diverse food scene, I often found myself missing the specific tastes of home. I longed for the comfort of my mother's cooking, the rich flavors of Beijing's street food, and the unique blend of spices and sauces that had been a staple in my life. The food courts offered variety, but they couldn't replace the familiar taste of home.

The longer I stayed, the more I realized that it wasn't just about missing home; it was about the deeper sense of cultural belonging that I had left behind. In China, I understood my place in the world — my identity was tied to the people, the customs, and the history that surrounded me. But here, in Singapore, I felt untethered. I was an outsider, navigating a new culture that I didn't fully understand, and it was exhausting. Every interaction was a reminder that I didn't quite belong, and that feeling of being out of place seeped into every aspect of my life.

As time passed, I began to better understand Singapore's political structure and the philosophy that shaped its government. The system was built on the belief that paying high salaries to government officials would foster integrity and prevent corruption, ensuring that the best and brightest served the country. The government wasn't just a body of representatives; it was a collective few, chosen elites who were thought to know what was best for society. In this, it was a dictatorship of sorts, but a benevolent one — loved by the people and admired for the way it ran the country with such remarkable efficiency. Singapore was a society that thrived on order and control. Even something as simple as chewing gum was banned because of the inconvenience it posed to public cleanliness.

Life in Singapore was practical, efficient, and — at times — lifeless. The government-issued HDB flats where we lived, while well-maintained and functional, lacked personality. They were sterile, devoid of the quirks and individuality I had once known in the alleys of Beijing or the traditional homes of old China. The TV shows, filled with pop culture, felt shallow, and local news only seemed to reflect the carefully polished image of a country always striving for perfection.

But this perfection came at a price. Singapore had no mountains to climb, no valleys to explore, no Great Wall stretching across the horizon. There were no ancient temples to discover, no Summer Palaces filled with the echoes of history. The seasons never changed — there were no autumn leaves falling like fiery rain, no winters to brace for, no spring blossoms. Even as an island, Singapore didn't boast the golden sand beaches that might have made up for its lack of historical culture. Instead, everything felt the same, day in and day out.

In an effort to shake off the gnawing sense of loneliness, I began exploring more of what Singapore had to offer. One weekend, I decided to visit Sentosa, a popular island destination that promised sun, entertainment, and a brief escape from the everyday routine. It was well-known for its attractions — beaches, resorts, and amusement parks — and I thought maybe a day spent by the water would help lift my spirits.

Sentosa, though marketed as a tropical paradise, felt oddly sterile. It was beautifully maintained, like everything else in Singapore, but I couldn't shake the feeling that it was more of an engineered experience than a natural one. The beaches weren't the sandy expanses I had imagined; instead, they felt man-made, with meticulously groomed sand and artificial waves. The palm trees swayed in the breeze, but there was something almost too perfect about the setting, as if it were designed for a postcard rather than real life. I wandered along the shore, watching families play in the water and tourists snapping photos of the sea.

As I walked, I found myself longing for the rugged coastline of China's beaches, where the waves crashed against the shore in unpredictable rhythms and the sand was rough underfoot. Sentosa was beautiful, yes, but in a way that felt distant and disconnected. It was a reminder of how much I missed the imperfections of home — the natural beauty that couldn't be manufactured.

But amidst this overwhelming sense of sameness, there was one place that truly impressed me — Sentosa's Sea World. It was unlike anything I had ever seen, and it took my breath away. The moment I stepped into the underwater world, I felt as though I had been transported into a realm where the boundaries between land and sea blurred. Massive aquariums stretched out before me, their glass walls holding back the vibrant, pulsating world of the ocean. Schools of fish swam gracefully through the water, their silvery bodies catching the light in mesmerizing patterns. Coral reefs, with their stunning array of colors, created an underwater landscape that seemed almost too beautiful to be real. I could have stood there for hours, completely entranced by the beauty and mystery of the ocean world. It was as though Sentosa's Sea World had captured a slice of the planet's most vibrant and awe-inspiring ecosystems, bringing them to life in a way that felt both intimate and grand.

One of the most magical parts of Sentosa's Sea World was the underwater tunnel. Stepping into it felt like entering another world entirely. The curved glass arched above and around me, creating the sensation that I was walking beneath the ocean, surrounded by sea life on all sides. As I moved through the tunnel, sea creatures swam above, to my left, and to my right, their movements graceful and mesmerizing. Giant rays glided overhead, their wide, elegant wings spreading like silent shadows. Schools of vibrant fish darted playfully beside me, their shimmering colors reflecting the soft light filtering through the water. Sharks cruised just beyond the glass, their powerful forms both awe-inspiring and fearsome. The entire experience felt surreal, as if I had been transported into the very heart of the ocean, surrounded by the beauty and mystery of marine life. It was a serene, immersive world that made me forget the bustling city outside.

I didn't know it at the time, but Sentosa's Sea World would set the bar for every aquarium I would visit in the future. In years to come, I would visit the Sea World in San Diego, touted as one of the best in the world, and I would feel a pang of disappointment. London's famed aquarium left me feeling the same way. None of them could quite compare to the magic I had felt at Sentosa, where the sea felt closer than it ever had before, where each creature seemed more alive and every color more vibrant. It was a place of wonder that stood out starkly against the otherwise monotonous landscape of Singapore.

The trip to Sentosa had been meant as an escape, but instead, it made me confront the reality of my displacement even more. I was a tourist in this city, not just in the literal sense, but in the deeper sense of belonging. I could visit all the attractions, enjoy the perfectly manicured parks, and marvel at the city's efficiency, but it wasn't mine. Singapore was a place I lived in, but it wasn't a place I felt rooted to.

Despite the beauty of places like Sentosa, there was an undeniable loneliness that followed me. Singapore, for all its efficiency and safety, wasn't home. It lacked the warmth of familiarity, the deep cultural ties that I had once taken for granted. Each day felt like a repetition of the last, and as much as I tried to adapt, there were moments when I longed for something more. The structured order that had first impressed me now felt suffocating at times, as if there was no room for the spontaneity or the messiness that life needed to truly thrive.

These moments of displacement, of feeling disconnected from the world around me, came and went like the ebb and flow of the tide. I missed the chaos of Beijing, the history, and the culture that had shaped my identity. In Singapore, everything was modern, forward-thinking, and efficient — but it lacked the deep roots that I so desperately craved.

Sentosa, with its stunning Sea World, was a rare escape. Yet even in the midst of such beauty, there was a longing inside me. It was as though the underwater world, with all its vibrant life, mirrored the isolation I felt on the surface. I was surrounded by people, by the hum of a city that never stopped moving, but deep down, I felt alone.

This chapter of my life, like so many others, was one of transition. I was building a new life, but it came with its fair share of struggles. As much as I tried to embrace Singapore, there were times when the loneliness was overwhelming, and I couldn't help but feel like a stranger in this meticulously organized land.

Singapore was a small island, just 20 by 30 kilometers. It was a city of practicality, a place where every square kilometer was planned and utilized, but it lacked the natural beauty and historical depth that I had taken for granted in China. The result was a growing sense of cultural displacement that left me feeling adrift, yearning for the familiarity of home.

Loneliness wasn't just about missing my family or the familiar rhythms of my life in China; it was about feeling out of sync with the world around me. I missed the sense of depth that came with living in a place steeped in centuries of tradition. Here, life felt surface-level, practical, and organized, but it lacked the character and texture I had once taken for granted.

But amidst the loneliness and cultural displacement, there was also growth. The struggle to find my footing in this new life forced me to confront parts of myself that I had never questioned before. It made me more self-reliant, more introspective, and more aware of my own resilience. Slowly, I began to see that displacement, while painful, also brought with it the possibility of transformation. I wasn't the same person I had been when I left China, and perhaps that was part of the journey. I was learning to redefine what home meant, not as a physical place, but as something I carried within me.

Singapore, with all its differences, was teaching me new ways to adapt, new ways to understand myself and the world around me. The isolation, while difficult, was also a space for reflection, a place where I could begin to shape a new sense of belonging — not tied to a country or a culture, but to the life I was building for myself. And though the feeling of being adrift remained, there was a flicker of hope that maybe, just maybe, I could find my place in this new world after all.

Chapter 16: Thoughts of Family and China

As the months turned into years, Singapore became more familiar, but the ache of separation from my family in China never faded. No matter how much I settled into my new life, the thoughts of my family, my son, and the life I had left behind remained constant companions. On quiet nights, my mind often wandered back to simpler times in China, to moments that were deeply rooted in my family's history.

I remembered a particular winter break during my time at Peking University. It was around Spring Festival — the Chinese New Year, the most important holiday in China — when I visited my grandparents in Zhejiang. My mother had joined me, using her rare one-month vacation to visit her parents. For her, this was a rare reunion. She had spent most of her life in Xinjiang, far from her family, and had only visited her parents a handful of times since she left home at 18. On that trip, I saw the ritual to honor our ancestors for the first time — a simple ceremony, but one filled with deep meaning. My grandparents lit incense and offered symbolic gifts, maintaining a connection to the past even as the world around them changed.

What made this ritual even more poignant was the fact that my grandparents' house itself had survived through the turbulence of Chinese history. It had been inherited from my great-grandfather, passed down through generations. It was a miracle that the house never had been confiscated, even during the Cultural Revolution, when so many families lost everything. Somehow, it had remained a sanctuary for my family — a place where our history lived on, despite the upheaval. The house stood as a testament to survival, to the resilience of my ancestors in the face of uncertainty and political chaos.

The house was modest but filled with pride. My grandmother, in particular, was proud of the fact that it had a private bathroom — a rare luxury in China at the time. I remember her expressing disdain for the poverty that forced many to use public bathrooms without doors between toilets, an indignity she never had to face. The private bathroom in her home was something she valued deeply, as a symbol of dignity, also as a reflection of the life she had always known. The house was a mark of her status, of a family that had weathered China's changing tides without losing its footing.

In contrast, life in Xinjiang, where I grew up, had been different. We didn't have private bathrooms — public ones with open toilets served the whole community, and at night, we used chamber pots. I could now see how much that private space meant to my grandmother. It wasn't just about comfort; it was about holding onto dignity in a world that often stripped it away.

As I settled into life in Singapore, memories like these from my past would surface, reminding me of the contrasts between the life I had left behind and the life I was trying to build. Singapore was a land of efficiency and modern comforts, but it often felt detached from the deeply rooted traditions and family history that defined my identity. Life here was polished, structured, almost too perfect. But it lacked the warmth of my grandmother's house, the stories my parents told, and the history that had survived in the walls of that old house in Zhejiang.

I often thought of my son. He was growing up without me, under the care of my mother, and though I knew he was in good hands, it pained me to think of the milestones I was missing. His first words, his first steps — these were the precious moments of his childhood that I would only hear about secondhand. Every letter my mother sent was bittersweet, filled with updates about his growth, his developing personality, and how much he had begun to resemble me. They were a reminder of what I was missing.

China was still home in my heart, even though I had made a life in Singapore. The sense of belonging I felt there, the deep connection to its culture and history, was irreplaceable. Here, everything felt polished, but it also felt sterile. There were no bustling hutongs, no old men playing chess on street corners, no women selling homemade dumplings from small carts. The traditions and daily rhythms I had taken for granted were gone, replaced by the structured, orderly pace of Singapore.

I found myself thinking more about my parents as well. My mother had always been a strong, stoic figure in my life. She had raised me to be independent, to prioritize my work and responsibilities, but now I wondered if she ever regretted encouraging me to leave. Did she miss me as much as I missed her? Or was she simply proud of the life I was building for myself, even from afar? My father had always been quieter, more reserved, but I knew he cared deeply. I thought of him often, wondering if he felt the same void that I did, separated by thousands of miles from the family we both cherished.

The decision to leave China had always been an easy one, in spite of all the challenges that would come with starting a new life in a foreign country. I had been raised to seize opportunities, to step out into the world when the right moment presented itself. My mother's own experiences shaped that outlook. She often spoke about how leaving home for Xinjiang had impacted her life, and those stories were ingrained in me. Back in her youth, China operated under a much more rigid system. There were six workdays a week, with only Sunday as a rest day, and no concept of annual vacation days as we know them now. For workers like my mother, who had left their hometown to work in another region, there was only one precious month of vacation to visit parents every ten years.

My mother had left home at 18, filled with the same sense of determination that she passed down to me. But because of those strict rules, she only managed to visit her own parents twice before she turned 40. By the time I was born, she had already accepted that her time with family would be rare and limited. That was simply life in those days. Things changed in China later on — there was a policy update that granted one month of vacation for visiting parents every four years for married workers, and every year for unmarried workers. But for my mother, the damage had already been done. By the time I graduated from Peking University, she had only visited her parents four times since she was 18.

When I reflected on that, I realized how different my life had been, even before moving to Singapore. I had already visited my parents three times before I got married, something my mother could never have done at my age. I had also spent my nine-month maternity leave at my mom's house after my son was born, which brought us even closer together. It was a luxury of time that my mother had never experienced with her own parents, and she was incredibly happy that we were able to see each other so often before I left for Singapore. Our relationship, though still shaped by distance, was different from the one she had shared with her family.

When I returned to China with my son, just one month after arriving in Singapore, my mother was thrilled. The joy in her eyes, the way she held my son — those moments made the distance seem more bearable. I remember thinking how fortunate we were to have these opportunities to see each other, to remain connected even as our lives were pulled in different directions. She hadn't known when she'd see me again after I left for Singapore, but now she had her grandson to cherish, a piece of me to hold onto.

Still, even though the decision to leave China had been easy, it didn't mean the path that followed wasn't filled with complexities. As much as I had taken the opportunity to move abroad without hesitation, the ties that bound me to my family were strong, and I carried the weight of those connections with me, always. China was more than just a country; it was a part of me, a part of my family's history, and it influenced every decision I made, every reflection I had about my life in Singapore.

The reality of that decision sometimes hit me hardest in quiet moments. The distance from home, while chosen freely, still created a sense of displacement. No amount of independence or new experiences could erase the feeling that I was away from the people who mattered most. I had my work, but the absence of my parents and my son, and the familiar comfort of my mother's presence, lingered in my thoughts.

I reflected on my path often. I wondered about the sacrifices my mother had made and compared them to my own choices. She had seen her parents so few times throughout her adult life, and yet, her resilience never wavered. It gave me strength, knowing that despite the distance, we were still connected. That bond was unbreakable, even as we lived in different worlds. My mother's happiness at seeing my son during my visit reaffirmed that I had made the right decision. Even in the most difficult times, the love we shared bridged the gap between us.

My journey, though different from my mother's, was a continuation of the choices women in our family had made for generations — the choice to seek something better, to create a life beyond the confines of what was expected. Yet, in doing so, there was always the tug of home, of family, and the bittersweet reality of what was left behind.

Looking back, the decision to leave China had been easy, but the journey of reconciling that choice with the distance from my family was far more complex. And yet, through it all, the one constant was the love we shared — across borders, across time, and across the many paths we had chosen.

Chapter 17: Moving to America

The decision to leave Singapore and move to the United States wasn't made overnight. Going to America had always been a dream — not just for me, but for many people I knew. The country stood as a symbol of opportunity, the place where anything seemed possible, where fortunes were made, and lives were transformed. But the idea of uprooting ourselves once again, after having built a life in Singapore, was daunting. It meant leaving behind the familiar, venturing into the unknown, and starting from scratch all over again.

Wayne received an offer from Northwestern University as a research staff member, and that opportunity set everything in motion. The excitement in his voice when he told me about it was infectious. It was an incredible achievement, the kind of opportunity we had only talked about in passing, never fully believing it would happen so soon. However, reality settled in quickly — we had a life in Singapore. I had a stable job and friends we had made over the years, and our son was still in China with my parents. It wasn't an easy decision, but we both knew this was a chance we couldn't pass up.

Wayne left Singapore in the summer to start his new life in Chicago. As soon as he left, I threw myself into the endless tasks that came with preparing for a move of this magnitude. For the first three months after Wayne's departure, I kept myself occupied by helping my parents get passports and applying for their visas to visit Singapore. The process was tedious, and the days felt long as I navigated the bureaucracy involved in securing their visit. I was excited at the thought of seeing my son again, who had just turned three, and having my parents visit me in Singapore for the first time. The anticipation of their arrival became the light at the end of the tunnel during those months when Wayne was absent, and the house felt quieter than ever.

Finally, after weeks of waiting, their visas were granted. The day my parents arrived at Changi Airport with my son felt like a dream. I remember watching them walk through the gates, my heart pounding with excitement as my son, full of energy and innocence, ran toward me. He had grown since I last saw him — his face slightly fuller, his eyes bright with curiosity. My mother and father, though travel-worn, were equally thrilled to be in Singapore, a place they had only heard about in my letters and phone calls. It was a rare reunion, especially for my mother, who had spent much of her life in Xinjiang, far from her own parents.

With my parents in Singapore, the three months that followed were filled with joy, laughter, and a sense of togetherness that I had missed deeply. We spent our days exploring the city, visiting its landmarks, and most importantly, enjoying time together as a family. One of the most memorable days was the one we spent in **Sentosa**, an island that seemed to embody the very essence of paradise. I had taken my parents and son there, hoping to show them the beauty and luxury of Singapore's famous resort island.

The moment we arrived, Sentosa felt like a world apart from the bustling streets of the city. The air was warm and fragrant, carrying the scent of the ocean and blooming tropical flowers. As we walked along the manicured pathways, the lush greenery enveloped us, with palm trees swaying gently in the breeze and vibrant flowers lining the streets. The island was alive with color and energy, but there was also a sense of peace, as if time had slowed down to allow us to savor each moment.

I watched my son's eyes widen in awe as we explored the island, and my parents, though reserved, couldn't hide their amazement either. We strolled through immaculate gardens with water features that sparkled in the sunlight, and the laughter of families enjoying their day echoed around us. My son ran ahead, giggling as he tried to catch the birds that flitted around us, their bright feathers reflecting the vibrant surroundings.

We spent much of our day by the sea. The beach at Sentosa, though man-made, was stunning. The soft white sand stretched out before us, meeting the crystal-clear waters that sparkled like diamonds under the sunlight. My son was captivated by the waves, his tiny feet sinking into the sand as he chased after the foam that bubbled up onto the shore. My parents sat under the shade of a palm tree, watching him with contentment in their eyes. It was moments like these — watching my son play, seeing the joy on my parents' faces — that made the months of preparation worth it.

We also visited **S.E.A. Aquarium**. It felt like stepping into another world, one where the boundaries between land and sea blurred into one magical experience. The immense tanks stretched out before us, filled with the most breathtaking marine life. My son pressed his tiny hands against the glass, his eyes wide with wonder as he watched the sea creatures move gracefully, almost as if they were performing just for him.

The highlight, of course, was the **underwater tunnel**, where the glass walls and ceiling arched above us, creating a 360-degree view of the marine world. We walked through it as if we were submerged beneath the ocean itself, with sea creatures swimming above us, to the left, and to the right. My parents and son were mesmerized, and for a moment, I could forget the upcoming move to America and simply enjoy the beauty and tranquility of that underwater world.

Those three months with my parents and son were filled with moments like these — simple, beautiful days spent in each other's company. It was as if we were creating memories to hold onto before the next chapter of our lives began. But no matter how much joy we experienced, I always knew that we would soon be parting ways again. Saying goodbye to my parents at **Changi Airport** was one of the hardest things I had ever done. I could hardly hold my tears as I tried to hold back my emotions. My mother looked at me with her usual strength, her eyes filled with pride and love, while my father patted my back, his quiet presence offering me comfort. When I finally let go and watched them walk away, my tears broke free. I wasn't used to crying in public, but this was different — this was saying goodbye to a piece of home, knowing I wouldn't see them for a long time.

As soon as my parents left, I turned my attention to preparing for my own departure to the United States. The idea of going to America still felt like a dream — back in China, I had often fantasized about visiting New York, even for just a month, to see how the country looked. Now, I was about to embark on an entirely new life in a foreign land. Wayne had already rented an apartment in **Evanston**, close to **Northwestern University**, and had even gotten his **driver's license** in preparation for our arrival.

It was on the last day of 1997, New Year's Eve, that my son and I boarded the flight to Chicago, I felt a whirlwind of emotions — excitement, fear, anticipation, and sadness all mingling together. The flight itself was long, but my son, being a curious and energetic three-year-old, was fascinated by everything — the plane, the flight attendants, the tiny meal trays, and the clouds outside the window. I, on the other hand, felt a deep sense of the unknown. What would life in America be like? Could we truly build a future there? These questions haunted me throughout the journey.

When we finally arrived in **Chicago**, Wayne was there to greet us at **O'Hare International Airport**. Seeing his familiar face amidst the crowd of strangers was a relief beyond words. He smiled as he embraced us, and for a moment, everything felt right again, as though the distance between us had never existed.

The apartment building in **Evanston** felt vastly different from the **HDB flats** we had become accustomed to in Singapore. The first thing that struck me as we walked in were the **carpeted stairs**, which were unlike anything I had seen in the Singaporean public housing system. In Singapore, the HDB flats had hard concrete or tiled floors — sturdy, practical, but devoid of any warmth. Here in Evanston, the plush carpet that lined the stairs gave the entire building a cozy, homely feeling. With each step, the carpet seemed to cushion our movements, and it had a sense of quiet luxury that immediately contrasted with the more utilitarian design back in Singapore.

As we walked up the stairs, I noticed the distinct **wooden floors** in the hallways, which added another layer of warmth to the apartment building. The polished wood gleamed under the soft lighting, a far cry from the cold, tiled corridors of Singapore's HDB flats. In Singapore, everything felt meticulously maintained but impersonal. Here, there was a softness and a lived-in feeling that made the apartment building feel like a true home.

When Wayne opened the door to our new apartment, the first thing I noticed was the **bathroom**. It was another stark contrast to the minimalist bathrooms we had back in Singapore. In our HDB flat, the bathroom was a simple affair — just a shower stall with a small, basic washing basin. There was no bathtub, no fancy fixtures, just the essentials. In fact, most apartments in Singapore were designed this way — practical and functional, but far from luxurious. But here, in America, even the most common apartment came with a **bathtub**, a large sink with ample counter space, and more storage than I had ever seen in a Singaporean bathroom. It felt almost extravagant in comparison.

The **bathroom in Evanston** reminded me of the expensive, private apartments I had occasionally seen in Singapore, the kind reserved for wealthy expatriates or those who could afford luxury living. The tiled floors were sleek, the fixtures gleamed, and there was even a large mirror above the sink that gave the room an open, airy feeling. As I turned on the faucet, I couldn't help but smile at the warm water that poured out effortlessly — here, even the most mundane act of washing up felt like a small luxury.

The **living space** was equally impressive. The **hardwood floors** continued throughout the apartment, a beautiful rich brown that contrasted with the white walls. The living room had large windows that let in plenty of natural light, and as I looked out, I could see the tree-lined streets of Evanston. It was a quiet neighborhood, peaceful in a way that felt entirely different from the hustle and bustle of Singapore.

The apartment, though modest by American standards, felt far more spacious than our home in Singapore. In Singapore, every square meter of space was accounted for, with little room for extras or luxuries. But here, the rooms were larger, the ceilings higher, and there was an openness to the layout that made the space feel like a place we could truly settle into. There was a **kitchen** with full appliances — something that felt rare in the small kitchens of Singapore's public housing. In our HDB flat, the kitchen had been functional but tiny, with just enough space for basic cooking. Here, in America, the kitchen was spacious, with more counter space than I knew what to do with.

The carpeted bedrooms gave the apartment an added sense of comfort, especially for my son, who immediately took to running across the soft flooring. He seemed to love the apartment right away, and I could tell that the cozy, homey atmosphere made him feel safe and secure. Watching him explore his new home, I felt a sense of relief — this place, as unfamiliar as it was, felt like the beginning of something new, something hopeful.

As I unpacked, I reflected on the differences between Singapore and America. In many ways, Singapore had offered us a high standard of living — clean streets, organized systems, and a safe environment — but there had always been a sense of formality and restriction, especially in the way homes were designed. The HDB flats, while practical, lacked the warmth and individuality that this new apartment exuded. In Singapore, everything was standardized, regulated, and designed for efficiency. Here in America, there was room for personal expression, for comfort, for making a space truly your own.

In those early days, the apartment became our sanctuary. Wayne and I would often sit together in the living room, marveling at how different life already felt in America.

I quickly discovered that life in America was different from the structured, orderly pace of Singapore. There was more freedom, more flexibility, but there was also a sense of unpredictability that I wasn't used to. In Singapore, everything ran like clockwork — the buses were always on time, the streets were immaculate, and life followed a predictable routine. Here in Evanston, things were more relaxed, but also less efficient. I found myself missing the cleanliness and organization of Singapore, even as I embraced the more laid-back atmosphere of American life.

In many ways, our apartment in Evanston symbolized the new life we were building. It was a place where we could settle down, where our son could grow up, and where we could begin to carve out our own space in this vast, unfamiliar country. The cozy **carpeted stairs**, the **wooden floors**, and the **luxurious bathroom** were all markers of a different life, one that was filled with both possibilities and uncertainties. It wasn't always easy to adjust, but every day brought something new — a new challenge, a new discovery, and a new step toward making America our home.

Moving to America was a leap of faith, a decision that came with both excitement and uncertainty. But as I stood in our new apartment, watching the snow fall gently outside, I felt a sense of peace. This was our new beginning, a chance to build a new life together, and though the road ahead was unknown, I was ready for whatever it would bring.

Chapter 18: Settling in Evanston, IL

The first few months in America felt like a whirlwind of emotions, logistics, and constant adjustment. After the initial excitement of moving into our new apartment in Evanston, reality set in. We weren't just visiting; this was our new home. Everything felt new and unfamiliar, from the language to the customs, to the way people lived their daily lives. Despite all the preparation, nothing could have fully equipped us for the cultural and emotional transition that came with settling in the U.S.

Wayne adapted more quickly than I did. His role at Northwestern University provided him with a sense of purpose and routine. His colleagues welcomed him warmly, and he quickly found his place in the academic environment. For me, the adjustment was more complex. I had left behind a job in Singapore, and with my philosophy degree from China, finding work here proved nearly impossible. I realized I would need to go back to school to pursue another major, something more practical in the American job market.

Like many other Chinese immigrants with liberal arts degrees, I had to choose between common fields like accounting or computer science. Computer studies seemed like the best option, but by the time I arrived in America, I had already missed the deadline for spring semester enrollment at Northwestern University. Still, I decided to visit the admissions office anyway, hoping for a chance. Unexpectedly, they asked me if I would write an essay right there on the spot. Of course, I accepted the challenge and passed. That essay turned out to be my ticket into a certificate program in computer studies.

On the first day of my C programming class, I encountered my next challenge: the professor was African American, and I could barely understand his accent. Even simple phrases like "Let's take a break" eluded me. I only realized class was over when I saw other students stand up and leave. It was an overwhelming start, and I knew I had to find a way to keep up.

I taught myself by reading each chapter before attending class, trying to grasp the technical concepts on my own. When I sat in class, I could follow the lecture only because I had already familiarized myself with the content. I would listen carefully for key phrases, hoping to pick up on a few words that confirmed what

I had studied. It was a challenging process, but I persisted, determined to succeed.

One particular incident stood out during the course. I had received a B on an assignment but didn't understand where I had gone wrong. During a break, I approached the professor and asked for clarification. He told me he had changed the assignment and announced it during class. I explained to him that while I could engage in one-on-one conversations with him, I could barely understand what he said when addressing the whole class. He seemed genuinely surprised and apologized. From that day forward, he would write down any changes to assignments, ensuring that I could follow along. By the end of the semester, only seven students remained in the class, and I was one of them, with an A on my final exam.

Life in America, however, wasn't just about academic challenges. Wayne and I had decided early on that if we were going to truly adapt to American life, we needed to fully immerse ourselves in the culture. Unlike many Chinese immigrants, we made a conscious effort not to watch Chinese TV, read Chinese newspapers, or engage with Chinese media at home. The only exception was our language — we still spoke Chinese to each other. Speaking English felt too awkward between us, but in every other aspect of life, we embraced American culture.

It took more than two years for me to reach a point where I could attend classes without needing to read the chapters in advance. By the time I finished the certificate program, I could understand most of what was being said in real-time, and my confidence in navigating American life had grown immensely. However, it wasn't until another eight years later that I felt comfortable enough to go back to Chinese media. I finally allowed myself to read Chinese newspapers and watch Chinese TV programs again, realizing that I could now comfortably straddle both cultures.

The cultural differences didn't stop at language and education. I vividly remember my second visit to the dentist's office. As soon as I walked in, both the receptionist and the dentist greeted me warmly, calling me by name and asking about my son. I was touched by their warmth and care, amazed that they remembered such personal details from my last visit. But very quickly, I realized that they didn't actually remember me — they had simply read the notes from my previous appointment. At first, I felt a bit foolish for having been moved by what seemed like an insincere gesture. But as I reflected on it, I realized they weren't pretending. They truly cared about their patients, even if their knowledge was based on notes rather than memory.

This type of "indifferentiable love" was a foreign concept in Chinese culture. In China, relationships are built on deep personal connections, and warmth is earned through long-term familiarity. Here, in America, people showed care for others, even strangers, in ways that felt impersonal but were genuine, nonetheless. This was, perhaps, the biggest culture shock for me — understanding that people could sincerely care without needing to know you deeply. It challenged my preconceived notions of how love and kindness were expressed, and it made me appreciate the subtle, yet profound differences in cultural attitudes toward human connection.

One evening, during a quiet conversation with Wayne, he sighed and said something that struck me deeply. "We, Chinese Americans, will always be marginal people no matter how successful we might become in our careers. The cultural differences are just too immense to overcome." I could sense the weight of this realization in his words, a kind of resignation that we might never fully belong. In that moment, however, I made a determination. I refused to accept that fate for myself. I wasn't going to stay marginal. I had a goal in mind, a determination that burned within me.

When I started the certificate program, I had just turned 30. As I stood in front of my first computer class, feeling like an outsider who could barely understand her professor, I made a vow to myself: I was going to reach the same career level as someone who had studied computer science after high school and entered the field right after college. These people had a ten-year head start on me, but I was determined to close that gap. It was a daunting challenge, but one that I embraced with the same tenacity that had carried me through every other stage of my life.

As I immersed myself in my studies, that determination became my driving force. While other students might have had years of experience and training, I had the willpower to push through, to work harder and catch up. Every assignment I completed, every lecture I attended, felt like a step closer to that goal. I knew it wouldn't be easy, but I was ready for the long journey ahead. I wasn't just chasing a career — I was proving to myself that I could overcome the obstacles that came with being a Chinese immigrant in America.

Yet, settling in America was more than just adapting to daily life. It was about understanding the culture — something that went far deeper than just learning a new language or navigating new systems. In Singapore, there had been a shared understanding of traditions and customs, even in the melting pot of cultures that the country represented. Here, in the U.S., everything felt different. The individualism that pervaded American culture was new to me. People here were friendly, but they kept a certain distance, a personal space that wasn't present in the more communal way of life I was used to. In Singapore, there was always a sense of community — people looked out for each other in small ways, whether it was in the shared spaces of the HDB flats or in casual conversations at the hawker centers. In America, there was a polite distance that, while respectful, often left me feeling more isolated.

One of the cultural shocks came when I attended a community event in Evanston. It was a local fair, and I thought it would be a good way to meet people and learn more about the neighborhood. As I walked around, I noticed how self-sufficient everyone seemed. Families stayed within their own circles, exchanging polite smiles but not much more. I had expected more warmth, more interaction, but I realized that people here were different. It wasn't that they were unfriendly — it was just a different way of relating to each other. In Singapore, neighbors would drop by unannounced, and conversations flowed easily. Here, there were boundaries that weren't meant to be crossed.

Despite these challenges, there were moments of wonder as well. I remember the first time I saw snow in Evanston. In Beijing, snow had been a rarity, and in Singapore, it was nonexistent. But here, in Evanston, winter brought with it a blanket of white that transformed the world. The first snowfall was magical — my son and I stood by the window, watching as the delicate flakes drifted down from the sky, covering the ground in a soft, pristine layer. We bundled up in thick coats, scarves, and gloves, and stepped outside into the cold. My son was thrilled — he ran around, his laughter echoing in the crisp air, his tiny hands trying to catch the falling snowflakes. For a moment, the challenges of immigration faded away, and all that mattered was the beauty of that snowy day.

As the weeks turned into months, I began to develop a routine. Wayne's work at the university kept him busy, but he always made time for us in the evenings. We would sit together in the cozy living room of our apartment, with its carpeted floors and soft lighting, and talk about our day. Slowly, I started to feel less like a stranger in this new land. The apartment itself became a symbol of our new beginning. It was a place of warmth and security, a stark contrast to the cold, impersonal buildings I had left behind in Singapore. The wooden floors, the cozy carpeted stairs, the fully equipped kitchen — all of it made me feel like we were starting to build a home again.

I also began to explore the area around Evanston. There was something comforting about the tree-lined streets, the small parks where families gathered, and the local shops that had a personal touch to them. The neighborhood had its own rhythm, slower than the fast-paced life of Singapore, but more intimate in its own way. I would take long walks with my son, discovering new paths, new places, and slowly, the unfamiliar started to feel more familiar.

But no matter how much I adapted, the sense of displacement lingered. I missed the vibrancy of Singapore, the food, the culture, the friends I had made. There were days when I longed for the comfort of a hawker center meal, for the familiarity of the streets I had walked for years. I missed the sense of belonging that came from living in a place where I understood every nuance, every cultural reference. In America, everything was still new, still foreign, and while I was learning to navigate it, there was a part of me that always felt out of place.

Slowly but surely, America started to feel less like a foreign land and more like a place we could call home. It wasn't easy, and there were days when the challenges felt overwhelming. But there were also moments of joy, of discovery, and of growth. We were building a new life, one step at a time, and even though the path was uncertain, I knew we were moving forward.

As I looked out the window at the snow-covered streets of Evanston, I felt a mixture of emotions. The road ahead was long, but we had come so far already. Settling in the U.S. wasn't just about adapting to a new culture or learning a new language — it was about finding a way to carry the past with us while embracing the future. It was about creating a home in a place that was still unfamiliar, and learning to thrive in a world that was vastly different from the one we had known. And as I watched my son play in the snow, his laughter filling the air, I realized that we were doing just that. Slowly, we were finding our place in this new world.

Chapter 19: Early Success and Stability

The move to Evanston wasn't just about adapting to American culture and life — it became the backdrop to a deeper transformation in both our personal lives and our sense of belonging. Shortly after arriving in Evanston, Wayne and I were approached by campus missionaries. Their warmth and kindness were our first real human connections in this new place, and their invitation to join a Chinese Bible study group was an opportunity we welcomed. At the time, we had two main reasons for joining. The first was for our son to have a chance to play with other children, and the second was the weekly Chinese potluck. Every family brought their favorite dish to share, and those meals became the highlight of our week.

The group was primarily made up of other Chinese immigrants, people like us who were trying to find their way in a foreign land. The husband, Sam, graduated from University of Science and Technology of China and held a top technical position at a company. The wife, Sara, was a housewife. The gathering quickly became a source of comfort and community. Wayne, though more reserved, came along mostly for the social aspects, while I found myself drawn to the teachings. The Bible study group wasn't just a weekly gathering for scripture discussion; it was a lifeline that connected us to people with similar backgrounds and experiences. We shared stories of our struggles, exchanged advice, and, most importantly, we supported one another. I had never been particularly religious before, but there was something about this group — the sense of unity, faith, and hope — that resonated with me deeply.

In the year 2000, after months of contemplation, I decided to get baptized. It was Mother's Day — a fitting moment, as I stood at a crossroads both in faith and in my new life in America. The baptism was a turning point, not just spiritually but symbolically, as I had recently completed my certificate in Computer Studies. It felt like the start of a new chapter. I was no longer the same person who had first arrived in America, unsure of her place or her future. I had found a career path, a supportive community, and a renewed sense of self. Yet, looking back, I realize I wasn't truly born again until 2015. At the time, I thought I had undergone a transformation, but I didn't fully understand what it meant until much later.

Around the same time, I received two job offers — one as an Internet Specialist at Hadley School for the Blind in Winnetka, Illinois, and the other from a consulting company in Boston. Both were significant opportunities, but the decision wasn't easy. Moving to Boston felt too much disruption, especially when I was just starting to find my footing. On top of that, my spoken English was still far from fluent, and I doubted my ability to succeed in such a fast-paced environment.

I chose Hadley, partly because it allowed me to stay in the familiar environment of Illinois, and partly because I wasn't ready to take on the challenge of a big move again. It was a role where I could apply what I had learned, grow my skills, and continue building the life we were starting to shape. Meanwhile, Wayne was also at a turning point in his career, which brought with it its own challenges and revelations.

While I was settling into my role at Hadley, Wayne's career was also evolving, though in a different direction. Despite his success at Northwestern — receiving best paper awards year after year — academia wasn't fulfilling him. Wayne had never wanted to be a scholar. He had followed the academic path largely out of necessity, having earned his degrees in mechanical engineering because, in China, it was nearly impossible to switch majors once you were on a particular track.

As a result, Wayne felt trapped in a field that he hadn't truly chosen. In China, students didn't have the freedom to explore different fields the way they did in America. After earning his bachelor's degree, he had no choice but to continue his education in mechanical engineering, eventually leading to a postdoctoral position. But now that he was in America, the land of opportunities, he could finally pursue what he had always wanted — entrepreneurship. This dream had been simmering for years, and America seemed like the place where he could make it happen.

That entrepreneurial spirit led him to apply for jobs outside of academia, and soon, he received an offer from a Japanese company in Los Angeles, California. The job offer was tempting for many reasons. Los Angeles represented a fresh start, a new city, and the opportunity for Wayne to explore business ventures.

But the decision to move wasn't straightforward. We had begun to settle in Evanston, and uprooting ourselves once again — especially with me just starting my new job at Hadley — felt daunting. There were also cultural aspects to consider. Wayne had once sighed to me, "We, Chinese Americans, will always be marginal people, no matter how successful we might become in our careers." That comment weighed heavily on me. Was it true? Could we ever fully integrate into American society? Or would we always be seen as outsiders, as perpetual foreigners in the land of opportunity? It was a question that gnawed at us, even as we pursued our individual ambitions. The Chinese Bible study group had been our only social connection.

After a year of working at Hadley, I made the decision to quit my job and move with Wayne to Los Angeles. He rented a U-Haul truck and drove across the country to secure an apartment for our arrival, while my son and I stayed behind for one more month. When we finally boarded the plane to California, it felt like another chapter was closing and a new one was beginning.

As much as we had been trying to adapt, there had been an undeniable sense of being on the outside looking in. Although we had been physically in America, there had been an invisible barrier separating us from the broader society. We hadn't been involved in any American political or social activities, and the truth had been, neither Wayne nor I had known where to start, nor had we felt like we had belonged in those spheres.

From 1998 to 2001, there was so much happening in America — politically, socially, and culturally — and yet, we were largely disconnected from it all. I remember hearing about major national events, political movements, and social conversations, but they felt distant, as though they were happening in a world that wasn't ours. It wasn't just that we were immigrants adjusting to a new culture; it was that we didn't have a sense of how to engage with this new country beyond our immediate survival needs — getting a job, raising our child, and establishing ourselves economically.

When Wayne expressed his frustration that "Chinese Americans will always be marginal people," it wasn't just a reflection of his personal career trajectory. It was a statement about our collective experience as immigrants. Most of the Chinese families we knew, both through Wayne's work and our Bible study group, were just like us — focused on building stable lives for their families, staying within our own circles, and keeping our heads down. We weren't encouraged to get involved in civic life or politics. The idea of participating in American social or political movements was foreign to us.

For many Chinese Americans, including us, there was a long-standing sense of separation from the political fabric of this country. We had been raised in a culture where politics was seen as something distant, controlled by higher powers, something that ordinary people didn't participate in directly. In China, the government was centralized and far removed from the daily lives of citizens. As immigrants in America, we carried some of that mindset with us. The idea of participating in local or national politics — of voting, organizing, or even protesting — felt unfamiliar, even intimidating.

Even when we heard about events like the 2000 U.S. presidential election, the controversy over the recount in Florida, or the policies that were shaping America at the time, it felt like we were mere observers rather than active participants. We would read about these things in the news, but there was always a sense that it was someone else's issue to solve, someone else's country to govern. It wasn't that we didn't care; we just didn't feel like we had a place in it. We didn't know how to make our voices heard in a system that felt so far removed from the realities of our lives as immigrants.

Our social circles were almost entirely Chinese. The Bible study group, while comforting, was also insular. It provided a space where we could be with people who understood our struggles and spoke our language, but it also reinforced the separation from the broader American experience. We weren't discussing American politics in these groups. We weren't talking about social movements or national events. We were focused on our own struggles — adjusting to life here, navigating jobs, and raising our children. The larger conversations happening in America didn't seem to touch us.

Looking back now, I can see that part of the reason for this disconnect was the sheer difficulty of adapting to life in a new country. For many immigrants, survival comes first. It's about finding stable work, learning the language, and making sure your children are safe and educated. There isn't much energy left to think about getting involved in civic life, especially when you feel like an outsider in the society around you. We weren't raised with the same sense of civic responsibility that might have been instilled in American-born citizens. We didn't grow up with the idea that our voices mattered in political discussions or that we could influence change.

Moreover, we didn't see ourselves represented in American politics or media. There were few, if any, Chinese American politicians or public figures who could show us that it was possible for people like us to have a say in shaping this country. The image of the American politician was almost always white, and often male. The issues being discussed in political debates didn't seem to reflect the concerns of immigrants, especially Asian immigrants. And so, we continued to feel marginal — not because we didn't care, but because we didn't see a way to bridge the gap between our lives and the broader American society.

Even though we were building a life in America, it often felt like we were living parallel lives to those of our American neighbors. We worked alongside them, our children played together at school, but there was still a gulf between us. The conversations at work rarely touched on the issues that truly mattered to us, and the social events we were invited to felt more like surface-level interactions than deep connections.

When I accepted the job at Hadley School for the Blind, it felt like a personal victory, but I also realized how isolated we still were from the larger American story. We weren't integrating into the political or social fabric of the country; we were simply navigating it as best we could, trying to carve out a space for ourselves without truly being a part of it.

In hindsight, I realize that the feeling of marginalization Wayne expressed reflected the larger issue facing many Chinese Americans at the time. We were living in the shadows, contributing to the economy, raising families, and succeeding professionally, but we weren't part of the social and political conversations shaping the nation. We didn't know how to be part of them, and in many ways, we didn't feel like we had the right to be.

The move to Los Angeles marked another chapter in our journey, but even as we changed cities, the sense of marginalization persisted. It would take years, and many personal transformations, before I would begin to understand how deeply this feeling of being on the periphery affected not just our personal lives but our community as a whole.

As we settled into life in Los Angeles, I couldn't help but reflect on the journey that had brought us here. From Singapore to Evanston and now to California, each place had changed us in profound ways. Our time in Evanston, with its Bible study group, its small community, and my first steps into a new career, had laid the foundation for this next phase. But the road ahead was still filled with uncertainty. Would Los Angeles finally be the place where we could find our footing? Or would we continue to feel like outsiders, always on the margins of American society?

The next chapter of our lives would answer these questions — in ways I never could have anticipated.

Chapter 20: Los Angeles, Change, and Reflections

After we moved to Los Angeles in June 2001, I landed a job at a startup company as a web developer in a towering skyscraper near LAX Airport. The new role felt like a fresh start, especially after the uncertainties of the past few years. I remember how exhilarating it was to stand in front of the floor-to-ceiling windows, overlooking the sprawling city below, with its highways weaving in and out like veins through the concrete landscape. From that height, it was easy to believe that Los Angeles, with its sunny skies and seemingly endless opportunities, would be the place where we could finally plant roots.

But that sense of optimism was short-lived. On the morning of September 11, 2001, just three months after I started the job, I received a call from the company's administrative assistant. It was early, and her voice was tense. She told me not to come to the office and urged me to turn on the TV. I did as she said, and like millions of people around the world, I watched in horror as the events of 9/11 unfolded. The world seemed to change in an instant. The attacks shook the foundation of not just America but also the world, and the economic ripple effects soon hit our small company. In the weeks that followed, contracts were canceled, clients disappeared, and the startup could no longer sustain its operations. I was laid off, along with many others.

I found myself jobless at a time when the job market was tightening, and without a bachelor's degree, my prospects were even slimmer. Though I had a certificate in computer studies, it wasn't enough to secure a stable job, especially given my short employment history in the U.S. The weight of this uncertainty pressed down on me. For over a year, I searched for work, sending out countless résumés, and facing rejection after rejection. All the while, Wayne's dissatisfaction with his own job grew, adding strain to our already fragile relationship.

There were deeper issues between Wayne and me that had been building for years. After much reflection, I concluded that the best thing for everyone involved was for us to part ways. Wayne didn't want a divorce, but I convinced him that it was the right decision for us and for our son, David. Our separation was amicable, and despite the end of our marriage, I still cared about Wayne's happiness. In fact, I helped him find a new wife. He began dating again, and I often offered my opinion on the women he was seeing. It became a running joke between us that while I wasn't the best wife, I was undoubtedly the best ex-wife. When he started dating a woman in San Francisco, I even drove him to the airport and picked him up after his trips. Eventually, they got married, and I was genuinely happy for him.

His new wife, a principal developer at Oracle, enabled him to quit his job and pursue his dream of starting a tech company in China. She was supportive of his ambitions, and together, they made the decision for Wayne to return to China to build his business. Despite our separation, Wayne was still very much involved in David's life. He didn't want to leave our son in my care while I was unemployed, and I didn't want David to return to China with Wayne, so I decided to move to Pittsburgh, where the cost of living was lower. Until then, David stayed with Wayne in Los Angeles, and I visited him on weekends. Wayne's job was stable, and it was convenient for him to take David to school on his way to work and pick him up afterward.

Los Angeles was a city unlike any other I had lived in. The sheer size of it was overwhelming at times. From the downtown skyscrapers to the sun-soaked beaches of Santa Monica, and the sprawling suburbs that stretched out endlessly, Los Angeles seemed like a patchwork of different worlds stitched together by freeways. The contrast between the wealth in neighborhoods like Beverly Hills and the economic struggles in other areas was stark. But what stood out most to me was the city's vibrant Chinese community.

Chinatown, located just a short drive from downtown, was like a city within a city. Stretching over several districts along the I-10 Interstate, it felt like an enclave of culture that had been transported directly from China. Walking down the streets of Chinatown, you could easily forget you were in America. Storefronts were adorned with bright red Chinese characters, and the scent of roasted duck and dumplings filled the air. Restaurants didn't offer forks unless you asked for them, and everyone spoke Chinese, creating a bubble of familiarity in the vastness of Los Angeles. I remember thinking that it was both a comfort and a reminder of the cultural divide that still existed.

Wayne once shared a conversation he had with his barber, a man who had come to America from Eastern Europe decades earlier. The barber commented that when immigrants like himself had arrived in America, they were forced to assimilate, to blend into the cultural fabric of their new country. But when the Chinese arrived, they built Chinatowns, refusing to assimilate fully. The barber asked Wayne why Chinese people even bothered to come to America if they were so intent on holding on to their traditions. It was a question that resonated with me, one I found myself pondering in the weeks that followed.

Why had we come to America? We came, like many others, for the promise of better opportunities, a brighter future. But did we really want to be assimilated? Or did we hope to change America, to make it more accepting of who we were? I knew we didn't want to change America into the place we had left behind, but perhaps we wanted more influence, more acceptance as ourselves. In Evanston, the Chinese population was small, and we didn't have enough numbers to make an impact. But in Los Angeles, the Chinese community was large enough that, if mobilized, it could make a difference in elections and politics. However, despite the potential power of the Chinese American vote, I saw little political action. I wondered why.

In Los Angeles, I saw a vibrant Chinese culture, but it existed parallel to American culture. The community wasn't integrated into the political fabric of the city in the way I expected. Even in Chinatown, where the streets bustled with life, there was a sense that it was an isolated world. We were contributing to the economy, raising families, and succeeding professionally, but politically, we seemed invisible. I didn't hear about any Chinese American social movements or significant political efforts at the time. It was as though we were living in our own separate sphere, detached from the larger currents shaping the country.

As Wayne began dating again and I helped him navigate his new relationships, I also experienced a few short-lived romances. One became serious. He was a French American who had been through a unique life journey. His ex-wife had met him in France while she was an exchange student, and he was attending a culinary academy to become a chef. They married and moved to America, where he worked as a chef at Palm Springs Resort, having served high-profile clients like Michael Jackson and President Clinton. For years, he supported his wife as she pursued her PhD, eventually becoming a high school principal. But when he decided he wanted to become a math teacher, she mocked him, dismissing his ambitions. That was the breaking point for him, and he divorced her.

When I met him, he was in his senior year as a math major at a community college, trying to rebuild his life. I helped him with his homework, and though it was clear math wasn't his strength, I admired his determination. We enjoyed each other's company, and despite his struggles, I didn't mind that he wasn't the smartest in math. We grew close, but when he proposed, I hesitated. He wanted a prenuptial agreement, which struck me as odd, considering he was the poorest man I had ever dated. The request made me laugh, and ultimately, I couldn't accept his proposal. When the relationship ended, as with others, I felt a sense of excitement for the unknown — for the possibility of who I might meet next.

In the year following my job loss, I often found myself reflecting on what it meant to be Chinese American in a city like Los Angeles. Despite the large Chinese population, we seemed politically and socially marginalized. Our community, though thriving economically, wasn't represented in the broader American narrative. We weren't part of the discussions shaping the country, and I didn't see any efforts from within the community to change that. It was as though we were content to remain in our separate world, disconnected from the political and social movements of the time.

Even as I was immersed in my personal struggles, the question of our place in American society loomed large. Wayne's comment from years earlier, that "Chinese Americans will always be marginal people," echoed in my mind. Was he right? Would we always be outsiders in this country, no matter how successful we became? The more time I spent in Los Angeles, the more I began to see that, in many ways, we had accepted this marginalization. We were thriving within our own communities, but we weren't integrated into the larger fabric of American life.

As I prepared to move to Pittsburgh with David, I couldn't help but feel a sense of unfinished business in Los Angeles. The city had offered so much potential, but there was also a lingering sense of disconnection. We were there, but not fully present in the larger societal conversation. We were building lives, contributing to the economy, and raising families, but we weren't making our mark politically or socially. The Chinese community, despite its size, remained a quiet presence in the city, powerful in numbers but lacking in visibility.

When I finally packed up and left Los Angeles, I knew that this chapter of my life was closing. But the questions it raised — about identity, belonging, and the role of immigrants in shaping America — would stay with me for years to come. The move to Pittsburgh offered a fresh start, but had also left me feeling like I was still searching for my place in this new world. Los Angeles had forced me to confront not just who I was but who I wanted to be. It was a city of contradictions, where the promise of the American Dream was both tantalizingly close and frustratingly out of reach. Los Angeles had laid the groundwork, setting the stage for the next chapter in my journey — one where I would continue to search for answers to the questions that had followed me across continents and through the many phases of my life.

Political Realities and Cultural Reflection in 2000s Los Angeles

The early 2000s in Los Angeles were marked by a combination of political upheaval and cultural reflection, particularly in the wake of 9/11. National security took precedence over most other political conversations, and the passage of the Patriot Act led to increased surveillance and scrutiny of immigrant communities. For Chinese Americans, this meant that even though we were not the direct targets of these new policies, the atmosphere of suspicion and heightened nationalism was palpable. We became more aware of our status as immigrants, as outsiders in a country that was now even more wary of those it perceived as different.

Chinatown itself, while thriving in its own way, began to feel the effects of these political changes. The community, which had once been a symbol of Chinese resilience and cultural pride, now seemed more isolated than ever. While the streets still bustled with activity, there was an underlying sense of unease. Business owners worried about declining tourism, and families like mine questioned what it truly meant to belong in a country where the conversation around national identity had shifted so dramatically.

This was the backdrop against which my personal journey played out — a time of both great opportunity and great uncertainty. The decision to move to Pittsburgh, to leave behind the familiarity of Los Angeles and its Chinatown, was not an easy one. But I knew that, just as I had done before, I needed to embrace change, to move forward even in the face of uncertainty. And so, with David by my side, I set off once again, ready to face whatever the next chapter of our lives would bring.

Chapter 21: Moving to Pittsburgh

When I was ready to leave Los Angeles, David was staying in San Francisco with his dad. I drove up to pick him up before heading east. Our route would take us along the I-90 Interstate Highway, which I had heard was renowned for its scenic beauty. As we left San Francisco and set out on the journey to Pittsburgh, the first leg of the drive took us through winding valleys that seemed to stretch on forever. The scenery was breathtaking, with golden hills rolling like waves, punctuated by clusters of oak trees standing tall and proud, their branches twisted and shaped by years of weather and time. The sunlight filtered through the leaves, casting dappled shadows across the valley floor, creating an almost otherworldly, ethereal glow.

I had always loved road trips, but this one felt different — heavier somehow. There was quietness in the car, an unspoken understanding between David and me about the significance of this journey. These valleys, so vast and empty, reflected the open and uncertain road ahead. I had no job waiting for me in Pittsburgh, no guarantee that things would work out as planned. The beauty of the landscape couldn't erase the tight knot of anxiety growing inside me. Each bend in the road felt like another question mark, another unknown challenge waiting to unfold.

As David sat quietly beside me, lost in his own thoughts, I couldn't help but think of Wayne. Although we had been separated for two years and he had remarried, the fact that he was about to leave for China made this trip feel like a final severing of ties. For the first time, I was truly on my own. There were no more shared responsibilities, no more safety net. I was embarking on a new life as an unemployed single mother with a 9-year-old son. The thought of it all made my stomach churn.

The valleys outside the car window were serene, peaceful, and steady, while my emotions were anything but. The silence in the car, though comforting at times, weighed heavily on me. I could tell David felt the weight of the journey too, although he said nothing. The vastness of the landscape mirrored the vastness of the uncertainties I faced. The open road, with its endless horizon, was both daunting and liberating. For the first time in a long while, I realized that I was completely in control of my own fate. While that terrified me, it also filled me with quiet determination.

As we continued eastward, the valleys gave way to long stretches of desert. The transition was subtle at first, the golden hills slowly flattening into barren, sun-scorched earth. The sky above was vast and endless, a brilliant blue expanse that seemed to go on forever. It reminded me of how small we were in the grand scheme of things, and in the face of such vastness, perhaps my worries weren't as insurmountable as they felt. I could do this. I had to do this — for David, and for myself.

The landscape around us was beautiful, but my emotions were raw. Every mile brought me closer to the realization that I was stepping into a new chapter of my life. For the first time, I wasn't just a wife or a mother — I was my own person, navigating the world on my own terms. But that realization also came with the burden of responsibility. I had to make it work. There was no other option. David sensed my anxiety, I think, though I tried to hide it. He was quiet for most of the drive, watching the scenery pass by, his small hands resting in his lap. I glanced over at him from time to time, feeling a surge of protectiveness. He was my anchor, my reason for pushing forward, even when the road ahead seemed uncertain.

Once we passed through the serene valleys, the road stretched out before us like a ribbon of endless possibilities, wide and smooth, almost inviting me to push the car a little faster. Without realizing it, I found myself driving at 100 miles per hour. It wasn't until I saw the flashing lights of a police car in my rearview mirror that I knew I was in trouble. Panic shot through me as I pulled over to the side of the road. The officer, a young man, approached the car and asked me to step out. As soon as I opened the door, I couldn't hold back my emotions — I burst into tears. I handed him my registration and insurance cards, still crying. He looked at David, sitting quietly in the passenger seat, and at the back seat filled with our belongings. Perhaps he saw that we were on a long journey, that I was overwhelmed, or maybe he was just feeling generous that day, but instead of giving me a ticket, he let me off with a warning. I was beyond relieved and thanked him profusely.

After that, I was careful to watch my speed, but the long stretches of highway still seemed to blur together as I drove. We drove all day, stopping only when I was too exhausted to continue. I'd pull into rest areas along the highway to sleep for a few hours before getting back on the road. Wayne had suggested that we stay in hotels along the way, worried about our safety, but I didn't want to take the time to find a hotel, nor did I want to spend the money. It wasn't that we couldn't afford it, but I had developed a habit of saving every dollar I could. Wayne had also asked me to call him once we'd stopped for the night, but I didn't want him to worry about the fact that we were sleeping at rest stops, so I told David not to mention it. David, being the honest boy he was, struggled with keeping the secret. I reassured him that as long as he didn't say anything, he wasn't lying.

The journey wasn't all hardship. Each day, I made sure to stop for lunch at a sit-in restaurant, a small luxury that allowed us to rest and recharge. These moments gave me a chance to sit back, have a meal, and take in the enormity of what we were doing. I would look at David, and although I knew he was nervous about the move, I could tell he was also excited about what lay ahead.

We passed through countless small towns, their quiet streets and old buildings standing as reminders of lives lived in quiet contentment. I wondered what my life would be like in Pittsburgh. Would I find that same contentment? Would I be able to give David the stability he needed? The road stretched on, and with every mile, the questions in my mind multiplied.

The days of driving were long and tiring, but they also gave me time to reflect. With every mile we covered, I felt like I was shedding a layer of my old self. The woman who had lived in Los Angeles, who had been married to Wayne, who had once relied on others for support — she was slowly fading away. In her place, a new version of me was emerging. A woman who was ready to face the challenges ahead, who would do whatever it took to build a new life for her son.

By the time we reached Pittsburgh, I was exhausted but also strangely calm. The panic I had felt at the beginning of the journey had subsided, replaced by a quiet determination. Yes, I was anxious about the future, but I was also ready for it. I had driven across valleys and deserts, through long stretches of uncertainty, and I had arrived. Now, it was time to take the next step — to start building the life I had envisioned for myself and for David.

In those quiet, scenic valleys, I had learned that even in the face of uncertainty, there was beauty to be found. And as I stepped into the unknown future waiting for me in Pittsburgh, I carried that lesson with me. The road ahead would be long, and there would be more valleys to navigate, but I knew I could make it through. After all, I had made it this far.

After three days of driving, we arrived in Pittsburgh in the late afternoon. I had printed step-by-step instructions for how to get to our destination, but in my exhaustion, I took the wrong exit. The city felt like a maze of unfamiliar streets, and I quickly became lost. David began to panic, which only fueled my frustration. I snapped at him, even though I knew it wasn't his fault. He fell silent, and guilt washed over me. I knew I shouldn't have taken my frustration out on him. After a few moments, I took a deep breath and called my friend, who was waiting for us. Her husband came to meet us at a gas station, and I followed him back to their house.

Their home was small and modest. They had set up a room for us with two mattresses on the floor, which I appreciated, but I could tell David felt uneasy. He wasn't used to this kind of living arrangement. My friend was a PhD student at Carnegie Mellon University, while her husband worked long hours at a Chinese restaurant. Her mother lived with them and helped take care of their two young daughters. It was a full house, but they were kind and welcoming, and I was grateful for their hospitality.

The next day, I wasted no time. I needed to find an apartment quickly so that David and I could settle in before school started. Fortunately, I found a two-bedroom apartment in a highly rated school district that was within my budget. It was perfect — two full bathrooms and located in a safe, quiet neighborhood. The move-in date was set for two weeks later, and I breathed a sigh of relief, knowing that we would soon have our own space.

Pittsburgh was different from any city I had lived in before. It wasn't the sprawling metropolis of Los Angeles or the intellectual hub of Evanston. It had its own unique charm — a mix of old-world industrial grit and pockets of vibrant, modern culture. The city was nestled in a valley, surrounded by hills that turned brilliant shades of red and orange in the fall. The rivers that cut through the city seemed to mirror the winding paths my life had taken, unpredictable and ever-changing.

As I navigated this new chapter in Pittsburgh, I was determined to find a new direction for myself. The move wasn't just about starting over geographically; it was about reassessing my goals and finding a path that would give me both stability and fulfillment. For too long, I had been swept up in the current, reacting to life's changes rather than directing them. Now, in this new city, I had the opportunity to carve out a future that felt more aligned with who I had become.

With David settled in his new school and the apartment lease secured, I started looking into programs that would allow me to further my education. I wanted to pursue something more substantial than a certificate, something that would open more doors for me in the future. Pittsburgh had a number of universities with strong programs, and I knew this was my chance to go beyond what I had previously achieved.

It was in this period of transition, in a city so different from the ones I had lived in before, that I found clarity. The uncertainty of the journey from Los Angeles to Pittsburgh had mirrored the uncertainty I had felt for so long about my own path. But now, with a stable home, a supportive community, and a clearer sense of purpose, I began to feel that Pittsburgh would be a place where I could finally put down roots — not just for David, but for myself as well.

Looking back, the move to Pittsburgh was a defining moment. It marked the beginning of a new chapter where I took control of my future and set a new course for both my personal and professional life. The road ahead would still have its challenges, but for the first time in a long while, I felt hopeful, grounded, and ready to embrace whatever came next, again.

Chapter 22: Raising a Son as a Single Mother

Raising David as a single mother was both the most rewarding and the most challenging chapter of my life. From the moment we settled into our new apartment in Pittsburgh, it was clear that life was going to be different — not just for me, but for David as well. The apartment, though modest, represented a fresh start, a space where we could begin to build our new lives. But as we unpacked our belongings, the reality of the situation began to settle in: I was now solely responsible for my son's upbringing, education, and well-being, all while trying to navigate my own career and personal growth.

One of the first things I had to do was apply for Medicaid for David and me. I had never imagined myself in this position, but there I was, sitting in a government office, filling out paperwork for assistance. The woman who helped me was incredibly kind, offering not just Medicaid but also food stamps. She mentioned that I could also qualify for cash assistance if I applied. For some reason, though, I couldn't bring myself to do it. There was something about the idea of receiving cash assistance that I couldn't fully understand but that made me feel uneasy. Sometimes I wondered if I was being foolish about not accepting all the help I could get, but most of the time, I felt at peace with the decision. It was as if, by not applying for cash, I was holding on to a small piece of independence, however symbolic it may have been.

I knew the cost of living in Pittsburgh was lower than in many other places, but I didn't realize that it had some of the highest tuition rates in the country. When I investigated furthering my education, the only school I could afford was the community college. I went to the admissions office, determined to find a program that would help me land a stable job as soon as possible. I made it clear that my only goal was to find employment upon completion of the program. They recommended either the nuclear medicine technologist or the nursing program, both of which had high job placement rates. Nuclear medicine was a harder field, but that also made it less competitive. They happened to offer a compact nuclear medicine technologist program designed for people with a bachelor's degree. I had always enjoyed challenging myself with difficult subjects, so I chose the nuclear medicine technologist program and applied for a student loan.

The program was intense. Many of my classes started early in the morning, long before David was up for school. I had to leave the apartment before he even took the school bus, so I created a checklist for him. Each morning, David would follow the list I had made: turn off the TV, turn off the lights, put on his backpack, and lock the door before heading out. I set the alarm every day before leaving, and David, ever responsible, never missed the school bus. It wasn't ideal, but it was the best I could do under the circumstances. I was proud of how independent David was becoming.

To make ends meet, I looked for part-time jobs that fit around my class schedule. I got a position at a food court during lunchtime, thinking it would be an easy way to bring in some extra money while David was at school. But after a month, I was fired for being too slow. It was a humiliating blow. Still, I kept searching and found another job with an e-commerce company, where I applied shipping labels to packages. Yet again, I was let go because I couldn't keep up with the pace. It felt like a string of failures, and each time, the weight of single motherhood became heavier.

Eventually, I found a job at a small Chinese restaurant, answering phone calls and helping out where I could. The owner didn't know any English, so in addition to taking orders, I helped them with reading their mail and handling other small administrative tasks. They had a son who was David's age, and I often brought David with me to the restaurant. He and the boy played together, running around the restaurant while I worked. It brought me comfort knowing that David was happy and had a companion. Sometimes, the restaurant owners would even let David stay for the whole weekend, giving me a much-needed break — and the occasional chance to go on a date.

The small Chinese restaurant was a simple, modest establishment, but it had a warmth to it that made me feel almost at home. The restaurant offered a buffet with just a few dishes, not a wide variety like some of the bigger places, but each dish was prepared with care. The food was fresh and appealing, with dishes like fried rice, stir-fried vegetables, and sweet and sour chicken. The flavors were simple but comforting, the kind of food that didn't need to be extravagant to satisfy.

The lighting in the restaurant was soft and inviting, casting a warm glow over the tables, making the space feel cozy despite its modest size. On one wall, there was a large Chinese drawing — a traditional landscape painting with mountains, rivers, and bamboo trees swaying gently in the wind. It added a touch of elegance to the room. The seating was comfortable, simple wooden chairs with soft cushions, making it easy for customers to linger over their meals without feeling rushed.

David and the restaurant owner's son spent many weekends together there. The restaurant's buffet was perfect for the boys — they could simply take food whenever they were hungry, and it didn't seem to cause any trouble when David stayed overnight on weekends. They would run back and forth between the tables and the small play area in the corner, their laughter filling the restaurant. It was a relief knowing that David was happy and safe, especially when I needed a break to catch my breath.

Working at the restaurant didn't feel like a burden. In fact, I found comfort in the routine of it. I enjoyed small talk with the owner's wife, who always had a kind word or a funny story to share. She made me feel welcomed, and those conversations helped ease the loneliness that came with my new life in Pittsburgh. The restaurant became more than just a place of work for me — it was a refuge, a space where I could feel at ease, even if just for a few hours. The more time I spent there, the more it started to feel like home.

Between the soft lighting, the simple but satisfying food, and the company of the restaurant owners, I found a sense of peace in my work that I hadn't expected. It was in those quiet moments, amidst the clattering of dishes and the warm chatter of customers, that I realized how important it was to find small joys in the everyday, no matter how challenging life seemed at times.

One day, a boy from the fourth floor came down to our apartment on the second floor to play games with David. They took the same school bus and attended the same school. David later told me, "The boy said his mom told him the reason they didn't buy a house was because she didn't want the government to know she had money." I couldn't help but laugh. I didn't know if the boy had overheard his mother talking or if it was something she had actually told him, but I couldn't imagine why anyone would say that to a child. It amused me at the time, but it also made me wonder how much children absorb from their parents, whether intentional or not.

That sense of amusement quickly turned into a different kind of concern when I stumbled upon one of David's writing assignments from school. He had written, "I hope my mom will finish school and find a job so that she can pay off her debt and won't go to jail." At first, I laughed at the innocence of his words, but then a wave of sadness washed over me. I couldn't imagine how insecure David must have felt to write something like that. I hadn't realized just how much my financial struggles and our situation had impacted him. I sat down with David that evening and promised him that everything would be fine, that he didn't need to worry. I reassured him that no matter what, we would be okay — and that I would never let him face that kind of fear again.

The job at the restaurant wasn't glamorous, but it was steady work. It reminded me of how many Chinese immigrants had made a life for themselves in America through sheer hard work and determination. In the Chinese immigrant community, there were generally two kinds of people. The first kind was people like myself — well educated, often from top universities in China, coming to America with the hope of pursuing new opportunities and achieving something greater. The second kind were those with little formal education, who didn't speak much English and often came through human smuggling routes, paying hefty sums to underground networks just to make it to America. Many of them opened small Chinese restaurants or laundromats, working tirelessly to create a stable life for their families.

Despite their lack of education, they held on to the deeply rooted Chinese value of placing a high priority on education for the next generation. These families poured everything they had into ensuring their children's success. Even if the parents couldn't speak a word of English, their children often went on to excel in school and build impressive careers. It was a silent yet powerful testament to the resilience and determination of Chinese immigrants. Education was the great equalizer, and no matter how poor a family was, they knew it was the key to a better future.

I saw this same determination in myself as I balanced school, work, and motherhood. It wasn't easy. There were days when I felt like I was drowning under the weight of all my responsibilities. But I kept going. I had to. David was depending on me, and more than anything, I wanted to give him a better life.

The classes for the nuclear medicine technologist program were demanding, but I found solace in the challenge. I had always thrived when faced with difficult subjects, and this was no different. As I worked my way through the program, I began to see a future that wasn't defined by struggle but by opportunity. I was building something, step by step, that would eventually lead to stability for both David and me.

Looking back, I realize that the struggles I faced as a single mother were shaping me into a stronger, more resilient person. I was learning how to manage my time, how to prioritize what really mattered, and how to find joy in the small victories — like David never missing the school bus, or landing a job, however small, that allowed me to support us. The balance between raising a son and building a career wasn't perfect, but it was ours, and we were making it work, one day at a time.

The challenges of single motherhood were not going to define me — they were going to empower me. I was raising a son on my own, but I wasn't doing it alone. David and I were in this together, and no matter what obstacles we faced, we would overcome them, side by side.

Chapter 23: Studying Nuclear Medicine

The journey of learning nuclear medicine opened up a whole new world for me. The program was intellectually stimulating, and I loved diving into the intricacies of how radiation could be used for medical diagnosis and treatment. It felt empowering to be in a position where I could blend science with practical applications that could help people. As a single mom returning to school, I felt a sense of pride and fulfillment. It wasn't just about expanding my knowledge — it was about reclaiming a part of myself that had been lost in the daily grind of survival.

In many ways, my decision to return to school mirrored the journey of countless Chinese American immigrants who view education as the most powerful tool for upward mobility. I wasn't just reclaiming my intellectual identity — I was participating in a broader narrative of perseverance that resonated with the Chinese American experience. Education had always been the cornerstone of advancement in Chinese culture, and here, it represented a way to secure not only my own future but also the future of my family.

During my time in the Nuclear Medicine program, I met Dylan. He was a technical writer with a degree in Electrical Engineering, a man who valued precision and discipline in every aspect of his life. Our connection wasn't immediate, but it grew over time, fueled by mutual respect. Dylan admired my decision to go back to school. He had been considering returning to school himself for a second degree in computer science, but it wasn't until he heard my story — how I had gone back to school as a single mom — that he finally took the leap.

Dylan often praised my intellect, which I appreciated. My computer science knowledge was solid, even though I didn't earn a full BS degree. The certificate program I completed covered all the necessary courses; the only difference was that it didn't include general education. I had even helped others along the way, like the French chef with his math homework, and now, I found myself tutoring Dylan in his computer science courses.

I suppose part of what drew Dylan to me was that we shared a similar drive for excellence. We both had a kind of self-discipline that pushed us to seek perfection in everything we did, whether it was academics, work, or even our personal lives. But Dylan's idea of perfection was different from mine, as I'd soon learn.

One early memory of our relationship still lingers vividly in my mind. Dylan took me to Macy's, straight to the cosmetics counter. I had barely worn makeup throughout my life, except for the occasional use of lipstick and an eyebrow pencil. The first time I had experimented with makeup was at Peking University, mimicking my roommates. It had felt strange then, like I was trying to be someone else. The foundation and rouge made me look different, not necessarily prettier, and I quickly gave up on the idea. Simplicity suited me better.

At Macy's, however, Dylan had other ideas. He asked the girl at the counter to apply makeup on me, and when it was done, he asked me to look at myself in the mirror. I nodded, unsure how I felt about the transformation. To my surprise, he told the girl to pack everything she had used on me, along with the products needed for removal. The total came to about $400. I had never received a gift like that before, and it overwhelmed me. At dinner afterward, Dylan smiled, clearly pleased with himself. "It's critical for a successful relationship for a guy to act quickly to claim a girl before someone else does," he said, half-joking, half-serious.

I appreciated his gesture, but part of me wondered if he truly understood who I was. Was the makeup for me, or was it for the version of me he wanted to see? I had always preferred simplicity — perhaps because of the cultural norms I grew up with, where even a hint of personal vanity was labeled as bourgeois sentiment. Wearing makeup felt like stepping outside of myself, and yet here I was, indulging in it for the sake of this new relationship. The experience at Macy's, though seemingly trivial, opened a window into the intersection of cultural and gender expectations. As a Chinese American woman, I had grown up with a sense of simplicity and practicality when it came to appearance — yet here I was, navigating a different cultural landscape that valued outward expressions of beauty. In that moment, I realized that the immigrant journey isn't just about adapting to new political or social environments — it's also about negotiating cultural and personal identity, constantly redefining what it means to belong.

That summer, David went to China to spend time with his dad, Wayne, who was running a tech company with a team of programmers. It was during this time that Dylan introduced me to

American football. He took me to two Steelers games at Heinz Field, and those outings became a transformative experience for me.

I had never been able to connect with football when watching it on TV. The rules seemed confusing, and the endless commentary made it difficult to follow. But being in Heinz Field was entirely different. The roar of the crowd, the sea of black and gold jerseys, the palpable energy in the air — it was exhilarating. The stadium seemed to pulse with excitement, and for the first time, I understood the appeal of the sport. It wasn't just about the game itself; it was about the community, the camaraderie, the shared sense of pride and belonging. I felt like I had been given a direct window into American culture. From that moment, I became a Steelers fan.

Attending those Steelers games was more than just enjoying a sport — it marked a turning point in my relationship with American culture. For many immigrants, there is a delicate balance between maintaining one's cultural roots and fully participating in the customs of a new country. In that moment, surrounded by the roar of the crowd, I felt a sense of belonging that had previously eluded me. It was through these seemingly small moments that I began to understand how cultural integration could lead to a broader acceptance and involvement in American society. Those games were more than just entertainment; they marked my first real, personal experience with American culture. It wasn't through academics or the workplace but through something as simple as a football game that I began to feel more connected to the world around me. It was as if I had crossed a threshold, not just as a student or a mother, but as someone finding their place in a new country.

When David returned from China, I introduced him to Dylan over dinner at a restaurant. David, being his energetic self, couldn't sit still. He had ADHD, which made dinner outings unpredictable. While we were waiting for our food, he slipped under the table, crawled out of the booth, and wandered around the restaurant. Most patrons were kind and tolerant, ignoring him or offering polite smiles. A few seemed surprised, but none appeared truly bothered. Eventually, a waitress gently brought David back to our table. I had promised David a new game after dinner, something he had been looking forward to, but Dylan wasn't amused by David's behavior. He thought it was an embarrassment and insisted that David should be punished.

I had always considered myself strict with David, except when it came to his ADHD. Even my mother had commented on how patient I was with him. I had tried various methods of correction, including punishment, but nothing seemed to work. If punishment wasn't helping, I saw no reason to keep enforcing it. I believed that, over time, David would grow out of his impulsive behavior. I stuck to my promise and bought him the game after Dylan left.

My approach to parenting David was deeply influenced by my upbringing and cultural background. In Chinese culture, discipline is often viewed through a collective lens — children are expected to conform for the sake of the family and society. Yet, as I navigated American expectations of individualism and child autonomy, I found myself at a crossroads. Parenting David, especially with his ADHD, forced me to redefine my role not just as a mother, but as someone balancing the values of two cultures. The choices I made reflected a growing understanding of how my identity as a Chinese American immigrant informed my views on family and child-rearing in a society that valued different approaches.

David had been struggling at school, especially with his home-class teacher, who wouldn't listen to him unless he was calm, something David found impossible to achieve on his own. I sided with his teacher, convinced that discipline was the right approach. It wasn't until much later that I realized how wrong I had been. I had let David feel all alone, without any support, not even from me — his own mother. That guilt stayed with me for a long time.

Fortunately, things changed when David entered fifth grade. He had a new home class teacher who understood him. This teacher had a gentle approach, handling David's hyperactivity with ease. He said everything was fine in class and suggested that David be evaluated for his overall well-being. I followed through, and the results surprised me: David's IQ was 129, just one point away from the threshold of being considered a genius. I didn't know that students with IQs of 130 or higher were required by law to be placed in special education programs designed to help them explore their potential. In addition to his high IQ, David was officially diagnosed with ADHD, which also required special education intervention.

With that diagnosis, David was placed in a special education program, and a special education teacher, Suzanne, came to our apartment every day after school to spend an hour with him. This dedicated attention made a world of difference. David began to improve, both academically and emotionally. I was so grateful for her patience and the school's decision to provide this support. For the first time in a long while, I felt like David wasn't struggling alone.

Suzanne became a significant presence in our lives. She was an older woman, perhaps in her early 50s, with kind eyes and a gentle but firm demeanor. There was patience about her that put David at ease, and she seemed to have a natural ability to connect with him, even on his most restless days. Her hair, streaked with gray, was always neatly pulled back, and she often wore simple, comfortable clothes — loose blouses, soft sweaters, and practical shoes.

She wasn't just a teacher; she was someone who genuinely cared about David's progress. Over time, she became more than an educator to us — she became a family friend. Her visits to our home, initially all business, gradually turned into conversations over tea after the lessons, where she would tell me about her own life, her past experiences working with children, and her love for helping those with special needs.

One day, she joined us for grocery shopping, something that made me realize how much she had become part of our lives. David, being his usual energetic self, decided to explore in his unique way. While we were walking down the frozen foods aisle, he spotted one of the large freezers, the kind with glass doors, and without a word, he opened one, stepped inside, and closed the door behind him.

I stood there, frozen for a moment, unsure of how to react, but Suzanne didn't miss a beat. With the same calmness she used during their lessons, she simply walked over, opened the freezer door, and pulled David out as if nothing unusual had happened. David, unfazed, gave her a sheepish smile, and she returned it with an amused shake of her head. It was moments like these that made me grateful for her presence — not just for the help she provided David but for the way she handled life's little surprises with grace and understanding.

Her steady influence wasn't just in the classroom; it extended to our everyday lives. She seemed to understand David in ways even I sometimes couldn't, and she helped me see the world from his perspective.

Dylan, however, couldn't see things the same way. He continued to express frustration with David's behavior, finding it stressful to be around him. It became clear to me that Dylan, despite his kindness and meticulous nature, wasn't the right fit for our family. David didn't need another dominating figure in his life — he needed understanding and support. Eventually, Dylan and I parted ways.

Though my relationship with Dylan didn't last, the experience left me with valuable lessons. I realized that intellectual compatibility wasn't enough if emotional understanding was missing. Dylan's meticulous nature and desire for perfection, while admirable, didn't align with the fluid, sometimes chaotic reality of raising a child with ADHD. I needed to protect David's emotional well-being, and that meant choosing partners who could handle the unpredictability that came with our life.

Reflecting on that period, I saw it as a time of tremendous personal growth. I was learning nuclear medicine, expanding my intellectual horizons, and at the same time, navigating the complexities of motherhood and relationships. I had found a new part of myself at Heinz Field, embraced a piece of American culture, and solidified my resolve to put David first, even when it was difficult.

In many ways, my journey in nuclear medicine, my role as a mother, and my experience with Dylan were microcosms of the immigrant experience itself — filled with moments of adaptation, resilience, and self-discovery. As Chinese Americans, we often find ourselves navigating between worlds — balancing old traditions with new possibilities. And yet, it is through these very challenges that we carve out our own space in American society, transforming not just ourselves but the communities we are part of.

In the end, I emerged stronger, more confident in my abilities, both as a mother and a woman forging her own path.

Chapter 24: Realizing a Change of Heart

The excitement of learning nuclear medicine started to fade during my internship at various hospitals. I had enjoyed the study — the intricate science of how radiation could be harnessed for diagnostic purposes, the detailed protocols for each scan, and the delicate balancing act of using this powerful technology for medical good. But working with terminally ill patients every day began to weigh heavily on me. The reality of seeing people at the end stages of their lives, suffering and often beyond help, left a deeper impact than I had anticipated. No one had warned me how draining it would be, not just for the patients but for those who worked around them. I saw it in the faces of the nurses, in the fatigue of the technologists — this constant exposure to people who were slowly fading away.

One patient stood out in my memory. She was in her late 50s, with a warm smile despite her frailty. Every time she came in for a scan, she would ask me how I was doing, her voice light, as if it were her job to put *me* at ease. I admired her resilience, but I could see in her eyes that she knew her time was limited. The scans confirmed it, and yet, there was nothing I could do except follow the doctor's orders, make sure the machines were calibrated correctly, and print the results.

One day, I worked with a young man in his early 30s, much younger than most patients I had encountered. His face was gaunt, his skin pale, but his eyes were still sharp, as if he was determined to fight against the inevitable. His wife sat beside him, holding his hand, her face a mask of forced optimism. They had two young children, and when I looked at them, I couldn't help but feel a lump in my throat. He smiled at me as I prepared the machine for his scan, but there was a quiet sadness behind his eyes. Even though I followed protocol, I felt powerless. It was moments like these that chipped away at my resolve.

I found myself watching the other technologists, some of whom had been in the field for years, and I didn't see myself in them. They followed orders without question, went through the motions, and then clocked out at the end of the day.

Another realization dawned on me during this time: despite all the knowledge I had gained, I was still just a technician following orders. This realization hit me hard. The work I had been so excited about now felt hollow. I wasn't part of the solution — just a small cog in a larger machine, necessary but not integral to decision-making. The limitations of my role became glaringly obvious. As a nuclear medicine technologist, my role was to perform the scan, not to interpret or engage in the bigger picture of patient care. That sense of disillusionment began to grow. I had always been a top student, used to excelling, pushing boundaries, and asking questions. But in this role, none of that mattered. My intellect and curiosity had no place. I would be limited to a strictly defined task, performing scans. There was a day when a patient's results didn't seem right to me. The numbers were off, and something about the scan didn't match what I had studied. I wanted to ask questions, to dig deeper, but that wasn't my role. The technologists weren't supposed to question the doctors' orders or the results. I was there to perform a task, and nothing more. That stifling realization left me feeling powerless and frustrated. What good was my knowledge if I couldn't apply it in a meaningful way?

Just as I was starting to realize that my role in nuclear medicine wasn't what I had envisioned, I began to understand that many Chinese immigrants face similar disappointments in the American workforce. We are taught that hard work and education will open doors, but the reality is often more complex. Social dynamics, networking, and cultural adaptation are just as important as skills and dedication. In that sense, my experience wasn't unique — it was part of a broader immigrant narrative where expectations clash with the nuances of the American workplace.

One of my classmates, a cheerful woman who always seemed to have pastries or treats for the nurses and technologists, effortlessly blended into the workplace culture. She was friendly and sociable, always making small talk and fitting in seamlessly. Even before our program ended, she had secured a job offer. Her ability to network and make herself liked by everyone around her was the key, more than her technical abilities or knowledge. I began to notice the subtle rules of the hospital workplace. It wasn't just about doing your job well; it was about who you knew, who liked you, and how well you fit into the social dynamics. The nurses and technologists formed cliques, and those who brought in homemade pastries or chatted with the doctors over coffee breaks seemed to be rewarded with better shifts or recommendations for promotions. I couldn't understand how my skills and dedication could be overshadowed by something so trivial as small talk over coffee. It wasn't that I was anti-social, but I didn't want to rely on such methods to advance in my career. I had always believed that hard work, knowledge, and skills would be the defining factors. The hospital setting showed me something different, something I wasn't comfortable with. It was a place where personal connections, not performance, opened doors. This didn't sit right with me, and I started to question whether I truly wanted to stay on this path. Would I ever feel fulfilled in an environment where my abilities weren't fully valued? Navigating the workplace politics in the hospital was a reminder that the American workplace isn't always a meritocracy. For many immigrants, learning how to maneuver these informal social rules can be a challenge. We are often at a disadvantage, not because we lack ability, but because we are unfamiliar with the hidden dynamics that drive professional advancement. This experience made me reflect on how many Chinese American immigrants face similar barriers in their own careers, and how overcoming them requires not just skill but a deep understanding of the culture we are working in.

The realization that I couldn't advance my career in such settings only deepened my doubts. It was a difficult realization. My drive for academic excellence had no bearing here. The hospital setting wasn't a meritocracy. In the hospital environment, social connections often carried more weight than skills or intelligence.

One late afternoon, after a long and busy day, I found myself alone in the scan room. It was a rare moment of calm. The day had been filled with back-to-back patients, and for once, there were no new orders coming in. The machines were quiet, the room still. I put my arms on the desk, rested my head on them, and closed my eyes for just a moment, hoping to steal a brief rest before the day's work was picked up again.

I wasn't asleep — just taking a pause, something I thought would be harmless in an empty room. But a few minutes later, I heard footsteps approaching. I lifted my head to see the supervisor standing in the doorway, looking at me with concern.

"Are you feeling sick?" he asked, his voice surprisingly gentle.

I shook my head, a little embarrassed to have been caught resting. "No, I'm fine," I replied.

But instead of moving on, he gave me a look that immediately made me feel uneasy. "It's inappropriate to rest like this during work hours," he said firmly. His tone had changed, and I could feel the weight of his judgment.

In that moment, I felt a wave of frustration and sadness. I had been working hard all day, giving my best to every patient and to the job. I wasn't slacking off; I was simply taking a moment to breathe. But now, it felt as though all my effort had been reduced to this one instance — like all the dedication I had shown meant nothing.

Without warning, tears welled up in my eyes, and I burst into tears right there in the scan room. I felt so wronged, like I had been reprimanded for something so small, so human. The weight of the situation — of the internship, of working with terminal patients, of feeling out of place in this environment — hit me all at once. The supervisor seemed surprised by my reaction, offering a few awkward words of comfort before leaving the room.

Later, I learned that it wasn't just the supervisor's own observation that had led to the confrontation. One of my classmates had told on me. He had been eyeing a job offer from this hospital, and he must have felt threatened by the possibility that I might be more preferred. Telling the supervisor about my brief rest had been his way of gaining favor, of making sure he was seen as the more dedicated candidate.

As the supervisor walked away, a knot of resentment formed in my chest. I had worked tirelessly that day, and in one moment, it felt like all my efforts had been reduced to a single perceived mistake. What hurt more was learning that it wasn't just a random observation — it was a deliberate act by someone I had considered a peer. I never imagined that the competition for job offers would lead to such underhanded tactics. That was when I realized that this environment wasn't just exhausting — it was toxic.

That realization stung. The hospital environment was already starting to feel suffocating, with its rigid hierarchy and relentless pace. But this? This petty betrayal over a potential job offer? It made me question everything. Was this what my career would look like in the future — struggling not only against the emotional toll of the job but also against the petty, underhanded tactics of colleagues?

The incident confirmed what I had already begun to suspect: this wasn't the right path for me. I couldn't see myself thriving in a setting where politics and favoritism seemed to matter more than skill or dedication. The work itself was emotionally draining enough, but the added burden of navigating these kinds of interpersonal dynamics made it clear that I didn't belong here.

In the weeks that followed, I spent a lot of time thinking about the future. Was this really where I saw myself — working in an environment where the emotional and political dynamics overshadowed my passion for learning and my drive to excel? I had always believed that hard work and intelligence would lead me to success, but I was beginning to see that the world didn't always work that way. I didn't want to spend the next 20 years feeling like a cog in a machine. I wanted more — more freedom, more intellectual engagement, more purpose.

Despite all of this, I remained determined to finish what I had started. I passed the board exam at the end of the program, not because I still wanted to pursue a career as a nuclear medicine technologist, but because I needed the sense of closure. I wasn't someone who gave up easily, and I wasn't going to let this experience define me. But I knew, deep down, that I had to find another path.

As the stress from the hospital began to weigh on me, I found myself withdrawing from other parts of my life. My relationship with David was strained, and I often felt too tired to engage fully with him at the end of the day. I wondered if this was the kind of life I wanted to lead — constantly drained and emotionally distant from those I loved. When I met Paul, it was like a breath of fresh air. He offered a new perspective, a different way of life that wasn't weighed down by the same pressures. He was looking for a bookkeeper for his small advertising company, and I decided to take a break from the medical field and explore a different path. I started working for him, helping to build an intranet for his company while keeping his books in order. It felt like a way to reset my course and explore new possibilities.

Leaving nuclear medicine wasn't just about changing careers — it was about redefining what success meant to me. As an immigrant, I had always believed that finding a stable, respected profession was the ultimate goal. But my journey taught me that adaptability is just as important as ambition. Many Chinese American immigrants face similar moments of redirection, where the paths we had originally planned for ourselves shift, and we must learn to embrace new opportunities. In that sense, my decision to leave nuclear medicine wasn't a failure — it was a moment of transformation, an opportunity to find what truly mattered to me, a chance to find fulfillment in a new direction and to pursue something that feels right, even if it wasn't part of the original plan.

When I began working for Paul, it wasn't just about leaving behind a career in nuclear medicine — it was about finding more control and purpose in my life. For many Chinese American immigrants, the search for autonomy and independence is a central part of our journey in this country. Whether it's through starting a small business or finding a profession that gives us more freedom, we seek out paths that allow us to define our own success. In taking this new direction, I was reclaiming that sense of control, a sentiment shared by so many immigrants who come to America in search of a better future. Working for Paul was a sharp contrast to the hospital's setting. Here, I had control over the work I did, and I could see the immediate impact of my contributions. It wasn't the work I had originally envisioned for myself, but it was fulfilling in a way that my internship never had been.

Looking back on my decision to leave nuclear medicine, I realized that it was more than just a career change — it was a lesson in resilience. The path I had envisioned for myself wasn't the one I ended up on, but that didn't mean I had failed. Like many Chinese American immigrants, I had to learn to adapt, to find strength in moments of uncertainty, and to keep pushing forward even when the road ahead seemed unclear. This resilience, this ability to transform and grow, is at the heart of the immigrant experience.

Chapter 25: Meeting Her Future Husband

The first time I brought David to meet Paul is a memory that still stands out vividly. As we drove to Paul's house, I could sense David's nervousness. He fidgeted in his seat, stretching his hand down to lightly tap the plastic container of rotisserie chicken I had placed on the floor in front of him. After a while, he asked, "May I put the chicken on my lap so that I can smell it?" His request puzzled me, but I agreed. "Yes, you may, but don't open it. I don't want you to make a mess in the car."

There was a long pause before David voiced his real concern. "What if Paul doesn't like me?" His voice was small and filled with uncertainty. I turned to him, understanding how vulnerable he felt. Meeting someone new, especially someone who could become a permanent figure in our lives, was intimidating. "Whoever doesn't like you, I will break up with him," I reassured him. His face relaxed, and I could see the relief wash over him.

When we arrived, Paul greeted David with a big, warm hug. This was a simple gesture, but it taught me something profound about cultural norms in family life. In Chinese culture, physical affection isn't displayed so openly, and I had unknowingly mirrored that with David. Watching Paul interact with David so easily made me realize that, as immigrants, we must adapt our family dynamics to fit the cultural framework of our new environment. The transition to this different way of showing love and care reflected the larger journey of Chinese American immigrants — learning to balance the traditions of our heritage while embracing new cultural practices.

Paul's affection reminded me how different things had been in my upbringing. In Chinese culture, we didn't hug like that. In fact, I couldn't remember my mother ever hugging me. I hadn't hugged David as much as I should have either. Physical affection had never been a priority for me, and it was only when I saw David's need for it that I realized how important it was. I remembered a time after we had moved to Pittsburgh, when David came home from school one day and asked, "Could you gain some weight?" Startled, I asked, "Why?" He explained, "Our teacher said one can carry as much as half of one's weight." Thinking back, I realized how I had been too focused on the practicalities of life to notice his need for physical closeness. Paul, however, naturally filled that gap, making David feel immediately comfortable.

David quickly grew attached to Paul. Paul's gentle, loving nature extended to everyone, especially children. His kindness wasn't something forced; it was simply who he was. It wasn't just David who noticed this — I did too. There was something special about how Paul treated every child as if they were his own, and that made me realize how fortunate we were to have him in our lives.

One weekend, Paul suggested taking David and some other kids to Great Wolf Lodge in Ohio. Paul's company provided phone recordings for the resort, so we had the opportunity to enjoy it as part of his business perks. We invited the boy from the Chinese restaurant where I worked part-time, along with his baby sister, Anna. While David and his friend explored the water park, Paul spent most of his time looking after little Anna. I found myself growing upset as the day went on — why was Paul paying more attention to Anna than David? I had brought David to bond with him, yet here he was, seemingly ignoring my son.

But later, as I reflected on the day, I realized something important about Paul: his love wasn't selective. He treated all children with the same affection and care, not because he had to, but because that was simply who he was. The very reason Paul could love David as his own was because of that same boundless love. He didn't divide his attention; he shared it freely with everyone. That moment taught me a valuable lesson in understanding Paul's character — there was no favoritism in his heart. I shouldn't have felt hurt by his attention toward Anna because that love was what made him who he was.

In many ways, blending our lives together reflected my journey as an immigrant. Just as I had to learn how to navigate American society, I had to learn how to integrate new family dynamics. Paul's way of showing love and care for children, whether it was David or Anna, was different from the way I had been raised. But over time, I learned that these differences didn't mean one approach was better than the other. Instead, they represented how immigrant families must merge their cultural traditions while embracing new ways of being a family in America.

Paul worked long hours every day, dedicating himself to his small advertising company. His business focused on designing call flows and creating phone recording messages for clients, including banks, auto shops, restaurants, theaters, and resorts. Many of the local businesses had in-trade services with him, which meant Paul received perks like maintenance for his lawn equipment, meals at restaurants, and tickets to local theater productions. His entire kitchen set was furnished on trade, and although his company wasn't turning a profit, Paul remained content. He hadn't paid himself for years, as the company's revenue went directly to covering bills, but Paul never let financial stress diminish his optimism.

Paul was 13 years older than me, but his youthful appearance often surprised people. Even my mother once commented that he looked younger than my older brother, Tony, who was five years older than me. Paul was energetic and healthy, with a vibrant enthusiasm for life that I admired. He had a way of staying active even when I found myself struggling to keep up. His energy and youthful spirit were contagious.

There was one thing about Paul that challenged my perceptions — his weight. By my standards, Paul was overweight. I had always maintained strict discipline when it came to my appearance, keeping a perfect weight and never straying far from my routine. To me, being overweight symbolized a lack of self-discipline. I believed that if someone couldn't control their weight, they wouldn't be able to control other aspects of their life either. But Paul made me question that assumption. Despite his size, he was disciplined in his work, his love, and his care for others. It was a reminder that outward appearances don't always reflect inner strength or character.

I knew Paul was going to propose, but I had my reservations. I spoke to my mother about it, expressing my concerns. "He's poor," I told her. "And he's older than me... and he's fat." My mom listened patiently before offering her perspective. "Hasn't he been living a comfortable life? Then there's nothing to worry about being poor. He looks young, so age isn't an issue. And although he's fat, he's handsome. He says it's all muscle."

Her words reassured me, and a year later, in 2006, Paul and I got married. He became the perfect stepfather to David, showing the same love and care that he had from the beginning.

Paul's proposal came on a day that Suzanne, David's special education teacher, was visiting. She had become an important part of our lives, having seen firsthand how David and Paul interacted. Suzanne, always gentle and observant, was thrilled when Paul got down on one knee. Her face lit up with joy, and I could see how happy she was for David and me. She had watched our little family grow, and it was clear that she knew how much this proposal meant for all of us. Suzanne even attended our wedding, sharing in the celebration of this new chapter in our lives.

When David and I moved into Paul's house, it felt like a new beginning. Paul's small brick house had three bedrooms, two stories, and a basement. It wasn't large, but it was sturdy and well-maintained, with a small back porch and a neatly kept front yard. The house was always clean and organized, ready for guests at any moment. Paul took pride in his plants, which he called "his babies," and though he missed his two sons who lived with their mother, I could see that his plants offered him a different kind of nurturing outlet.

David seemed to settle in quickly. The security of Paul's home, combined with Paul's steady presence, gave David a sense of stability that he hadn't felt before. The solid walls of Paul's house mirrored the safety David felt within our new family. As we began our life together, I knew this was the start of a new chapter, not just for me but for David as well.

Our marriage wasn't without its challenges. Whenever I got angry, Paul would withdraw, avoiding conflict at all costs. He considered any form of argument negative, and he believed my anger was out of control. I had to tell him, again and again, that my anger was never out of control. I expressed it because I wanted him to face the issues that upset me. Ignoring our problems wouldn't help us grow. I told him that if we didn't face these issues together, our marriage wouldn't last. Eventually, he realized I wasn't making empty threats. We started to talk through our problems, and with each heated discussion, we gained a deeper understanding of each other. Over time, our relationship grew stronger.

However, living in Paul's house presented a different kind of challenge. His house was full — everywhere. I had always wanted simplicity and hated clutter, but Paul would never throw anything away. I remember standing in the kitchen, surrounded by piles of old magazines and shelves packed with knick-knacks. No matter how much I tidied, the house seemed to resist my efforts for simplicity. I accepted that I would never feel completely at home there, but I made peace with it.

The truth was, feeling at home had not been a priority for a long time. When I returned to China in 2002, for the first time since leaving for Singapore in 1995, I realized how deep my sense of homelessness ran. My first stop was Hangzhou, where my mother had retired and bought an apartment I had never lived in. It didn't feel like home. In Beijing, where I had spent my adult life, I had no relatives, and staying in a hotel only heightened the feeling of estrangement. Even in Xinjiang, where I was born and lived until I was 17, staying at my sister's apartment didn't offer the comfort of home, despite being close to my sister. When I returned to Los Angeles, faced with the need to find a cheaper place to live after the lease on my apartment near Wilshire Blvd ended, I felt the same — adrift, without a sense of home. For a short while, I felt sad, realizing I had been moving every three years since I was 17. But I couldn't afford to dwell on it. I made a conscious decision that I didn't need to feel at home anywhere. Perhaps this constant movement had become my only form of stability.

Despite the challenges, we continued to build our life together. We got married in August, just in time for David to start junior high school. At the parent orientation, Paul and I insisted that David remain in the special education program. My primary goal was simple: I wanted David to be allowed to doodle during lessons without being punished. Navigating the American educational system for David's needs was an eye-opening experience. It wasn't just about securing special services for David — it was about understanding the broader social and political framework that governed those rights. In advocating for David, I became more aware of the mechanisms that shaped our lives as immigrants, and the ways in which we must actively participate in these systems to ensure a better future.

David was popular at school. He was smart, funny, and the kind of kid who made friends easily. Despite being one of only three Chinese students in a predominantly white school, he never struggled socially.

Marrying Paul wasn't just about our personal relationship — it was about how my life as an immigrant was evolving in America. Through our marriage, I learned to navigate new ways of being a family, merging the values I grew up with into the broader cultural framework of American life. This journey mirrors the experiences of many Chinese American immigrants, as we learn to balance our heritage with the new cultural practices we encounter. In doing so, we don't lose our identity; we expand it, creating new ways of understanding family, love, and belonging.

Paul's steady, loving presence transformed both of our lives for the better. David finally had the father figure he needed, and I had found a partner who would support me through the next chapter of our journey.

Chapter 26: Moving Forward with New Career Goals

Building a life with Paul was a continuous adventure, full of both opportunities and challenges. His skills and talents seemed endless, but so did his quirks. Whether it was plumbing, electrical work, or even legal matters, Paul handled everything at a professional level. I marveled at his ability to transform our basement into a fully functional recording studio, doing all the wiring and technical setup himself. I had never seen anything like it. Watching him work with such focus and precision was fascinating. I wasn't used to someone who could fix and build everything himself — no need for external help, just Paul and his tools.

One day, I asked him, "How did you learn all this?"

He smiled, wiping his hands on a rag, and said, "I just pick things up as I go along. If you want something done right, you've got to learn to do it yourself." That was Paul in a nutshell — self-reliant, confident, and driven by his own internal standards of excellence.

His self-reliance, while admirable, stood in contrast to my upbringing as an immigrant. I had grown up in China, where community was central to survival, and families often leaned on each other for support. But in America, particularly in my marriage to Paul, I was learning that individualism and self-reliance were often seen as the marks of success. Paul embodied this American ideal, while I had to adapt and reconcile these differences with my own cultural values. This gradual transformation reflected a larger shift experienced by many Chinese American immigrants: balancing the values of community with the pressures of independence in a new society.

Even when it came to legal matters, Paul took control. His attorney was a long-time friend who trusted Paul to write all the necessary documents. All the attorney had to do was sign them, charging only for the time it took. I admired Paul's resourcefulness in keeping his legal costs minimal while ensuring everything was done with precision. He always found a way to handle things himself, relying on his intelligence and knack for understanding complex tasks quickly.

However, as I reflected on his abilities, I couldn't help but think about the immigrant journey. For many Chinese Americans, the challenges of navigating legal, financial, and business systems in America were overwhelming. We often didn't have the advantage of long-time connections or the self-assurance that Paul had cultivated over time. Immigrants like myself had to learn to bridge the gap between the unfamiliar systems of our new home and the reliance on personal networks that sustained us back in China. Watching Paul manage everything with such ease made me wonder about how Chinese immigrants often face additional layers of complexity when building a life in America.

What amazed me most about Paul was his dedication to perfecting every aspect of his work. After finishing a production in the recording studio, he would spend hours listening to it on repeat, making the tiniest adjustments to get it just right. It wasn't enough for something to sound good — it had to be perfect in Paul's eyes. He'd often say, "Probably nobody could tell the difference except me," and he was right — I certainly couldn't hear what he was tweaking. I would listen with him, nodding along, but I never understood how he could hear those subtle variations.

I once attended a concert where we sat next to the principal of a music school. Paul's commentary on the performance impressed the principal, who marveled at his ability to hear the subtle differences in the music that no one else noticed. Paul wasn't just a musician or technician; he was a perfectionist in the truest sense. This pursuit of perfection extended beyond music — it infiltrated every part of his life. Whether it was the way he brewed coffee or arranged his office, Paul's life was a series of perfectly curated details. Watching him work could be both inspiring and frustrating.

Paul's history was just as fascinating. He had his own radio show at the age of 15, back when he only had a learner's permit to drive. His stage name was Boogiemann, and he became a DJ, choreographer, and the leading male dancer for touring performances up and down the East Coast. I could hardly believe it when he first told me. "You? A dancer?" I teased, but he showed me old pictures and even some videos. He was incredible. His parents were incredibly proud of him. I think they believed he could do anything.

When I met Paul, his parents had already relocated to Seattle to live with his sister. His father was in poor health, and his mother needed more support as they aged. Paul had refinanced his house a few years earlier to help cover the costs of their relocation, explaining why, despite living in his home for over a decade, he still had nearly 30 years left on the mortgage. When he told me this, I was surprised and concerned. A 30-year mortgage at his age? It didn't make sense to me.

This was yet another point where our different upbringings became clear. In Chinese culture, financial security and preparation for the future were paramount. Debt, particularly a long mortgage, was something to be avoided. I had grown up with the belief that one's responsibility to their family meant securing stability, saving for emergencies, and ensuring a legacy. Paul's carefree approach, while admirable in its simplicity, seemed foreign to me. For Chinese immigrants in America, this clash between financial cultures was something many families grappled with as they tried to reconcile traditional values with the new realities of American life.

When I suggested refinancing again to take advantage of lower interest rates, Paul wanted to take out the maximum loan available to free up more cash. I insisted on borrowing only the minimum amount necessary. I knew any extra cash would be squandered quickly, just as it always had been. That's how Paul lived — he didn't save for emergencies or retirement, and I knew that if we weren't careful, we could end up in financial trouble. I took control of the finances, and since the loan was under my name to secure the lowest rate possible, I made the decision to borrow just enough to pay off the existing loan.

I handled the refinancing just as I had learned to handle other financial matters after my first marriage ended. Back then, Wayne had managed everything — paying the bills, saving for the future, and investing. When we separated, I told him he didn't need to give me half of our savings since most of it had come from his contributions. But Wayne refused. He said he was grateful for the ten years of best years of my life we spent together and wanted to give me my share, even though I hadn't contributed financially in the same way. He also promised to cover David's college tuition, which was a huge relief. His promise gave me a sense of security and enabled me to worry free during a very uncertain time, and I would always be grateful for that.

After our separation, I had to learn quickly how to manage finances on my own. I remember the first time I opened a bank account in my name. It was daunting, but it was also empowering. I learned how to set up auto-payments for bills, manage my money, and even invest what little I had. Those experiences made me more self-reliant, and they served me well when I married Paul.

With Paul, I realized early on that I had to be the financial planner for our family. At first, I thought Paul was generous because he was poor, but I soon realized he was genuinely generous — he would spend his last penny on the people he loved without thinking twice. That was just who he was. His father passed away when we had just started dating, and his mom visited us once after his father's death. Paul was so attentive to her. He took her to visit her friends at the senior center, showed her around the places she used to frequent, and even took her on a cruise down the Allegheny River. It was an emotional trip for him — he said it might be the last time his mom would be in Pittsburgh. I remember watching him that day, deeply moved by the way he cared for her.

Paul often said, "I may be poor financially, but I'm rich in love." In Chinese culture, a man who is poor financially would often feel a deep sense of shame or failure. But Paul was different. His self-worth wasn't tied to his financial situation, and he never let money — or the lack of it — define him. He was always generous, always giving, never worrying about tomorrow's bills. That carefree attitude was something I both admired and feared.

When I acted as Paul's bookkeeper, I couldn't sleep at night knowing a bill was due the next day and there wasn't enough money to cover it. After I started my new job, I begged him not to tell me anything about his company's finances — good or bad. If he told me good news, I'd worry when I didn't hear anything, and if he told me bad news, I'd lose sleep over it. It was easier for my sanity not to know.

Paul's approach to life was focused entirely on the present. He never worried about tomorrow. This attitude was evident in how he handled money, but it also showed up in other areas of his life. For example, each month, as soon as a client paid him, Paul would go grocery shopping and stock the refrigerator for the entire month. He'd buy everything in abundance to make sure we didn't run out of anything. But by the end of the month, we'd end up throwing away spoiled food that had been forgotten in the back of the fridge. I hated the waste, but Paul shrugged it off, always saying, "There's always more where that came from." He wasn't bothered by the excess or the waste, but to me, it was a constant reminder that he wasn't thinking about the future.

For Paul, life was about enjoying the present moment — the food, the work, and the people around him. While I admired his ability to live in the moment, it made long-term planning nearly impossible. His lack of savings, his willingness to spend without considering tomorrow, and his refusal to think ahead worried me. I often wondered how we would manage emergencies or retirement. As much as I tried to steer our finances in a responsible direction, there was a part of me that realized this was another area where my Chinese upbringing and American life clashed.

As talented and intelligent as Paul was, he lacked long-term vision. I often wondered if he had ever set concrete goals for his company. He didn't seem to think about profitability or sustainability, and even though I wasn't a business expert, I understood the 80/20 rule and the importance of efficiency. Paul, on the other hand, was a perfectionist. He spent endless hours perfecting things, but to grow a business, one needed to know when to stop. I used to tell him, "Paul, you're spending too much time on that last 20%. Just finish it. It's good enough." He would smile, shake his head, and say, "Not for me."

That was Paul — always striving for perfection, even if it meant never finishing. His brilliant mind was both a gift and a curse. While he was capable of so much, his pursuit of perfection often held him back. I knew that his upbringing, especially his mother's unwavering faith in him, had influenced this mindset. She believed he could do anything, which may have prevented him from pushing himself further. He peaked early, at 15, with his radio show and his dancing, and had been enjoying every moment of his life since. He attended college but didn't finish it because he was able to learn everything better and faster on his own.

I wasn't joking when I often said to Paul, "Lucky for me, you didn't have a mom like me, or you'd be as successful as Sean Hannity, and I'd never have had the chance to marry you." In truth, I believed that if someone had pushed Paul harder, he could have achieved much greater things. But at this point in our lives, I had accepted that Paul was who he was, and I couldn't change him. What I could do was focus on my own career and ensure that David and I had the stability we needed for the future.

When we first got married, I thought I could help Paul turn his company profitable. I threw myself into assisting him, streamlining operations, and helping wherever I could. But I quickly realized that Paul wasn't going to change his approach. He spent hours perfecting the tiniest details but lacked the strategic thinking needed to grow the business. It was frustrating to watch because I could see the potential for success, but Paul was too smart, too confident, and too wrapped up in his own genius to change. I had to accept that he wasn't going to take a different path, and I couldn't make him.

That's when I knew I needed to focus on my own career. After helping Paul build and maintain the intranet for his company, I realized I had the skills to pursue a full-time job in the computer field. It had been six years since I left the workforce, but I found an entry-level position as an application developer at a small trucking company. I was responsible for managing their sales intranet, and though the salary was the same as my first full-time job at Hadley School for the Blind, I was thrilled to be back doing what I loved. The sense of purpose I found in that job was something I hadn't felt in years, and it gave me the confidence I needed to move forward with my career.

With the stability of my new job, the first thing I did was refinance our home loan. When I met Paul, he had just refinanced to help his parents, and still had almost 30 years left on the mortgage. I found a way to reduce the interest rate from 8.99% to 4.99% and shortened the term from 30 years to 15. I refinanced again later, reducing the interest rate to 4.49% and the term to 10 years, with almost the same monthly payment. With my perfect credit score, like all the Chinese people I knew, I secured the lowest rate possible and ensured the house would be paid off much sooner.

This decision to take control of our finances wasn't just about financial security — it was about embracing the transformation I had undergone as a Chinese American immigrant. I had become adept at navigating these systems, understanding the complexities of loans, interest rates, and credit scores. For many immigrants, financial literacy isn't something we learn right away; it's something we acquire through necessity, through the process of adaptation. My ability to manage our finances became symbolic of my journey — from a new immigrant struggling to understand the American financial system to a confident woman making informed decisions for her family.

Paul's lack of financial planning wasn't malicious — it was just how he was. He didn't worry about the future, and he didn't let money stress him out. I, on the other hand, couldn't sleep at night if I knew a bill was due the next day. It was a constant balancing act — managing Paul's carefree attitude while trying to ensure we didn't end up in a financial hole. It wasn't easy, but over time, I learned to let go of some of the stress. Paul would always be who he was, and I couldn't change that. What I could do was manage the things I could control — our finances, my career, and the future I was building for myself and David.

This new chapter brought me a sense of fulfillment and direction. Even though Paul and I had different approaches to work and life, we found a balance. He supported me in my career, just as I had supported him in his. We didn't always see eye to eye, but there was a mutual respect that held us together. As I moved forward with my own career goals, I felt a renewed sense of purpose — not just as Paul's partner, but as someone carving out her own path.

In many ways, this chapter of my life mirrored the experience of countless Chinese American immigrants. We arrive in a new country, often unsure of how to navigate its systems, but over time we learn, we adapt, and we grow. Just as I learned to manage my career and finances, I learned to embrace both the challenges and the opportunities of living in America. My journey with Paul, though unique, was part of a larger story of transformation, one that reflected the resilience and determination that so many immigrants carry with them as they build their new lives.

Chapter 27: At Allegheny Freight Lines

Allegheny Freight Lines was located at 27th Street in Pittsburgh, just a short walk from the vibrant Strip District. The Strip District, a historical hub of trade and culture, buzzes with life at any time of day. The narrow streets were lined with ethnic grocery stores, cafes, and outdoor markets where you could catch the scent of fresh bread from Italian bakeries, the spices from Middle Eastern shops, and the sound of lively conversations in multiple languages. One of my favorite spots was the Farmer's Market, where vendors sold the freshest local produce. I often spent my lunch break there, selecting crisp vegetables for dinner, soaking in the aroma of freshly picked herbs, and enjoying the hum of the market.

On some days, I'd stroll to a small Chinese restaurant tucked into a corner of the district. It wasn't a fancy place, but the food had a certain warmth and authenticity that reminded me of earlier times. The gentle clatter of chopsticks and the comforting sound of the chef's wok sizzling in the kitchen created an inviting atmosphere where I could briefly escape from the demands of work. These small breaks gave me the opportunity to reconnect with my roots and reflect on the journey I had taken as a Chinese American immigrant. Balancing the demands of work with the solace I found in familiar cultural settings was emblematic of the broader immigrant experience — one where we continuously navigate two worlds.

At Allegheny Freight Lines, my primary responsibility initially centered around customer service issues, particularly those related to the sales intranet. The sales team heavily relied on the website, and yet, the platform was plagued with issues that were commonly dismissed as "user errors." I, however, refused to accept that term. To me, a website should be intuitive and user-friendly. If a user was consistently making errors, it was a design flaw, not a user error. This philosophy, in many ways, paralleled the immigrant experience. Just as I had to adapt to a new country, new customs, and new challenges, I believed that systems should adapt to people — not the other way around.

So, each time I received a support ticket, I went beyond just solving the immediate issue. Instead, I analyzed why the website allowed errors in the first place and fixed the root cause of the problem. This approach took time, but it was worth it. Over the course of a year, my workload from customer service tickets dropped by 90%. At first, the sales team was skeptical of me — many of them were used to their own workarounds and didn't believe I could fix the 'user errors' they constantly encountered. But slowly, as I began solving their issues at the root, they came to appreciate my approach. One salesperson, Mark, used to groan every time he had to open a ticket, but by the end of that year, he was stopping by my desk just to say, 'Thanks, the system's running smooth as silk.'

Moments like these, where my efforts were recognized, reminded me of how far I had come — not just in my career but as an immigrant navigating a new life in America. The desire for improvement, for perfection, and to constantly better myself mirrored the journey of many immigrants, particularly Chinese Americans like myself, who are driven by a desire to excel in every aspect of life.

The website had been written in ASP.net, a language I wasn't entirely familiar with when I first joined the company. I refused to let my lack of knowledge become a hindrance, so I dedicated my downtime to completing a full set of free online training courses from Microsoft. Learning ASP.net wasn't easy. Some nights, I found myself awake past midnight, scouring forums for solutions to bugs I couldn't seem to fix. But each time I solved a problem, no matter how small, I felt a sense of victory. Little by little, I became fluent in the language, and soon I was building systems from the ground up with confidence I hadn't felt before. It was a long road, but every challenge was a steppingstone.

My drive to never feel inadequate in my job again became a strong motivator, and I took every opportunity to expand my knowledge. Not only did I learn ASP.net, but I also began applying it in ways that streamlined the workflow for the entire sales team. This pursuit of continuous learning and self-improvement was something that had been instilled in me from my upbringing in China, where education and hard work were cornerstones of success. In many ways, it was also a reflection of the broader Chinese American immigrant experience — a relentless drive to overcome obstacles and seize opportunities in a new land.

Initially, Paul and I had talked about starting a family. We both wanted a baby, and for a while, it was something we hoped would happen naturally. But with each passing month, that hope seemed to slip further away. Instead of letting the disappointment weigh me down, I made a conscious choice to focus on something else — something within my control. Shifting my energy to advancing my career was a bittersweet decision, but it gave me a sense of empowerment. I wasn't just accepting the situation; I was actively taking charge of my future.

That's when I made the decision to pursue a master's degree in Information Science. I had always been passionate about learning, and I knew that furthering my education would open doors for me, especially in a field as rapidly evolving as technology. While the idea of having a baby together was still something I cared about, I also realized that building a solid career would give me more security and options for the future, both for myself and my family.

By early 2008, I enrolled in a part-time master's program in Database and Website Applications at the University of Pittsburgh. With a strong desire to keep growing professionally, I balanced work, studies, and my personal life, knowing that the education I was gaining would ensure I was never caught unprepared again.

Juggling a master's program and a full-time job was not for the faint of heart. There were nights when I was so exhausted, I wasn't sure how I'd make it through another day of work followed by hours of studying. But I kept reminding myself of the end goal — that with every project I completed, I was one step closer to securing my future. Some nights, I'd be at my computer until 2 a.m., only to wake up for work a few hours later. There were moments of doubt when I wondered if I was pushing myself too hard. But every time I learned something new or aced a class, it reignited the fire inside me to keep going.

As I pushed forward in my career, there was always this quiet question in the back of my mind: Was I trading one dream for another? I still wanted a new baby, but for the first time in a while, I felt in control of my future. The idea of being financially secure, of being someone who could provide for herself and any future family, gave me a sense of freedom I hadn't realized I needed. While the path I was taking wasn't what I had originally envisioned, it felt right.

Paul was supportive, but as I became more immersed in my career, there were times when we both wondered if we were drifting apart. Our conversations often turned to the future — what we envisioned for ourselves and our family. He understood my drive, but I could see that the focus on my career was taking time away from the moments we had once shared dreaming of a larger family. It wasn't an easy transition for us, but we both knew that investing in my future would ultimately benefit us all.

That summer, the company decided to develop a new Deal Flow application for the sales team, aimed at introducing more efficient processes. Typically, this project would have required a system analyst to gather business requirements from the sales team and translate them into technical specifications for an application developer to code. However, the system analyst position was vacant at the time. I saw an opportunity and took the initiative, volunteering to take on both roles as the system analyst and the application developer. My boss, relieved to avoid hiring another person, agreed.

The experience of wearing two hats — both analyst and developer — was reminiscent of the balancing act I had been doing in my personal life. As a Chinese American immigrant, I had long learned the importance of flexibility and the ability to adapt to multiple roles. This ability to shift between responsibilities was a skill I honed through my immigrant journey, where learning to navigate multiple cultural expectations and new environments was crucial for success.

I immersed myself in the project, working closely with the salespeople to understand their needs and building an application that would make their work easier. When the Deal Flow application was complete, it exceeded expectations. I was relentless in ensuring it was perfect, tweaking every detail until it functioned flawlessly. The sales team, now able to navigate the site with ease, was thrilled, and the customer service tickets became a rare occurrence. For the first time in a long while, I felt like I had truly mastered something in my career.

With the application running smoothly and the sales team happy, I knew it was time to address my own position. I approached my boss and said, "I accepted an entry-level position, but you know I'm not at entry level." I requested a promotion, confident that my hard work and results spoke for themselves. But it was 2009, and the aftermath of the 2008 financial crisis had left many companies, including ours, with a salary freeze. My boss explained that promoting me during a salary freeze would be meaningless, as it wouldn't come with any financial benefit. He suggested I wait, and reluctantly, I agreed.

A year passed, and the promotion was still on my mind. On the Friday before Memorial Day, I once again approached my boss. This time, his response shocked me. He explained that our company was small, with only two senior positions, and unless a vacancy opened, there was no opportunity for advancement. I felt betrayed, as if all my hard work had led to a dead end.

The experience of being told there was no room for advancement despite my efforts was a familiar one. It echoed the struggles of Chinese American immigrants who, despite hard work and determination, often find themselves hitting invisible barriers in their professional lives. Many of us, particularly immigrant women, face a ceiling that prevents us from moving up, no matter how qualified or capable we are. This was one of those moments that tested my resilience and made me reflect on how much further I had to go to truly carve out my space in this new world.

I had poured my heart into this job. When my boss told me that a promotion wasn't in the cards, it felt like a punch to the gut. I smiled and nodded as if I understood, but deep down, I felt completely unappreciated. It wasn't just about the money — it was the acknowledgment of the hard work, the long hours, and the dedication I'd given to this company. That weekend, as I clicked 'submit' on my resume, it felt like I was closing the door on an era of my life, one where I'd put others' needs ahead of my own. It was time to move on.

That weekend, feeling disillusioned, I updated my resume and submitted it online. I wasn't expecting much, but to my surprise, I received a phone call from Champion's Sports Warehouse on the Tuesday after Memorial Day. They wanted to interview me for a new position. The interview at Champion's Sports Warehouse felt like a breath of fresh air. Their offices were bright, modern, and bustling with energy. I immediately knew this was a place that valued innovation. The hiring manager seemed genuinely impressed by the systems I had developed at Allegheny, and by the end of the interview, I had a feeling this was where I was meant to be.

When I got the job offer, it felt like everything had fallen into place. As I looked back on my time at Allegheny Freight Lines, I realized how much I had grown. The challenges, the late nights, and the constant problem-solving had turned me into a more confident, capable person — not just in my career but in my personal life as well. I had learned the importance of advocating for myself and recognizing my own worth.

Moving on to Champion's Sports Warehouse felt like the right next step in my journey, but I would always carry the lessons from Allegheny with me. Every obstacle had been a learning experience, and I was ready to take on whatever came next. Moving on was necessary for my growth, and the change, though unexpected, proved to be one of the best decisions I ever made. I knew I was stepping into a future full of promise and potential. The process moved quickly, and by August, I had started a new job — one that nearly doubled my previous salary.

This chapter of my life, both professionally and personally, was yet another reflection of the Chinese American transformation. It's the story of hard work, resilience, and the pursuit of opportunities — a story of learning to assert oneself, to value one's contributions, and to never settle for less. The transformation was ongoing, but with each new step, I felt a deeper connection to the dual identities I carried as a Chinese American.

Chapter 28: Voting for the First Time

Section 1: My Personal Journey to Voting

I became an American citizen in April 2006, just a few months before Paul and I got married. Two years later, in 2008, I had the opportunity to vote in my first presidential election. Voting was a completely new experience for me, and I felt both excited and uncertain about it. In China, where I grew up, we didn't have the same political system or voting structure. Although the Chinese constitution granted the right to vote, I never really understood what that meant since I had never been given the chance to cast a ballot.

When I became a U.S. citizen, I still didn't fully grasp the significance of voting here. Like many Chinese American immigrants I knew, the idea of participating in an election felt distant and abstract. Voting seemed like a formality rather than a true opportunity to influence the future. However, I knew that my right to vote was what distinguished me from being a green card holder. It was the one thing that truly marked my transition to becoming an American citizen, so I wanted to exercise that right as soon as I became eligible.

Despite my enthusiasm, I knew very little about the political landscape. I had heard names and caught glimpses of debates on TV, but I didn't have a deep understanding of the differences between the Republican and Democratic candidates. What I knew was largely surface level. Barack Obama was young, energetic, and the first African American presidential candidate, while John McCain was an older, seasoned white politician. With that limited understanding, I cast my vote for Obama.

Paul, on the other hand, had a long history of voting. He told me that he had never missed a single election since turning 18. Although registered as a Democrat, Paul voted for McCain in 2008, a decision that surprised me. While I was still finding my footing in American politics, Paul's engagement in the process showed me the weight that voting carried. He took pride in participating, and his influence certainly deepened my appreciation for the privilege.

When I shared my experience of voting with an old friend, her reaction was not what I expected. She sneered, dismissing my excitement, and said, "I'm not interested in politics," as though staying uninvolved made her somehow superior. Her dismissiveness left me perplexed. Here I was, eager to exercise my new right — a right that had been denied to me in my country of origin — and her reaction implied that this participation was beneath her.

This response reminded me of something much deeper, a cultural mindset I had encountered in many Chinese intellectuals: an ingrained disinterest in political engagement, something I had to reflect on after that conversation.

Section 2: The Historical Context of Chinese Intellectualism

Her attitude was not unique; it resonated with a deep cultural belief ingrained in many Chinese intellectuals, one that is summed up in an old saying, "All things are inferior; only reading is superior" (万般皆下品, 唯有读书高). This phrase encapsulates a long-standing tradition in Chinese culture that placed intellectual pursuits far above the so-called "mundane" activities of life, particularly politics. Intellectuals were seen as lofty figures, scholars whose primary duty was to focus on academic and philosophical achievements, rather than engaging with the gritty realities of governance or politics, which were often viewed with suspicion or disdain.

This mindset has deep historical roots, steeped in contradictions that reveal the complex and often hypocritical nature of Chinese intellectuals throughout history. For centuries, intellectuals in China aspired to pass the imperial exams (科举), a grueling and highly competitive process that would allow them to secure coveted government positions. These exams were not merely a test of knowledge; they were a measure of a person's intellectual merit and a gateway to both social and political power. Passing the exam meant rising to a prestigious position, one that offered security, influence, and honor. However, the very intellectuals who devoted their lives to passing these exams often sneered at politicians and the political system itself.

The contradiction is glaring. On the one hand, intellectuals viewed themselves as above the fray of politics, adhering to the belief that "all things are inferior; only reading is superior." Yet, these same scholars devoted their lives to passing the imperial exam, the ultimate goal of which was to become a government official. This meant that despite their disdain for politics, they actively sought positions within the political system. The imperial exam, after all, was designed not to test one's ability to govern, but to assess one's mastery of the Confucian classics, poetry, and literature. Success in this exam allowed one to rise to the upper echelons of society, not through experience in governance, but through scholarly merit.

Lu Xun, one of China's most influential writers and thinkers, famously exposed this hypocrisy. He sharply criticized the intellectual class for their detachment from real societal issues and their self-aggrandizing pursuit of government positions through the imperial exams. In his essays, Lu Xun described how Chinese intellectuals cloaked themselves in the guise of superiority, preferring to sneer at the political system while secretly yearning for the power and prestige that came with being part of it. To Lu Xun, this revealed the moral weakness of the intellectual class: they despised the system, yet they sought to benefit from it.

The very idea that intellectuals could maintain a disdain for politics while simultaneously aspiring to the highest political offices is deeply hypocritical. The path to becoming a government official was arduous and filled with fierce competition, but it was the ultimate dream for generations of Chinese scholars. They viewed passing the exam as not only a personal achievement but a validation of their intellectual and moral superiority. Once in power, they saw themselves as moral arbiters, guiding society through the lens of Confucian values. However, the hypocrisy was that the route to this power was intertwined with the political system they claimed to disdain.

The imperial exams themselves symbolized this paradox. They were not designed to produce leaders with practical governance skills but to elevate scholars who could recite Confucian doctrine and compose elegant essays. Thus, the exam system reinforced the idea that intellectual superiority alone was the key to power, regardless of one's ability to govern effectively. This detachment from practical governance fostered a class of officials who were often ill-prepared for the complexities of political life but who believed their scholarly achievements gave them a moral right to rule.

Lu Xun's scathing critique of this system revealed a deep cynicism about the intellectual class. He saw them as complicit in the perpetuation of a system that valued form over function, theory over practice, and intellectualism over real engagement with societal problems. The intellectuals' obsession with passing the exam, despite their outward disdain for politics, epitomized the deep contradictions in Chinese society. These scholars sneered at politicians, believing themselves morally superior, yet their ultimate dream was to become the very officials they claimed to despise.

This hypocrisy was not just limited to individuals but was embedded in the broader cultural mindset. Intellectuals were seen as the moral conscience of society, yet their ambitions were driven by the desire for power and status. The imperial exam system, which they revered, allowed them to ascend to positions of influence, but it also kept them detached from the real responsibilities of governance. Their intellectual pursuits were seen as a way to transcend the corruption and compromises of politics, yet they could not resist the allure of the political power that came with success.

Historically, there were few intellectuals like Lu You, the famous Song dynasty poet, who despite holding a low position, felt deeply about the importance of national duty. He wrote, "Even though I am in a low position, I still dare not forget my country" (位卑未敢忘忧国). Patriots like him, who directly engaged with national concerns, were rare in the intellectual landscape. Even today, a higher percentage of college graduates in China seek government positions compared to their American counterparts, reflecting a continuation of the same values. Despite the respect for intellectualism, many Chinese still seek political power as the ultimate validation of their success.

Section 3: Voting and Civic Duty in America

In contrast to the Chinese mindset, in democratic societies like America, intellectualism and political engagement are often seen as intertwined. In the West, intellectuals are encouraged to participate in political discourse, to apply their knowledge and ideas to shape the policies and direction of their country. The idea that one can be both an intellectual and a political actor is not seen as contradictory but as complementary. Political engagement is viewed as a civic duty, an extension of one's intellectual and moral responsibilities.

My friend's dismissive reaction to voting brought all of these cultural nuances to the forefront of my mind. While in America, voting is seen as a powerful tool for change and a cornerstone of democracy, in China, even among those granted the right, voting never carried the same weight. It was seen as either a formality or something detached from the intellectual sphere. For many Chinese people, their concerns lay elsewhere — on their families, their careers, and their personal lives — rather than on the public responsibilities that came with citizenship.

Yet, even with this cultural backdrop, I couldn't shake the feeling of excitement I had about voting. Though I was unfamiliar with many of the political nuances at the time, voting represented something bigger than just choosing a candidate. It represented a new chapter of responsibility, one I was eager to embrace despite the unfamiliarity. To me, the act of voting wasn't just about selecting a president; it was about becoming an active participant in the society I now called home, taking part in shaping the future of a country that had welcomed me.

Conclusion: Balancing Two Worlds

As I stood in line to vote that day, I couldn't help but reflect on how different my journey had been compared to those who had grown up in this system. For me, voting wasn't just a civic duty — it was a privilege I had earned through the journey of immigration and naturalization. It was the ultimate expression of belonging to this new country, one that my old friend couldn't understand, but one that I cherished deeply.

Voting in America was an entirely different experience from what I had grown up with in China. There, the political system often felt distant and unchangeable, with limited avenues for ordinary citizens to have a say. But in the U.S., I was now part of a system that, while far from perfect, allowed for direct participation in shaping the government. For the first time, I understood the sense of duty that came with being a citizen. It wasn't just about exercising a right — it was about contributing to the future direction of the country.

That first election marked the beginning of my journey into American democracy. Over time, I would come to learn more about policies, political ideologies, and how deeply the act of voting could impact our society. But in 2008, my knowledge was limited, and yet, I felt a sense of accomplishment simply by participating. Voting was a way to assert my place in this new country, to embrace the privileges and responsibilities that came with being an American.

In reflecting on my voting experience, I also began to understand more clearly the significant differences between the Chinese intellectual tradition and American civic duty. The legacy of the imperial exam system in China fostered a detachment from politics, where intellectuals sought government positions but often disdained political engagement. In contrast, American intellectualism encourages active participation in the political process, viewing it as a civic duty and an extension of one's moral responsibility.

I realized that, unlike many Chinese intellectuals who viewed politics with disdain, in America, the democratic process depends on the active participation of its citizens. Here, political engagement is not seen as beneath one's dignity, but rather as an essential part of being an informed and active member of society.

As I stood in line to vote that day, I was reminded of how far I had come on this journey. Voting represented more than just a political act; it symbolized my full acceptance of the rights and responsibilities of citizenship. And though I may have been unfamiliar with the political nuances at the time, I knew that this act of voting was my way of shaping the future of the country that had become my home.

Chapter 29: Growing in the Tech Field at Champion's Sports Warehouse

Champion's Sports Warehouse was more than just a job; it was an environment designed to foster innovation and growth. As the largest sporting goods chain in the U.S., it chose Pittsburgh as its headquarters, a city known for its passionate sports culture with teams like the Steelers, Pirates, and Penguins. The company's campus itself was stunning. It felt more like a resort than an office, with indoor and outdoor sports fields, state-of-the-art gyms, and outdoor seating areas beside a three-layer waterfall that extended into a mile-long walking trail through the woods. On Fridays, when work wasn't too hectic, my coworkers and I would go out to nearby restaurants for lunch, enjoying the atmosphere of the surrounding shopping center.

The Signage project I was initially hired for was completed on time, and soon after, I was assigned to work under Scott, a newly hired senior project manager. Jason, a passionate senior application developer, also joined our team. The dynamic between us worked well — Jason loved coding and didn't want to be involved in anything else, while I gravitated toward more analytical tasks. This division of labor allowed me to take on system analyst responsibilities, and I saw an opportunity to expand my role. I approached Scott and suggested that since we had two developers but no system analyst, I could handle the system analysis work. He agreed, happy to delegate those tasks to me.

Around this time, Champion had hired Raj, a new VP in charge of the Innovation Team, which initially comprised just Scott, Jason, and me. Raj, a young Indian American without accent, had big ideas and several Proof of Concept (PoC) projects in mind. Raj, Scott, and I often met to brainstorm, and I ended up leading three of these PoC projects. I worked closely with business units to gather requirements and led application design, which was both a challenging and rewarding process. I was also responsible for writing detailed test cases and conducting thorough QA testing to ensure that each project phase met our standards. Scott trusted my testing so completely that he would sign off on a phase based solely on my word, often bypassing the official QA team entirely. I took pride in the fact that by the time I handed over the application to QA, I had already thoroughly tested every aspect of it.

Being the point of contact for vendors was another new responsibility I embraced. I worked on three significant initiatives: the RFID project with two vendors (an Israeli company and Verizon), the Microsoft Power BI project in collaboration with the Power BI team (at a time when Microsoft was considering acquiring a Canadian company for Power BI's UI), and a project involving Cassandra, the NoSQL database. My technical leadership grew as these projects progressed, and I found myself gaining confidence and expertise in areas I hadn't explored before.

Scott was frequently too busy to attend project meetings, so I stepped in as his surrogate. Every time he would ask, "Are you okay to hold the meeting?" I would almost always respond with an assured "Yes." Occasionally, when I wasn't sure, Scott would hold the meeting himself. The first time I led a meeting, which included project managers from various departments, I was amazed at how smoothly everything went. Despite my title as an application developer, nobody seemed to care about my formal rank — they valued my contributions and trusted my judgment. This experience showed me that titles were often secondary to the skills and results you brought to the table.

After a year in the system analyst role, my hard work paid off. I received a promotion and a pay raise, reaching a milestone I had set for myself years ago — to hold a position as though I had gone straight into computer science after high school and pursued a career without interruptions. It had taken me seven years, starting from an entry-level position at Allegheny Freight Lines, but I had finally achieved it. Scott later told me Raj had handpicked me for the innovation team, and I hadn't disappointed.

Among the three PoC projects, two successfully transitioned into full-scale production after the pilot phase, marking significant milestones for Champion's Sports Warehouse. One of the most impactful was our Power BI project, which revolutionized the company's approach to data and analytics. By integrating advanced analytics tools, we provided the management team with unprecedented visibility into critical areas such as sales trends, inventory efficiency, and customer behavior. This newfound transparency enabled data-driven decision-making that helped the company not only streamline operations but also sharpen its competitive edge in the rapidly evolving retail market. Witnessing the direct impact of my contributions on the company's overall performance made me realize that I wasn't just working on isolated tech projects — I was actively shaping the future of Champion's Sports Warehouse.

During the RFID project, we ran two parallel pilot applications — one with the small Israeli company and the other with Verizon. Both vendors were eager to secure the contract, and we carefully evaluated their solutions over several months. As part of the evaluation, I was responsible for sending daily reports of inventory counts to both vendors so they could track the performance of their RFID systems. I also developed a comparison matrix to measure the performance of each vendor's technology against key criteria, such as accuracy, ease of use, and scalability. I shared these criteria with both vendors to ensure transparency in the evaluation process.

After months of careful analysis, the decision was made to go with Verizon. Their solution demonstrated better reliability and scalability, which were crucial for our long-term objectives. Once the decision was finalized, Scott informed me that I no longer needed to send inventory reports to the Israeli company. It was a tough moment for me, as I had worked closely with both vendors throughout the pilot phase, and the Israeli company had put in considerable effort to win the project.

A few days after the decision, I received an email from the Israeli company asking why they had stopped receiving reports. I knew they must have realized the outcome by then, but it still felt difficult to break the news. With a heavy heart, I replied, "I was told not to send the reports to you anymore." Although they probably understood why Verizon was chosen, sending that email still saddened me. It was a reminder of the challenging decisions we had to make in business, where only one solution can move forward, even when both parties have invested significant time and resources.

The RFID project was initially rolled out in the firearm departments across all stores and proved to be transformative. Previously, staff had to manually count firearms twice a day, which was not only time-consuming but also prone to errors. With the introduction of RFID tags, this process became almost instantaneous, dramatically reducing the time and labor costs associated with inventory management. Later, the application rolled out to some high-end products. The accuracy of inventory records improved from approximately 70% to over 95%, which had a direct impact on operational efficiency.

Given the sensitive nature of firearms, I had to visit several stores to personally test the RFID tags and ensure they worked seamlessly within the unique environment. This was a completely new experience for me — I had never handled or even been close to real guns before. Learning about different types of firearms and how to work around them in a professional capacity added an unexpected dimension to my role. It broadened my understanding of the retail landscape, teaching me that technological solutions often require a deep, hands-on understanding of the physical products they're designed to support.

Ultimately, these projects were not just about implementing new technologies — they were about transforming how the company operated at its core. Whether by enabling better decision-making through Power BI or improving efficiency and accuracy with RFID, I felt a deep sense of accomplishment knowing that the work I had led was creating lasting, tangible value for Champion's Sports Warehouse.

As the PoC projects wrapped up, the entire team saw promotions. Scott became a director, Jason was promoted to principal developer, and Raj moved up to executive VP. Jason and I were reassigned to Nancy, a new project manager. With new team members and additional resources, my workload was significantly reduced, which left me feeling uneasy. I had grown accustomed to handling numerous tasks and the fast pace of leading PoC projects, so the slower pace made me feel insecure and reconsider my career path.

After some reflection, I decided to pursue a career in IT security. I saw it as an exciting field with ample growth opportunities. Scott supported my decision wholeheartedly, even purchasing a Pluralsight subscription for me so I could complete extensive IT security training. His encouragement meant a lot to me, especially since he said he'd rather see me stay at Champion's than leave for another company.

Feeling prepared, I applied for an IT security analyst position within Champion's. Despite Scott's glowing recommendation, the hiring manager decided not to interview me, citing my lack of direct experience in IT security. Though it was disappointing, I wasn't deterred. Through my research, I learned that the federal government had a higher demand for IT security professionals, and federal jobs offered the long-term stability I desired, particularly as I was already in my mid-40s. Paul and I discussed the possibility of moving to Washington, D.C., and he was surprisingly open to it.

The company's culture embraced the spirit of teamwork and achievement. After every successful project, the project manager would take the entire team to a Pirates game, complete with box seats. I never fully grew to appreciate baseball like I did football, but mingling with coworkers in the box seats was fun. These moments of camaraderie were part of what made my time at Champion's so memorable.

The sports culture at Champion's wasn't just a corporate branding exercise; it was woven into every part of our daily lives. Team-building events at Pirates games or Steelers tailgates were more than just social gatherings — they were where we bonded as a team. The company's emphasis on health and sports made it easy to develop close-knit relationships with colleagues. I remember the Friday afternoons when we'd head out to nearby restaurants, grabbing lunch and talking about everything from work challenges to the latest game scores. Before I left the company, Nancy even arranged a farewell party for our team at a restaurant, though I was surprised Scott didn't attend.

As I reflected on my career journey, from learning ASP.net at Allegheny Freight Lines to leading major projects at Champion's Sports Warehouse, I felt proud of how far I had come. I had transitioned from being an entry-level developer to leading critical projects and making strategic decisions that shaped the direction of the company's initiatives. I had learned to navigate complex business environments and build systems that had a lasting impact.

Balancing my professional growth with my personal life wasn't always easy. As my career advanced, Paul and I occasionally felt the strain. We had always been supportive of each other's ambitions, but there were moments when we both questioned whether my focus on work was pulling us apart. Yet, even with these challenges, we understood the importance of this chapter in my life. It was a time of immense growth for me, both professionally and personally, and I needed to see it through.

Champion's Sports Warehouse was a place where I truly hit my stride, pushing the boundaries of my knowledge and leadership capabilities. These were some of the most fulfilling years of my career. Even though my time there came with challenges, I learned valuable lessons that prepared me for the next stage of my journey. Looking back, I knew I had grown not only as a developer but as a leader, someone capable of driving projects and navigating complex business landscapes. It was a time of transformation, and I was ready for whatever came next.

Chapter 30: One-Way Relationships

When I first moved to Pittsburgh, I joined a Chinese church in Oakland. The pastor, a man about my age, had a remarkable story. He graduated from CMU and ran a successful tech company before closing it to follow his calling as a pastor. His journey fascinated me, and I introduced Henry, a graduate student in my class at the University of Pittsburgh, to the church. Like me, he had come from China, though much later. His spoken English was much better than mine had been when I first arrived in Evanston. The new generation of Chinese students was so different from ours. When Wayne and I came from Singapore, we were fortunate to have some savings, but many of our friends had to borrow money just to buy their plane tickets. Back then, China was still very poor. In contrast, the new generation like Henry was fully supported by their families — not only were their tuition and fees covered, but their housing, food, and other expenses were as well.

I brought Henry to the church and gave him a bilingual Chinese-English Bible as a gift. He hesitated to accept it, saying he didn't know how he could repay the favor. I told him there was no need to repay me directly — he could simply pay it forward. Yet his response highlighted a cultural value deeply embedded in Chinese tradition: relationships are often seen as reciprocal, a constant exchange of favors, where each good deed or gift must be returned in some way.

In Chinese culture, relationships thrive on reciprocity. The idea of unconditional love — giving without expecting anything in return — is foreign to many and even harder to practice. When love or help is given without expectation, it can sometimes be misunderstood, and the giver risks being hurt if their kindness isn't reciprocated. It's a mindset that has shaped how many Chinese, including myself, approach relationships. If someone doesn't return the love or favor, it's easy to feel slighted, and the relationship becomes strained. Only after I became a Christian did I begin to reflect and understand the concept of one-way relationships.

This became evident to me in multiple instances. For example, when David and I attended a Bible study hosted by a family from the Chinese church, many of the attendees weren't Christians yet, and it was clear they took the host family's generosity for granted just as I had done when I first came to America in Evanston. They showed up as if they were doing the hosts a favor by simply attending, with no thought on the effort involved in preparing the home, providing snacks, or leading the study. I could see the exhaustion on the wife's face, not just from physical work but from the emotional toll of feeling unappreciated. Eventually, they stopped hosting Bible study, burned out by the lack of acknowledgment or gratitude.

This reminded me of Sam and Sara, a Chinese campus missionary couple we had known in Evanston, Illinois. They were deeply involved in the Chinese Christian community, hosting Bible studies in their home for decades. I remember Sara telling us about the International Chinese Christian Conference held annually in Chicago. It was a free event, with all meals, lodging, and even children's services covered. She encouraged us to attend, treating it as a family vacation. Wayne and I, along with David, attended the conference, and it was a spiritual feast for us. It was unbelievable that we had been so naïve to believe the event was free. At the time, we hadn't considered how everything had been provided for at no cost to us, but later, when I became a Christian, I realized that someone had paid for those "free" gifts. Nothing is truly free — every gift is paid for by someone else's generosity.

When I was baptized, I received a bilingual Bible as a gift, just as I had given one to Henry. My hope was that someday, Henry would pass along the same gift to someone else, keeping the chain of generosity going. Over the two years that we attended Bible study at Sam and Sara's house, I witnessed many farewell parties for students who graduated and found jobs elsewhere. Sara would always say they were used to saying goodbye. They had seen countless students come and go over the decades, most of whom lost contact eventually. Yet they never wavered in their commitment. They only hoped the seeds they had planted would sprout somewhere, someday. Sam and Sara embodied the spirit of one-way relationships — they gave freely, without expectation of anything in return.

Christian values played a significant role in shaping my understanding of this mindset. In Christianity, love is seen as a gift that flows from the giver, independent of the recipient's actions. This is the essence of grace — undeserved, unearned, and given without expecting anything in return. As Christians, we are called to love others as Christ loved us, which is an expression of unconditional love. This concept of giving freely, without requiring reciprocity, was so different from what I had grown up with in Chinese culture, where every relationship was carefully measured and balanced. The Christian idea of love, rooted in grace, is liberating because it removes the burden of expectation from both sides. It allows you to give from a place of abundance, knowing that your worth and love do not depend on the recipient's response.

Jesus' teachings reinforce this perspective. In Luke 6:35, He said, "But love your enemies, do good to them, and lend to them without expecting to get anything back. Then your reward will be great, and you will be children of the Most High, because he is kind to the ungrateful and wicked." This scripture reveals a love that is radical in its selflessness, a love that doesn't tally favors or expect rewards in return. For many of us, this is a profound shift from the natural human instinct to ensure fairness in relationships, where we give only to those who give back. Yet, Jesus calls us to something higher — to give because it reflects the love of God, not because it benefits us.

I think of Paul as another example of this mindset. I remember how he took care of Anna at the Great Wolf Lodge water park. He didn't do it because Anna was particularly special or lovely — though she was — but because that's just who Paul is. He has an abundance of love to give. That's how he was able to love David as his own son. It wasn't about receiving anything back; it was simply his nature to give. Watching him love unconditionally made me realize that this was the kind of love Jesus called us to show.

Even professionals like the dentist and receptionist at our dental office in Evanston exemplified this. They cared for their patients with genuine kindness, without needing to know much about them personally. They didn't expect their patients to return the favor — it was their way of showing love and care in a professional setting, without expectation of reciprocity.

The Parable of the Good Samaritan is another example that shifted my thinking about love and reciprocity. In Chinese culture, it's often expected that kindness is reserved for those within your family or social circle. But the Good Samaritan helps someone who, by all social standards, is his enemy. This story shows that love isn't limited by societal boundaries, and it doesn't demand reciprocation — it's given freely, as a reflection of God's grace.

This understanding of one-way relationships brings freedom. Unconditional love, as described in the Bible, isn't contingent upon the actions of the recipient. Whether the other person reciprocates love or kindness doesn't matter. The giver might feel happiness if their love is returned, but they won't be bitter or hurt if it isn't. Their love is grounded in their own character and, ultimately, in their faith. It is rooted in the example of Christ's love — a love that sacrificed without the guarantee of return.

As I look around, I see so many relationships that are one-way relationships. When you help someone, they may never be able to repay you, and that's okay. When you receive help, you may never be able to return the favor, and that's okay too. For example, when we host Bible study at our house, we provide a space for others to gather and fellowship. Most likely, none of those attendees will ever invite us to their homes. But we're happy to host, without expecting anything in return. We don't feel bitter or resentful because we have never held any expectations to begin with. We've learned to embrace the one-way relationship, giving freely and finding joy in the act of giving itself.

The root cause of the differences in love between Chinese culture and American culture stems from Christian values. America, founded on Christian principles, has ingrained these ideas into its cultural fabric. Even non-Christians in America are often familiar with the one-way relationship mindset, whether they practice it or not. As Chinese Americans become more familiar with American culture, especially when they embrace Christianity, they start to understand and practice one-way relationships. This is something I experienced firsthand, and I saw it in Sam and Sara, and even in myself.

One of the ways these Christian values manifest in society is through acts of charity and service. In America, countless organizations are dedicated to helping those in need, regardless of their ability to give back. This is a direct reflection of the one-way love Jesus taught — to care for the vulnerable, the marginalized, and the forgotten. For example, the rise in adoption of children with disabilities or the homeless outreach programs in churches showcases how one-way relationships have the power to transform entire communities.

Christian faith transforms how we view relationships — not as exchanges of favors, but as opportunities to give from the heart. Jesus' teachings make it clear that our reward isn't in the recognition we receive from others, but in the knowledge that we are fulfilling God's will. In Matthew 6:3-4, Jesus said, "But when you give to the needy, do not let your left hand know what your right hand is doing, so that your giving may be in secret. Then your Father, who sees what is done in secret, will reward you." It's a way of loving that transforms how we view relationships — not as exchanges of favors, but as opportunities to give from the heart, without expecting anything in return from the recipient because we know our reward is in heaven.

Cultural Differences in Love for Children

One of the most striking differences between Chinese and American cultures lies in the way children are loved and cared for, especially children with disabilities or those seen as "unlovable." In Chinese culture, love for children can often be conditional, tied to societal expectations, obligation, and practical concerns. Parents may feel an intense pressure to raise children who will bring honor to the family, succeed in their studies, and provide for them in old age. If a child does not meet these expectations, particularly if the child has disabilities or challenges, it is not uncommon for the parents to feel shame, desperation, or even emotional distance. Raising a disabled or disadvantaged child is often viewed as a misfortune, and in extreme cases, families may choose to abandon these children or place them in orphanages.

In contrast, American families, many of whom are guided by Christian values, tend to view children, regardless of their circumstances, as gifts from God. These families often adopt children with disabilities, seeing beyond the physical or mental challenges to the inherent worth and beauty of each child. They believe that every life has a purpose, and that raising a disabled child is not a burden, but an opportunity to grow in patience, compassion, and love. This difference in perspective is deeply rooted in Christian teachings, which emphasize that every person is made in the image of God and is deserving of love and care, regardless of their abilities or challenges.

The idea of unconditional love, so central to Christian teachings, allows American parents — and often stepparents and adoptive parents — to embrace children who may be considered "unlovable" by societal standards. Stepparents in particular are encouraged to love their stepchildren as if they were their own, practicing one-way relationships where love is given freely, not because the child has earned it, but because the step-parent's love is a reflection of their own character and faith.

In Chinese culture, however, step-parenting can be more challenging because of the emphasis on reciprocity and obligation. A stepchild may be seen as a reminder of a former spouse or as someone who "belongs" to someone else. Without the practice of unconditional love, these relationships can struggle to flourish, and the lack of deep emotional connection can hinder the family dynamic.

American adoption of Chinese children, especially those with disabilities, highlights this contrast between the two cultures. Many abandoned or disadvantaged Chinese children have been adopted by American families, most of whom are motivated by their Christian faith. These parents see adoption as a calling to care for "the least of these" (Matthew 25:40). For them, adoption is a one-way relationship, where love and care are given freely without expecting anything in return from the child. The parents understand that their love is seen by God, and that is enough.

Part 3: Trials and Triumphs (2012–2020)

Chapter 31: Husband's Political Transformation

Paul had grown up in Pittsburgh, back when it was the steel heart of America. In the 1950s, Pittsburgh was a gritty, hard-working town dominated by laborers and mill workers. The values of that era and place were deeply ingrained in him from a young age: loyalty to unions, skepticism toward big business, and unwavering support for the Democratic Party. For most people like Paul, it wasn't even a question — Democrats stood for the working class, while Republicans were seen as champions of the wealthy. So when he became old enough to vote, it was no surprise that Paul checked the Democratic box without hesitation.

It went deeper than voting, though. Paul wasn't just a passive supporter; he was a voice for the party. As a spokesperson for local Democratic committees, he regularly took on the role of "the voice" at party events and polling nights. This was long before the internet or large-screen projectors, back when election results came in via phone calls. Paul would announce the incoming results over the loudspeaker, delivering updates to enthusiastic crowds who cheered and applauded. He felt proud to represent the party he believed truly fought for the people.

For years, Paul's loyalty to the Democratic Party never wavered — until 1985. It was a year that would mark a pivotal turning point in his political life. He had just finished working closely with local Democratic leaders, some of whom had become close friends over the years. These were people Paul respected deeply, but everything changed one day after they returned from a Democratic National Committee (DNC) meeting. The leaders gathered their support staff, including Paul, to brief them on the party's future direction. What he heard that day shook him to his core.

The leaders presented a new vision for the Democratic Party, one that included plans that some in the room fully embraced but which left Paul deeply disturbed. As the discussion unfolded, Paul became increasingly uncomfortable. They spoke of moving the country toward socialism, focusing on reducing divisions based on age, race, sex, and economic backgrounds. At first, this didn't sound so bad to Paul — after all, equality was a noble goal. But the more they talked, the darker the plan became.

The leaders spoke of decreasing the emphasis on nationalism in favor of globalism, explaining how they intended to indoctrinate younger generations into this worldview, starting at the school level. "We'll take over school boards across the country," they explained, "and shift the curriculum from American History to World History." They outlined a 30-year plan to reshape the American identity, starting with the youth. Paul listened in stunned silence, his mind struggling to process what he was hearing. But what came next changed everything for him.

One leader made the most shocking statement of all: "The hardest part," she said, "will be convincing the older generation to give up their freedoms. We know they'd rather die than let that happen." Paul, already feeling uneasy, hesitantly asked, "And how do you plan to accomplish that?" The reply sent a shiver down his spine: "We'll help them die."

Paul was horrified. When he asked for clarification, they explained a chilling idea — introducing a pandemic that would target the elderly and infirm, solving what they called the "problem" of Social Security and Medicare along the way. He couldn't believe what he was hearing. "You people are evil," he said, shaking his head. "I want no part of this." And with that, he walked out of the meeting, leaving behind the party he had supported his entire adult life.

For years afterward, Paul didn't tell anyone what he had heard that day. He didn't believe all Democrats were aware of these plans, and in his mind, many of them were still decent people. He stayed registered as a Democrat, voting for candidates he thought were well-meaning and hoping that the worst of the party's plans would never come to pass. But the memory of that meeting never left him.

It wasn't until 2023, during a campaign for a local county position, that Paul finally shared the story publicly. At a GOP gathering, he mentioned the 1985 meeting and its shocking revelations. To his surprise, a woman in the audience gasped. After the event, she approached Paul and said, "I heard the same thing back then." Like Paul, she had worked for the Democratic Party in another state, yet their experiences were eerily identical, confirming the disturbing plan he had learned about decades earlier.

Paul's departure from the Democratic Party became complete in 2012 after years of observing the internal workings of politics, especially following Hillary Clinton's presidential campaign. The more he learned about the Clintons, the more he distanced himself from the Democrats. In 2012, just three months after officially switching to the GOP, Paul received an email inviting him to join the White House Business Council under President Obama. At first, he thought it was a joke. After some investigation, he realized it was real. Despite his disdain for Obama's policies, he accepted the invitation, hoping to make a difference from the inside. His efforts were largely focused on resisting the push for Obamacare, which he saw as another step toward the socialist vision he had been warned about.

Then, in 2020, when the COVID-19 pandemic hit, Paul's suspicions were fully confirmed. The very pandemic strategy he had been told about in 1985 seemed to be unfolding in real time. The older generation, particularly the elderly and infirm, were the ones hardest hit by the virus. Paul saw it as a deliberate move to weaken the population, to push forward an agenda that had been quietly developing for decades. He felt a deep sense of foreboding as the country moved further along this dark path.

"They don't even hide their agenda anymore," Paul would say to anyone who would listen. "If you don't believe me, just look up the UN 2030 Initiative. They present it as a vision of utopia, but they don't tell you what happens to those who resist giving up their freedoms." For Paul, the political transformation had been one of gradual disillusionment followed by a complete break, and his journey from loyal Democrat to passionate Republican was driven by a desire to protect the freedoms he feared were being eroded.

With a mix of sadness and determination, Paul continued to advocate for the values he believed in, hoping that others would wake up before it was too late.

Paul's political awakening wasn't only fueled by his observations of party leadership. His personal experiences with Democratic leaders from his earlier years left a lasting impression on him. One moment that stood out was when Hurricane Agnes hit Pittsburgh in 1972. The Ohio River had breached its banks, flooding parts of the city, and Paul's neighborhood was heavily affected. Water surrounded his home, creeping all the way up to his front door. As Paul stood on his porch surveying the damage, a man in a yellow raincoat approached him through the waist-deep water. Paul was shocked to realize it was none other than Mayor Pete Flaherty (D), who had come to check on the residents himself, without a motorcade, police escort, or bodyguard.

Mayor Flaherty, soaked to the bone, asked Paul, "Do you have water in your basement?" Paul nodded and invited him inside to see. Together, they opened the basement door, revealing murky, smelly floodwater filling the lower level. The mayor thanked Paul for letting him inspect the damage and moved on to the next house, leaving Paul with a profound sense of respect for his dedication to the people. "At that moment," Paul would later say, "I felt he truly represented the Democratic Party." It was this hands-on, caring approach that Paul admired in leaders like Flaherty — a sharp contrast to what he had encountered in later years.

Another figure who embodied the integrity of the Democratic Party in Paul's eyes was Dr. Cyril Wecht, the chairman of the Democratic Committee of Allegheny County and Paul's boss at the time. Dr. Wecht was a respected juris doctor and medical pathologist, famed for having performed over 17,000 autopsies, including those of high-profile figures like John F. Kennedy, Robert Kennedy, and Elvis Presley. Men like Flaherty and Wecht reinforced Paul's belief that the Democratic Party once stood for something honorable.

But things started to change in the late 1990s when Paul took on a role under Pennsylvania Governor Tom Ridge. He was tasked with creating an inbound telephone program to explain the benefits of school choice. This project required Paul to research and present the Republican perspective on education, and in doing so, he gained a deep understanding of the Republican philosophy — a belief in competition among educators and wider choices for parents and students. This assignment became a pivotal moment for Paul, as it opened his eyes to the differences between the two parties.

Around the same time, nationally syndicated conservative talk radio, particularly Rush Limbaugh, was becoming more prominent. Paul listened regularly and found that the conservative arguments resonated with him more and more. Limbaugh's discussions on individual freedom, limited government, and competition in the marketplace aligned with Paul's evolving worldview. Through self-reflection, he realized that he identified better with Republican values than with the direction the Democratic Party seemed to be heading.

By the early 2000s, under the leadership of Governor Ed Rendell, Paul saw a stark contrast between the Democrats of his youth and the party that now existed. Compared to Tom Ridge, who Paul respected as a man of integrity, Rendell came across as sleazy, embodying the ethical decline that Paul now associated with the Democratic Party. It was becoming increasingly clear to Paul that the Democratic Party had shifted in a way that no longer represented his values.

As President Ronald Reagan once famously said, "I didn't leave the Democratic Party, the Democratic Party left me." That sentiment echoed deeply with Paul. His transformation from a loyal Democrat to a staunch Republican wasn't just a reaction to one meeting or one political scandal; it was a journey that spanned decades, shaped by both personal experiences and a changing political landscape. For Paul, it was no longer about party loyalty but about standing for what he believed was right — protecting the freedoms and values he held dear.

Chapter 32: Truly Reborn

It was spring in 2015, a time when everything seemed to have finally fallen into place in my life. One afternoon, on my way home from Champion's Sports Warehouse, I drove along highway I-279. The sun was gently setting in the distance, painting the sky in soft hues of gold. The trees and rolling hills outside the car window created a serene backdrop, and the warmth of the afternoon sun seeped through the glass, casting long shadows on the dashboard. Inside the car, there was a comforting stillness, broken only by the soft hum of the Christian radio station I had tuned into. I felt the gentle breeze through the slightly opened window, and everything around me seemed peaceful.

But as I listened to the program on the radio, a topic came up that stirred something deep within me — it was about pastors in China who were lacking basic training in the gospels. The serene scenery contrasted with the sudden conviction I felt.

The discussion on the radio pulled me back to 2002, a time when I had been unemployed and had gone on a short missionary trip to China. I had joined a group of medical professionals — doctors and nurses — as their interpreter. They had been participating in these trips annually for years, providing both medical aid and spiritual support. I remembered how, during that time, I had toyed with the idea of becoming a missionary myself. A pastor had even encouraged me to act on this calling. During the trip, we visited an English-language school where an American missionary was teaching English. She was single and had come to China after retirement, working without a salary in exchange for lodging and meals. I admired her dedication but questioned if I could ever make the same commitment. At the end of our trip, she returned to America with us, her mission completed.

Before we left, the medical group bought me a tapestry made of wool, decorated with Chinese characters that read, "A peaceful mind leads to longevity." It still hangs on the wall in our house, a symbol of that time and a reminder of the peace that I sought but hadn't yet found.

I remembered how the idea of becoming a missionary lingered in my mind during that time. Yet, something inside me hesitated. I feared that choosing to become a missionary while unemployed would feel like I had only taken that path because I hadn't succeeded in finding a "decent" job. I didn't want to be defined by failure, even in my own eyes. And so, I let the thought pass. I didn't choose the path of a missionary, and the idea faded into the background of my life.

All these years, I had been a faithful churchgoer, attending Sunday services and Bible study groups regularly. I considered myself a good Christian. I had admitted, like everyone else, that I was a sinner. But who wasn't? Sin felt like an abstract concept, something distant and theoretical, rather than a reflection of my daily life. I would list my sins in prayer, ask for forgiveness, but the confessions were always hollow. I didn't really feel the weight of what I had done, and repentance had never felt necessary because, in my mind, my sins weren't "that bad."

But on that drive home, something changed. As I listened to the radio and recalled my fleeting desire to become a missionary, it was as if a light suddenly struck me. In an instant, I saw filthiness in my thoughts, my actions, and my life. I was overwhelmed with shame. I felt exposed, not just for my sins but for the casual way I had treated my relationship with God. For the first time, I was deeply ashamed that people even knew me as a Christian. I had been living a life of pride, blind to the way I had been pushing God's grace aside, thinking I didn't need it as much as others.

God, however, had known my heart all along. Despite my blindness, He had loved me and protected me from the harm I could have inflicted upon myself. Even my reluctance to pursue a missionary life during unemployment had been rooted in pride. I couldn't see that God was at work in my life, guiding me, and paving the way for the success I had so longed for. At that moment, sitting behind the wheel of my car, I truly repented. For the first time, I felt the full weight of my sins, and I asked God for forgiveness — not out of routine, but from the depths of my heart. I knew I could be honest with God, because He knew me better than I knew myself.

At that time, I didn't have any desire to become a missionary again, and I wasn't sure if that would ever change. But what I did know was that I wanted to live a life that glorified God. In my prayer, I made a promise — a promise that, for years, I had been too embarrassed to say out loud. I vowed to live a holy life, a life that reflected God's love and grace in everything I did. When I got home, I shared this experience with Paul, and to my joy, he was completely on board. Together, we made a commitment to let Jesus be the Lord of our household.

From that day forward, we were dedicated to living a life that glorified God. I became eager to study God's Word more deeply, to learn and grow in ways I had never before considered. The best way I knew to do that was through formal courses, so I enrolled in the Christian Leaders Institute. My hunger for knowledge grew, and I poured myself into the study of theology, scripture, and ministry. The tuition at Christian Leaders Institute was free, but I couldn't bring myself to take the courses without contributing financially. I became a Vision Partner, donating to support the program. My picture was even featured in their 2017 calendar, representing their Asian students for January. Though I had discarded the calendar, Paul had picked it out of the recycling bin, framed the January page, and hung it on the wall. It still hangs there today, a reminder of that transformative time.

By the end of 2016, I had completed enough credits for a BA in Divinity. Interestingly, I hadn't initially set out to earn another degree. I just wanted to learn, to deepen my relationship with God and to live out the promise I had made. But with the credits in hand, I went through the paperwork and earned the degree, marking another chapter in my journey of faith.

When I was baptized on Mother's Day in 2000, it was a moment made even more special because my mom was baptized with me. She had retired the previous year, and we had invited her to Evanston to help us raise David. During her time with us, she joined our Bible study gatherings at Sam and Sara's house, but none of us had expected that she would ever want to get baptized herself. So, when I decided to take this step in my faith, I was surprised when my mom said, "Me too." Her announcement shocked everyone at the Bible study, but it was a joyful surprise. Her decision felt sudden, but it was clear that it came from a deep place within her heart.

After the baptism, my mom described the experience as nothing short of miraculous. She said that as soon as she was immersed in the water, she felt an overwhelming sense of heavenly peace — a kind of peace she had never felt before. It wasn't the fleeting peace that comes and goes with life's circumstances, but a profound inner peace, one that stayed with her and never left her again. She also recalled how, when she stepped out of the church that day, the sky looked unimaginably beautiful to her. She believed she had caught a glimpse of heaven in that moment, a divine reassurance that she was now walking in God's presence.

But for me, the experience was different. As much as I wanted to feel that overwhelming peace and joy, I didn't. The sky that day was blue, but it looked like any other day in Chicago to me. There were no overwhelming feelings, no visions of heaven. I couldn't help but feel a little envious of my mom's experience of God's presence. It had seemed so effortless to her. She hadn't read the Bible as fervently as I had, and while I felt the need to attend every church service, my mom was fine missing one if she didn't feel like going. She had only read through the Bible once from beginning to end since her baptism, yet she had this deep connection with God that I longed for.

For years, I asked God to grant me the kind of experience my mom had, but nothing happened. My prayers seemed to go unanswered, and I wondered why I couldn't feel God's presence in the same way. However, there was one thing I consistently did — whenever I woke up in the middle of the night, I would pray. It was a habit I had developed over time. Most nights, I would fall back asleep quickly, but if something was weighing on my mind, I would bring it before God in prayer.

After I interviewed for a job with The Library of Congress, my nightly prayers became focused on that. Every time I woke up during the night, I would pray for a job offer. It was a role I deeply wanted, and I kept asking God for it. Then, two weeks before I got the official call offering me the position, something extraordinary happened. I woke up, ready to pray for the job as I had done every night, but before I could even begin, I felt a distinct impression in my mind: "It's done." It wasn't a voice, but a certainty that was clearer than anything I had ever experienced. It was as if the message had been etched into my heart — God had already granted my request.

What struck me the most was how calm I felt. I wasn't shocked or overwhelmed. I simply accepted it, thinking, "Okay, I don't need to pray for the job anymore. I'll just praise God instead." That morning, I got up and told Paul, "I got the job." He looked at me, confused, and asked if I had already received a phone call. I explained to him the experience I had during the night and how I knew, without a doubt, that God had answered my prayer. Two weeks later, I received the official job offer from The Library of Congress.

That moment was when I realized that God had indeed answered my prayer to experience His presence. It wasn't in the same way as my mom's baptism experience, but it was just as real, if not more so. God had spoken to me in a way that was personal, quiet, and deeply profound. I had always thought that feeling God's presence required some dramatic moment of revelation, but now I understood that sometimes it comes in stillness, in a simple yet unshakable certainty that God is with you and hears your prayers.

Looking back, I see that moment when I was struck by the light in my car in 2015 as the true turning point in my spiritual life. It wasn't my baptism, my attendance at church, or even my outward declarations of faith that marked my rebirth. It was the day when I truly saw my sin for what it was, and it was the day when I truly surrendered my pride, my fear, and my control over to God. That was the day I truly repented and was reborn. From that point on, everything in my life — my faith, my marriage, my work — became a reflection of the grace I had received and the love I wanted to share with the world. I know I'm still deeply flawed, but with my faith in Jesus, I know He'll help me, guide me, and protect me. I have nothing to fear but God.

Chapter 33: Transitioning to Government Work

The interview with The Library of Congress for a system analyst position was scheduled for 1 PM. It seemed perfectly timed; I could leave Pittsburgh at a reasonable hour, drive to Washington, D.C., attend the interview, and then head back home. I wasn't nervous — just determined. After all, this was a step toward a new career in government, something I hadn't initially considered when I began applying for jobs.

Up until that point, I hadn't tried for IT security analyst positions. After all, the hiring manager at Champion's Sports Warehouse had dismissed me without even an interview for their security team, and it had discouraged me. So, I stuck to submitting resumes for system analyst roles, which felt like a safer bet.

There were three people interviewing me that day: the chief, who would be my future boss; the technical lead; and an HR representative. The interview began smoothly, with typical questions about my experience and how I approached tasks. I felt at ease answering them, explaining the projects I had worked on and how I had managed them. Then, the technical lead threw in an unusual question: "How do you know when a project is done?"

I paused for a moment, then responded confidently, "I set the criteria for each test case as complete. When each test case is completed, the project is done."

The room was quiet for a second, and I could see that my answer had impressed them. But then something remarkable happened. The chief, leaning forward, said, "Although we posted this job as a system analyst position, we didn't bother to update the job description. What we're actually looking for are two candidates — one for testing and one for an IT security analyst."

As soon as I heard this, I knew God's hand was in that moment. It felt like I was exactly where I was meant to be. I told them my story, my journey in pursuing an IT security role, and how the job had felt just out of reach until now. I promised them that I wouldn't disappoint them, and they seemed convinced. They even commented on the short-sightedness of the hiring manager at Champion's Sports Warehouse for not recognizing how transferable my skills were.

I had always heard that getting a federal government job was difficult and that the process could take years. Yet, within about six months — about the same time it took for private sector jobs — I was offered the position. I knew this was God's favor shining on me, and it only strengthened my resolve to live a holy life, keeping the promise I had made.

Once I accepted the offer, I began searching for a place to live near D.C. Initially, I looked for apartments to rent, but the rent prices were astronomical. After some consideration, I decided it made more sense to buy an apartment instead. While I searched, I rented a room from a Chinese family. On weekends, Paul would come down from Pittsburgh to help me look for places to buy, and we'd stay at a hotel.

One Friday, we saw a new listing for an apartment that immediately caught my attention. It was in the Parkside Condominium in North Bethesda, Maryland. The community's name spoke for itself — it was like living in a park. Trees lined the streets, lush green grass was carefully maintained, and the benches throughout the grounds were spotless. It was a peaceful oasis in the midst of the bustling D.C. metro area.

The apartment was on the first floor but had a balcony that faced a bamboo grove. The moment I stepped inside and looked out at the sliding door from the living room, I was captivated by the view. All you could see were the tall, swaying bamboo stalks bathed in the soft light of the setting sun. When you sat on the balcony, it felt like you were in the heart of the woods. It was the kind of experience only a first-floor apartment could offer, with that connection to the surrounding nature.

Without hesitation, I decided to make an offer at the asking price. I waived all contingencies for loan approval and inspection, knowing my excellent credit score would ensure no issues with financing. And with Paul's expertise, I felt confident that we didn't need a formal inspection. My only condition was that the seller cancel the upcoming open house. My real estate agent suggested I could have negotiated for $5,000 less, but I didn't want to take any chances or compete with other buyers. The seller agreed, and the apartment was mine.

Paul rented a U-Haul truck to bring down the bedroom furniture from our house in Pittsburgh. I handpicked each piece of furniture and decor with care. The apartment was the largest one-bedroom unit in the complex, and I wanted it to be a comfortable space for Paul when he visited on weekends. I even gave him 50% of the closet space — despite the fact that he only stayed there on weekends and, well, he was a guy! I was determined to keep the apartment uncluttered, so I made it clear that if Paul wanted to bring anything else from our Pittsburgh house, he would need my approval before it could enter the common areas. I was determined that this apartment would remain an organized, peaceful retreat.

The Capitol Hill building loomed before me, its gleaming marble facade and towering white columns commanding attention. It stood as both a monument to democracy and a symbol of the profound responsibilities carried out within its walls. As I prepared to embark on my onboarding orientation tour as a congressional staff member, excitement and nervousness coursed through me. The grandeur of the place was overwhelming, a constant reminder of the magnitude of the work done here and the history it embodied.

I paused for a moment, taking in my surroundings. While the Capitol's imposing structure dominated the landscape, the natural beauty around it softened its edges. Trees dotted the ground, providing refreshing bursts of greenery amidst the sea of stone. The gentle rustling of leaves in the wind offered a soothing contrast to the bustling activity around me. The sun shone brightly, casting long, golden rays that bounced off the white marble, creating a sense of warmth even in this formal setting.

Visitors from all walks of life milled about — some dressed in casual clothes, others in business attire — each snapping photos, chatting, and talking in the atmosphere. The Capitol attracted everyone, from curious tourists to seasoned professionals, all drawn to this place that shapes the lives of millions. It was clear that this was no ordinary building; it was the epicenter of critical decisions, where laws were crafted, and history was made.

A cool breeze picked up, sweeping across the landscape and carrying with it a refreshing chill that cut through the warmth of the day. I closed my eyes for a moment, appreciating the serenity of the breeze and the peacefulness it brought. Overhead, the sky was a vibrant blue, with fluffy white clouds drifting lazily, as if in no hurry at all, creating a picturesque scene against the backdrop of power and significance.

As I stood there, my thoughts returned to a time only a few years ago when I had visited Capitol Hill as a tourist. Back then, I had walked through these very grounds, listening intently to the tour guide as they recounted stories of the building's rich history and the pivotal moments that had unfolded here. The Capitol had felt distant and untouchable — a place I never imagined I'd be a part of. Yet here I was, no longer just an observer but a participant, about to step into a role that connected me directly to the decision-making processes that shaped the future of this nation.

I felt a surge of pride and awe as I stood on the steps of the Capitol, now not as a visitor but as a congressional staff member. This building, this place, once seemed like a distant monument of history, but now it was a living, breathing entity — vibrant with the energy of people working inside it to shape laws, policies, and the direction of the country. It felt humbling, even surreal, to be part of this complex machine. A sense of responsibility settled heavily on my shoulders. I gazed out at the visitors milling around, each unaware of the impact the work inside these walls had on their lives. It was a weighty realization, but one that I embraced with both gratitude and pride.

The orientation tour began, and I eagerly absorbed every detail being shared. The Capitol's corridors echoed with the footsteps of those who came before me, people who had debated, disagreed, and shaped the country's path. I walked through these halls, conscious of the immense history embedded in every corner. The stories of governance, compromise, and leadership were palpable. I knew that I had much to learn, but I was ready for the challenge.

As we moved through different rooms and offices, I glanced out the windows, catching glimpses of the trees swaying in the breeze, the visitors below continuing their exploration, and the steady drift of clouds across the sky. It was a constant reminder that this place was more than just a building; it was a beacon of democracy and hope. The white dome of the Capitol rose above, symbolizing the enduring promise of a government by the people, for the people.

I reflected on how far I had come, from my life in China to now, standing at the heart of American democracy. A close cousin of Paul's had worked for the Pentagon his entire life as a computer programmer and had proudly retired at the rank of GS-12. When I entered my government role at GS-13, Paul was incredibly proud of me, and it felt like a significant personal achievement. My journey, filled with its own struggles and triumphs, had led me here, and now I was part of something much bigger than myself.

As the tour continued, the magnitude of the moment sank in. This was where history was made, where the future was shaped, and where I now had the opportunity to contribute to the process. I was filled with awe and a sense of duty, knowing that I was part of something that would leave a lasting impact on countless lives.

Looking out at the Capitol building, the trees, the visitors, the wind-swept clouds, I realized that this was more than just a job — it was a calling. This place, with all its beauty and significance, was where I was meant to be. I felt more connected to this country and its democratic ideals than ever before. The transition into government work was not just a career change; it was the beginning of a new chapter in my life, one that carried both the weight of history and the promise of the future.

When I drove through the Basin Tidal on my way home to Bethesda, I didn't mind the heavy traffic at all. Instead, I found myself enjoying the scenery outside my window, taking in the iconic sights of Washington, D.C. as they unfolded around me. The Potomac River shimmered in the soft light of dusk, reflecting the monuments and trees that lined its banks. The majestic Washington Monument stood tall in the distance, a symbol of the nation's enduring strength and resilience. For the first time, I truly felt like I belonged here.

That evening, as I sat on my couch watching the news on TV, a profound realization washed over me. Suddenly, everything being discussed — politics, laws, national events — felt deeply relevant to me. I was no longer an outsider, no longer on the margins, observing a country I admired but wasn't fully a part of. The news wasn't just stories about distant people and events; it was about my country, my home, my community.

It was a moment I hadn't anticipated. For so long, I had struggled with the feeling of not quite fitting in. Since coming back from my trip to China in 2002, I had subconsciously given up the idea of ever feeling truly at home. As a Chinese immigrant, I had assumed I would always be on the periphery, forever carrying the weight of my past and my foreignness. But now, something had shifted. The sense of being "in between" cultures had dissolved, replaced by an overwhelming feeling of belonging.

For the first time, I felt it in my bones: this is my home. This is my country. I am no longer just a visitor or an immigrant. I am a Chinese American, part of the fabric of this nation. The sense of pride and connection I had longed for had finally arrived, and with it, a peace I had never fully known before.

Chapter 34: Working in Washington, DC

Living in Washington, D.C. felt like stepping into the heart of the nation's political and cultural life. Every morning as I walked past the towering Capitol Building or the majestic National Mall, I was reminded of the weight of the work being done here. I could feel the pulse of the city, the constant hum of discussions about policy and governance. In some ways, it was overwhelming, but in others, it gave me a deep sense of purpose. I wasn't just working in any city — I was contributing to a machine that shaped the very laws of this country.

Starting my career at The Library of Congress was a significant milestone, but the real challenges soon followed. Shortly after I began, my boss, Mark, the chief of my division, sent me to a week-long training course for the CISSP certification, one of the most prestigious and demanding certifications in cybersecurity. This was unexpected and daunting, given that the certification typically required five years of full-time IT security experience. I had just started the fulltime job, so I felt the pressure immediately. But there was no option but to face the challenge head-on.

The training was rigorous, designed specifically to prepare candidates for the exam. I gave it my full attention, thinking that if I aced the course, I could certainly pass the exam. Each day in class, I immersed myself in the material, tackling the practice tests with determination. By the end of the week, I felt confident. The six-hour exam awaited me (at the time, the CISSP exam was still six hours long; it has since been reduced to three). I went into the testing center with a sense of readiness, but my confidence was shattered when the results appeared on the screen: I had failed by a single point.

The failure hit me harder than I could have anticipated. On the drive home from the testing center, I felt overwhelmed with disappointment. I had never failed an exam before in my life, and this felt like not just a personal failure, but a failure of the trust Mark had placed in me. I replayed the test in my mind, wondering what went wrong. Adding to my distress, the exam had cost $600, which had been paid by the Library. I felt guilty about the financial cost as well. Determined to right this wrong, I told Mark I would pay for the second attempt out of my own pocket, but he assured me that the cost would be covered, encouraging me to focus on passing next time.

Failing the CISSP exam by a single point wasn't just a personal disappointment — it felt like a professional crisis. For the first time in my life, I was faced with a failure that seemed to eclipse all my previous achievements. I questioned whether I truly belonged in the cybersecurity field, whether I was cut out for the high standards set by Mark and my colleagues. But amidst self-doubt, I also found a new layer of resilience. This failure didn't break me. Instead, it fueled a determination I hadn't known before. I realized that success wasn't just about acing every exam or nailing every project — it was about how I responded to setbacks. For the next three months, I studied harder than I had ever studied before, even harder than when I had prepared for my college admission exam for Peking University. I immersed myself in textbooks, practice exams, and online resources, dedicating every spare moment to mastering the material. I didn't visit Pittsburgh during those months, sacrificing personal time for the sake of my professional goal. This time, when I took the exam again, I passed. The relief and pride I felt were overwhelming, not just because I had achieved something difficult, but because I had persevered through my first professional failure and come out stronger on the other side. When I passed the exam on my second attempt, it wasn't just about redemption; it was proof that failure could be the catalyst for growth.

Mark was thrilled with the news and soon after sent me for another certification, this time the CCSP (Certified Cloud Security Professional). This was another challenging credential, but with the experience of the CISSP exam behind me, I was ready. I passed it on the first attempt, much to Mark's delight. During my annual performance review, I received an "Outstanding" rating, along with glowing feedback on my work and contributions. It was a great feeling to know that my hard work and dedication were recognized and appreciated.

Working under Mark's guidance at The Library of Congress was more than just a professional opportunity — it was a turning point in my career. Mark was more than a boss; he was a mentor who believed in my potential, even when I doubted myself. His decision to send me for the CISSP certification training so early in my tenure was a testament to his confidence in me. That belief pushed me beyond my comfort zone, but it also unlocked new skills and a deeper understanding of cybersecurity in the governmental context. I began to see how the work I was doing, whether on securing systems or improving network protocols, had a direct impact on the preservation of the nation's most sensitive information.

However, about a year later, there was a significant restructuring at the Library of Congress. When I was initially hired, I was part of the IT group under the NLS (National Library Service) division. With the restructuring, all IT professionals were being reassigned to different divisions under the House's CIO (Chief Information Officer). Security professionals were among the first to be reassigned, but because my formal title was IT Specialist (System Analyst), I was overlooked when the security staff were transferred to the CISO (Chief Information Security Officer) office.

Mark, who had been a steadfast supporter of my career, explained that this oversight was beyond his control. He encouraged me to seek new opportunities. Armed with over two years of full-time IT security experience, my hard-earned CISSP and CCSP certifications, and a glowing recommendation from Mark, I began looking for a new role. It didn't take long. Within a few months, I was offered a position at the U.S. House of Representatives.

Soon after joining, a colleague told me that at the time of my hire, only four other people in the entire House held the CISSP certification. This revelation made me realize just how valued my expertise was in this new environment. Every contribution I made, no matter how small, was appreciated. It felt like I had found a place where my skills and knowledge were truly respected. I couldn't have been happier with the move, and I found myself thinking that if I could stay here for the rest of my career, I would be content.

Working at the House also brought new learning opportunities. I picked up new skills in cloud security, particularly in Azure. One of my proudest achievements was learning to create pipelines in YAML to streamline security processes in Azure. Learning cloud security and becoming proficient in Azure was like stepping into a new dimension of my career. There were moments when I felt out of my depth, grappling with the complexities of cloud infrastructure, but I thrived on the challenge. Mastering YAML pipelines to streamline security processes was a breakthrough for me, and seeing the results of my work directly improve our department's efficiency was incredibly rewarding. These new skills weren't just checkmarks on my resume — they were building blocks of expertise that would carry me forward in a rapidly evolving field.

Additionally, my CISSP and CCSP certifications opened new doors for me outside of my day-to-day work. I was invited by (ISC)², the organization responsible for the certifications, to participate in several Item Writing, Translating (Chinese), and Reviewing Workshops for both CISSP and CCSP exams. These workshops brought together cybersecurity professionals from all over the world to collaborate on developing new exam items, ensuring that the certifications remained relevant and challenging.

One of these workshops took place in Temple, Florida, at a Hilton hotel just before the COVID-19 pandemic. The workshop spanned three days, during which about 20 of us worked intensely to craft exam questions. The ISC² workshops were an eye-opening experience, not just for the intense work but for the opportunity to collaborate with cybersecurity professionals from around the world. Walking into a room full of experts, each with their own wealth of knowledge and perspectives, was both humbling and exhilarating. For three days, we worked in an enclosed environment, brainstorming, debating, and crafting new exam items that would challenge the next generation of security professionals. It wasn't just about writing questions — it was about ensuring the integrity of the certification process and keeping cybersecurity standards high. I felt privileged to be part of something bigger, knowing that my contributions were helping to shape the future of this field. It was a rare opportunity to engage with experts from different industries and countries, and the exchange of ideas was invaluable. We, the security professionals, weren't paid, but (ISC)² covered all travel, lodging, and meal expenses, and we were allowed to bring one guest at our own expense. Paul came along with me on that trip, excited for the chance to explore Florida while I attended the workshops during the day.

While I was in the thick of cybersecurity discussions and item writing, Paul enjoyed the warm Florida weather. He spent time at the hotel pool and had lunch with his niece, who lived nearby. In the evenings, we reunited to explore the city together. It was a lovely balance between professional and personal life, and Paul was beaming with pride over my accomplishments. He would often say how proud he was of everything I had achieved, from passing those grueling exams to now being involved in the very process of shaping them for future security professionals.

These experiences deepened my sense of belonging in the field of cybersecurity, and every new challenge pushed me to grow even further. I was no longer the person who worried about not meeting expectations or failing an exam. Instead, I was now part of a global network of professionals who were advancing cybersecurity and sharing knowledge across borders. Working at the U.S. House of Representatives gave me a profound sense of fulfillment. Knowing that the cybersecurity measures I helped implement were safeguarding some of the nation's most vital information systems made every challenge worthwhile. It wasn't just a job anymore — it was a mission. Every time I contributed to a project, no matter how small, I knew I was playing a role in protecting the very infrastructure that keeps the country running smoothly.

Throughout it all, Paul was my anchor. His pride in my accomplishments never wavered, and his support helped me navigate the most challenging moments of my career. After long days at work or stressful weeks of certification prep, he would always listen to my concerns, offering advice or simply lending an ear. Our weekends together became cherished times of relaxation and reflection. He would remind me that while my work was important, taking care of myself was equally essential. His words helped me find the balance between ambition and well-being.

Washington, D.C. had become more than just the city where I worked — it had become the backdrop to some of my most significant professional achievements and personal growth. I had adjusted to the fast pace of life here and was thriving in ways I had never imagined.

Looking ahead, I feel a deep sense of excitement about where my career in cybersecurity might take me next. The challenges I've faced and overcome, from passing the CISSP to navigating new roles in cloud security, have given me renewed confidence in my abilities. I'm eager to continue learning, growing, and contributing to the field in any way I can. As I settle further into my role at the House, I can't help but wonder what the next big project might be. The world of cybersecurity is always evolving, and I'm ready to evolve with it, embracing every new opportunity that comes my way.

Chapter 35: Becoming More Active in the Community

Settling into the Parkside Condominium felt like the beginning of a new chapter, not just in my professional life but also in my personal and communal life. Parkside was a quiet and unassuming community made up of three-story complexes that had been developed as affordable housing in the 1960s. Despite its age, the location and scenery were unparalleled. It was nestled in a peaceful, almost secluded part of Bethesda, surrounded by mature trees and lush greenery that gave it a natural, park-like feel. The apartment buildings, though old, were charming in their own way, with wide balconies and large windows that opened up to picturesque views of bamboo groves or well-maintained gardens. The prices were lower than nearby, newer apartments, but to me, that was part of its appeal — it felt like a hidden gem.

Another reason I had been drawn to Parkside was that Mark, my boss, the chief, also lived in the community. It was comforting to know that someone I respected had chosen to live there too. If it was good enough for Mark, it was certainly good enough for me. There was also plenty of free parking — an almost unheard-of luxury in the D.C. area — and I loved that I wouldn't have to deal with the hassle or expense of paying for parking permits or garages.

The only drawback, which I discovered almost immediately, was the thinness of the walls. You could hear the faint sound of water running through the pipes when your upstairs neighbors used their bathroom, and at times, it felt as if they were right in your apartment. At first, it was a little unsettling, but over time, it became one of those quirks you learned to live with in older buildings. After a while, I didn't even notice it anymore.

The community had a beautiful swimming pool — standard-sized, with four lanes — and I was eager to make use of it. When I first moved in during Labor Day weekend, the summer season was winding down, and the pool was about to close for the year. But the following summer, I was determined to take full advantage. Years earlier, when I moved to Pittsburgh, a friend had casually mentioned that it was nearly impossible for someone over 30 to learn how to swim. I was 35 at the time, and the comment stuck with me. Determined to prove her wrong, I taught myself to swim, and though I didn't stick with it at the time, I had managed to swim from one end of the lane to the other. Now, with easy access to such a beautiful pool, I decided to revisit swimming more seriously. By the following summer, I was swimming several times a week and even made some friends at the pool, finding both exercise and a sense of connection.

One of the unexpected joys of moving to Parkside was the community's active involvement in local governance. Every two years, there were elections for the board of directors, and when Paul noticed the nomination forms in our mailbox, he encouraged me to run. I would never have considered it on my own, but his suggestion intrigued me. Why not? With his help, I designed a small campaign. We created a postcard with my information and a photo, and I set about distributing it to my neighbors. I walked around the community, chatting with whoever I met, sharing my vision for improving the neighborhood. The experience was both fun and insightful, as I got to meet and engage with a wide range of residents. Even Mark, my boss, was amused by my candidacy and promised to vote for me.

I didn't win the election — an older, long-time resident was elected — but I didn't feel discouraged. I was new to the community, and it made sense that people would want someone familiar to represent them. What mattered more to me was that I had stepped out of my comfort zone and made an effort to engage with my neighbors. I was slowly becoming more involved in this community that was beginning to feel like home.

In addition to connecting with the residents at Parkside, I also began to engage more actively with the local Chinese American community, particularly through church. After marrying Paul in Pittsburgh, I had always attended his church so that our family could worship together. But now that I lived in Bethesda on my own during the week, I began attending a local Chinese church. It felt good to be around others who shared both my cultural background and faith.

When Paul visited on weekends, he would come with me to the English service at the church, which was designed mainly for second-generation Chinese Americans who spoke English more fluently than Chinese. We quickly became friends with another couple, Tony and Sally, who were about our age. Tony was also white and had a PhD in biology, while Sally was Chinese and worked as a Chinese language teacher at a public school. They had two children, Mike and Anne, who were still in high school, while David, my son, was already in his senior year of college. Despite the differences in our family dynamics, we grew close, bonded by our shared faith and mutual respect for each other's cultural backgrounds.

Sally and I both taught Sunday school at church, and it was through this service that I deepened my relationship with the community. I found joy in teaching the children, most of whom were second-generation Chinese Americans. Many of them could speak enough Chinese to carry on daily conversations with their parents but were more comfortable with English. It was a reminder of how the immigrant experience shapes identity and language, and it made me even more grateful for the cultural roots I could still pass down, even as I embraced my new life as an American.

Life at Parkside was peaceful and fulfilling. Between my work at the Library of Congress, my involvement in the community, and my growing connections through the church, I felt like I was truly becoming part of the fabric of Bethesda. I no longer felt like a newcomer or an outsider — I was becoming an active participant in the community around me, one step at a time.

Several people I met at the pool were also part of a local square dancing class, and after chatting for a while, they invited me to join them. I thought it might be fun, so I agreed. When Paul came to visit one weekend, I took him along to one of the classes. As soon as we arrived, the instructor immediately noticed Paul's natural grace and skill in dancing. He was a far better dancer than I had realized, and the instructor, clearly impressed, offered him a free pass to participate as a dancing partner for some of the other learners. Paul's enthusiasm was contagious, and it seemed like he was enjoying himself immensely.

As for me, I threw myself into learning the steps, but I soon realized that I didn't particularly enjoy square dancing. It felt more like a task than a source of joy. In fact, learning square dancing quickly became just another achievement in my life, something to check off a list rather than something I was passionate about. I completed the lessons anyway since I had already paid for the full semester, but each class felt like a chore.

That experience made me reflect on other things I had been doing, like swimming. Learning to swim had been an accomplishment, but I hadn't stuck with it because I didn't love it.

It felt like something I had done simply because I could, rather than because I wanted to. And now, square dancing was starting to feel the same way.

After some introspection, I realized that I didn't want my life to be a series of tasks or accomplishments. I didn't need another achievement. What I really wanted was to find activities that brought me joy and passion, not just ones that I could complete for the sake of it. I decided it was time to start living more authentically, to focus on what truly made me happy rather than what made me feel productive or successful.

So, after the square dancing lessons ended, I chose not to continue. I also stopped swimming regularly, opting instead to seek out things that brought me genuine fulfillment. It felt liberating to let go of the pressure to achieve and instead focus on simply enjoying life. That shift marked a turning point for me — a step toward finding my true passions and embracing the present, rather than constantly chasing the next goal.

In search of something more fulfilling, I decided to join the church choir. Singing had always been something I enjoyed, but I had never really thought about it as more than just a casual hobby. However, from the moment I joined, I felt an immediate sense of belonging. The camaraderie within the choir was infectious. We would rehearse weekly, and there was something so soothing about lifting our voices together in worship. It wasn't just about perfecting the notes; it was about coming together as a community, united in faith and song.

One experience stood out to me: our choir was asked to perform at the funeral of a longtime church member. I didn't know the person well, but the gravity of the moment and the role we were asked to play made it deeply meaningful. As we stood at the front of the church, singing hymns of comfort and hope, I could see how much our music meant to the grieving family and the congregation. There was an unspoken connection between all of us, as if the music was carrying both our sadness and our faith that the deceased was at peace. It was humbling and powerful.

In that moment, I realized how much I had been missing — not just the joy of singing, but the sense of purpose and community it brought. It wasn't about achieving something, like square dancing or swimming had been for me. It was about participating in something larger than myself, something that made a real difference in people's lives. Being part of the choir wasn't just fulfilling a task; it was feeding my soul.

After the funeral, I felt even more committed to the choir. I looked forward to each rehearsal, not because I was striving for perfection, but because it made me feel connected — to my faith, to the people around me, and to something much deeper. It was one of the first activities in a long time that I pursued simply because it brought me genuine joy.

The book of Revelation in the Bible had always fascinated me, with its vivid imagery, powerful symbolism, and mysterious prophecies. Yet, for years, I had never taken the step to seriously study it. There was always something else that demanded my time, or perhaps I was simply intimidated by the challenge of deciphering such a complex text. But now, with nothing pressing on my schedule after work, I decided to finally dive into it.

At first, it was a personal study — just me, my Bible, and some study materials. I poured over the verses, reading and rereading, trying to grasp the layers of meaning. But as I delved deeper, I realized how much more I was getting out of the experience than I had anticipated. The more I read, the more questions I had, and the more eager I became to understand the deeper significance of the text.

One evening, as I was reflecting on my progress, a thought came to me: "Now that I've made the effort to study this, maybe others could benefit too." Revelation was such a rich and challenging book, and I figured there must be other people who, like me, had always been intrigued but never really knew where to start.

With that in mind, I decided to reach out. I posted on WeChat, the popular Chinese social media platform, announcing, "If more than five people would like to join me in studying Revelation, I will hold a weekly Zoom meeting." To my surprise, about ten people responded almost immediately, eager to be part of this study group. Their enthusiasm was contagious, and I felt a new sense of purpose.

Each week, we gathered virtually to discuss our readings, ask questions, and share insights. What surprised me most was how much I learned through teaching and sharing my understanding with others. Explaining the intricacies of the book forced me to think more deeply, and the group's perspectives enriched my own.

It was more than just a study; it became a community of people hungry for spiritual growth and eager to explore this challenging part of Scripture together.

The experience was rewarding on multiple levels. Not only did I finally engage with a part of the Bible that had long fascinated me, but I also discovered how much more I could learn when I shared the journey with others.

Part 4: The Turning of a New Era (2020–2024)

Chapter 36: The COVID-19 Pandemic Begins

The early days of 2020 were filled with an eerie sense of uncertainty. News reports began trickling in about a mysterious virus spreading through parts of China, and within weeks, the world's focus shifted from isolated incidents to the rapid global spread of COVID-19. No one could have predicted how drastically life was about to change.

Just before the world was turned upside down, Paul and I had taken a significant step in our lives. After I started working for the U.S. House of Representatives, Paul was finally able to close his business in Pittsburgh and move to the Washington, D.C. area to be with me full-time. We had been living apart for too long, commuting back and forth, so this transition marked a new chapter for us as a couple. Finally, we were able to settle in the same city, and together, we decided it was time to find a home where we could build the next stage of our lives.

We began our search with the idea of finding a small house, something manageable for empty nesters like ourselves. However, nothing we saw seemed quite right. The houses we visited felt too cramped, too impersonal, or simply lacked the warmth we were looking for. After weeks of searching, we stumbled upon a larger house in Alexandria, Virginia, and scheduled a visit. The closing date was set for February 6, 2020 — just weeks before the pandemic swept across the country.

The house was impressive, much larger than what we had initially imagined for ourselves, and located in a beautiful community right next to Huntley Meadows Park, the largest wetland state park in Virginia. The neighborhood was quiet, filled with mature trees and greenery that created a serene environment, making it feel like a peaceful retreat from the city.

Despite our initial impressions, we dismissed the house due to its size. It felt excessive for two people, and we assumed it wouldn't be practical. But as we drove away, Paul couldn't stop thinking about it. "Let's go back and see it again," he said after a while. So we returned, took a second look, and something about it felt different this time.

When we had been there earlier with the seller's agent, it wasn't just the size or the layout that stood out to us — there was something about the atmosphere of the house that seemed to hold a story, a history that resonated deeply with both Paul and me. As we walked through the rooms once again, Paul asked the seller's agent if there was anything special about the house. She paused for a moment, almost as if deciding how much to reveal, and then she smiled. "Well," she said, "this used to be George Washington's backyard, along with Huntley Meadows Park."

We both stood there, taken aback. The idea that our potential new home was tied to such a significant piece of American history was an incredible thought. This land, which would soon become part of our daily lives, had once belonged to one of the country's founding figures. The connection to George Washington and the historical significance of the area added an unexpected, yet profound, weight to our decision. It felt as though we were stepping into something much larger than just a new house; we were becoming part of a legacy.

That revelation sealed the deal for us. It no longer mattered that the house was bigger than what we had initially envisioned. We knew it would become more than just a place to live — it would be a place where we could build our future, grounded in faith, history, and a commitment to advancing God's kingdom. From that moment on, the house felt like a gift, a space we were entrusted with, and we made a vow to use it for God's Kingdom.

The house had been the model home when the community was developed in 1988 — the largest in size and filled with character. While the interior was well maintained, the backyard was barren, neglected by the previous owner. Paul, with his love for creating beauty from nothing, saw the potential in the space and made it his mission to transform it into a garden that reflected the peace and joy we felt in our new home.

Over the following almost two years, Paul poured his heart and soul into the backyard. He built a stunning garden that included a two-tiered koi pond with a pretty white tiny bridge connecting the upper and lower ponds, complete with a water fountain at the center of the lower pond. He added a gazebo with a swing bench, two chairs, and a washing sink for convenience. A hot tub with jets became a perfect spot for Paul to relax, soaking in the serenity of the surroundings. He built a rotunda and installed a lion fountain, creating a centerpiece of calm and reflection. Paul's attention to detail was remarkable — he even cultivated a lush lawn that stayed green through the winter months, ensuring that our little oasis remained beautiful year-round. Several lounge chairs were scattered throughout the yard, inviting moments of rest and reflection under the shade of the trees.

The large deck became an extension of our living space, divided into three sections. There was a cozy sitting area with sofas and chairs, a fully screened gazebo that housed a second set of comfortable seating, and a picnic table with eight chairs underneath a large umbrella adorned with lights. The backyard became a sanctuary, a place where we could escape the chaos of the world and find peace in each other's company. Little did we know how much we would come to rely on this peaceful retreat once the pandemic took hold.

As we settled into our new home, the reality of the pandemic began to unfold. It was as if someone had pressed a pause on life. Schools closed their doors, offices sent employees home, and suddenly, the streets of Washington, D.C., once bustling with activity, were eerily quiet. I continued my work remotely, while Paul and I adjusted to our new routines within the confines of our home.

But amidst the growing public health crisis, something else began to stir — debates about government control, personal freedom, and the role of authority in times of crisis. As lockdowns and restrictions were imposed across states, people began to question how far the government could go in limiting freedoms in the name of public safety.

The inconsistencies in how these rules were applied only fueled suspicions and deepened the divide. Small shops and family-owned businesses were ordered to shut down, deemed "non-essential," while large chain stores like Walmart and Amazon continued operations as "essential services." Churches were told to close their doors, preventing people from gathering in worship, yet casinos and liquor stores were permitted to remain open. The contradictions were impossible to ignore, and they led to growing frustration and distrust in the government's decisions.

The vaccine mandates that were introduced later in the year added even more fuel to the fire. While many Americans were required to get vaccinated to keep their jobs, certain groups, such as congressional staffers, were exempt from these mandates.

Ironically, most of my colleagues chose to get vaccinated voluntarily, but the exemption highlighted the inconsistencies in the application of these policies. People couldn't help but question whether the mandates were truly about public health or part of a broader effort to exert control over the population.

Paul, in particular, found himself deeply conflicted. On one hand, he understood the need to control the spread of the virus and protect vulnerable populations, especially the elderly. On the other hand, he couldn't shake the feeling that this was exactly the kind of government overreach he had been concerned about for decades. The inconsistencies, the mandates, and the selective enforcement of rules felt too much like a slippery slope toward a loss of personal freedom.

The memory of the 1985 meeting — when Democratic leaders had discussed the idea of using a pandemic to eliminate the elderly and solve Social Security and Medicare issues — loomed large in his mind. The pandemic disproportionately affected the elderly, and the social and economic strain it placed on the country seemed to align with the unsettling discussions he had heard decades earlier.

As the months wore on, the country became even more divided. Protests erupted in several states, with people pushing back against extended lockdowns and government mandates. Others insisted that these measures were necessary to protect the public and save lives. It was a tension that seemed to deepen with each passing week.

From the sanctuary of our newly transformed backyard, Paul and I often discussed these events, contemplating the balance between public safety and personal freedom. The peaceful garden he had created became a place of solace, a reminder of the beauty that could still be found in uncertain times.

The year dragged on with no clear end in sight. The initial optimism that the pandemic would be short-lived had faded, and the world began to accept a new normal. But for us, this new normal came with a profound sense of unease. The political transformation Paul had experienced over the decades had brought him to this point — a deep skepticism of authority, a fear of government overreach, and a desire to protect the personal freedoms that we believed were being steadily chipped away.

"They don't even hide their agenda anymore," Paul would say, his voice filled with conviction. "If you don't believe me, just look up the UN 2030 Initiative. They present it as a vision of utopia, but they don't tell you what happens to those who resist giving up their freedoms."

I nodded in agreement, understanding the weight of his words. The pandemic was not just a health crisis — it was a test of how far governments could push people in the name of safety, and how much freedom people were willing to sacrifice in exchange for a sense of security.

When Paul and I moved into our new home in Alexandria, we were excited about this new chapter, but there were still practical matters to handle. The house in Pittsburgh hadn't sold yet, so Paul needed to travel back and forth to clear out his old belongings and get the house ready for sale. During this time, I found myself settling into our new home alone, at least part of the time. In February, I went to a nearby church by myself, hoping to find a community there, but shortly after, the church was shut down due to the pandemic. The pastor's online services didn't resonate with me either. His message felt distant, and I struggled to connect with the spirit of the service through the screen.

Now that physical attendance wasn't possible, and I wasn't confined by the distance, I began to explore other online services. I tried several churches, searching for one that spoke to me spiritually and emotionally. A friend recommended Cornerstone Chapel, and during Memorial Day weekend, Paul and I decided to give it a try. We watched the Sunday service together for the first time, and we were both blown away by Pastor Gary's powerful message. His words struck a chord in both of us, and we felt an immediate connection to the way he delivered the gospel. We decided then and there that Cornerstone Chapel would be our church home, even if it was online for the time being.

As the pandemic lockdown continued, I transitioned fully to working remotely. It was a sudden shift, but one that I embraced wholeheartedly. Without the daily commute or having to fight the notorious D.C. traffic, I found myself with more time — time that I had previously spent sitting in the car, navigating congested highways. Now, I could start my day more calmly, and I used those extra hours to focus on something I had long neglected: my health.

The lockdown, in some ways, gave me the gift of time, and I started incorporating regular exercise into my routine, and looked forward to it every day. I took advantage of the spacious backyard Paul had so lovingly transformed, doing stretches or yoga in the mornings and long walks through the Huntley Meadow State Park, just a stone's throw from our new home. I felt a sense of peace, even amidst the uncertainty of the world outside. The combination of spiritual nourishment from Cornerstone Chapel and the physical activity helped me stay grounded, despite the chaos the pandemic had caused.

Our home had become both a refuge and a place of reflection. The vow we made to use it for advancing God's kingdom felt more relevant than ever. We didn't know what the future held, but we were determined to face it together, grounded in our faith and committed to standing up for the values we held dear. As soon as Cornerstone Chapel reopened, we asked how we could start a Bible study group in our house.

Though the pandemic forced us into isolation in many ways, it also opened doors to new opportunities and deeper connections. It gave Paul and me a chance to slow down, reflect, and find joy in the simplest things. We were grateful for the time to grow closer to each other, our faith, and our new community, even if it was mostly online.

Chapter 37: Navigating the Pandemic

When we started searching for a new house at the end of 2019, Paul decided to buy an RV to assist with moving his belongings from the Pittsburgh house to our new home. This was especially helpful for transporting all his ceiling-tall plants, which had become a central feature of his life. The RV was a beautiful 2017 Class B+ Dodge Winnebago, and little did we know that it would become more than just a moving vehicle — it would be our escape from the restrictions imposed during the pandemic.

When we signed the contract for the new house, the previous owners offered to include all the furniture they had staged for selling the house. They had moved back to Puerto Rico after representing their government in the States for almost 30 years, and since they didn't need the furniture anymore, they suggested we keep it. It was a huge relief for us, as it meant we didn't have to bring any bulky furniture from the Pittsburgh house, leaving us free to focus on other aspects of the move.

Shortly after signing the contract, I put my apartment in Bethesda up for sale. Within a week, I received an offer, and the closing date was set for March 5th, 2020. However, just two days before the scheduled closing, the buyer's agent informed me that her loan application had been rejected. She had tried to secure a cosigner but had failed. The timing couldn't have been worse — the lockdown had begun, and my apartment was back on the market just as the world was shutting down. Nobody was coming for open houses anymore, and I couldn't afford to pay two mortgages without additional income. So, I made the decision to rent it out instead. Fortunately, due to the apartment's great location, I was able to find tenants quickly. Although every tenant moved out after just one year, the frequent turnover allowed me to adjust the rent according to market prices, which increased each year. In hindsight, it was a blessing in disguise. I learned the value of real estate as an investment, realizing that diversification was key to financial stability.

Looking back, I was so grateful that everything had worked together for the good of those who fear God, as it says in Romans 8:28. What initially seemed like setbacks were, in fact, opportunities for growth and blessing.

The RV also became our means of travel during a time when air travel and hotel stays were difficult, if not impossible, due to the lockdown. With the RV, Paul and I embarked on cross-country trips that took us all the way to California and Key West, Florida. We even decided to take the RV to Canada, which required us to get our one and only shot of the Johnson & Johnson vaccine so we could cross the border.

However, the trip to Canada didn't go entirely smoothly. At the border, we were asked if we had any firearms or weapons with us, including tasers. Paul, not thinking much of it, replied no, but the border patrol conducted a search of the RV and found a taser tucked away. Paul had completely forgotten about it and apologized sincerely, but the Canadian officials were not lenient. They fined us 500 Canadian dollars. Paul was frustrated, saying, "I could have thrown it away and bought a new one in Canada for less than $20. In the USA, people are more humane — this would never have happened."

As we cautiously made our way through Canada, we were stopped at each province for a COVID-19 swap test. Even at restaurants, people were scared, distancing themselves and wearing masks while waiting for their food. The atmosphere was tense, and we could sense the fear in everyone around us. When we finally crossed back into the U.S., we both let out a deep breath that we hadn't realized we had been holding. Being back on American soil felt like returning to freedom. We realized that, despite the restrictions we had experienced, America was still a free country, and that realization strengthened our resolve to defend it.

The contrast between Canada and the U.S. was stark. While in Canada, we felt the weight of government control with every test and restriction, but in the U.S., even amidst the pandemic, there was a sense of freedom that hadn't been fully lost. During our RV trips across the U.S., the roads were quieter due to light traffic, and we saw peaceful, serene landscapes. We stopped at local restaurants where people seemed relaxed, enjoying their meals without the fear that had permeated Canadian society.

At RV campsites, there were lively, heated discussions about the pandemic, but they weren't filled with fear. Instead, people were focused on living their lives, finding ways to navigate the situation without sacrificing their personal freedoms. It was a reminder that, despite the challenges of the pandemic, Americans had not given in to fear. They continued to hold onto their values and their rights.

Navigating the pandemic had been a challenge, but it had also given us a deeper appreciation for the freedoms we had always taken for granted. And while the world continued to grapple with uncertainty, Paul and I found peace in the knowledge that we would always stand for the values that mattered most: faith, freedom, and family.

The country had deeply divided. People from both sides seemed to live in two different worlds. The pandemic had exacerbated these divides, with people making decisions based on fear, political alignment, or personal belief. Once, when Paul and I visited Pittsburgh, I witnessed these divides firsthand. Paul wanted to spend some quality time alone with his sons, so I decided to reconnect with some old friends. It had been a while since I'd seen them, and I looked forward to rekindling those relationships.

I reached out to one of my old friends first. She sounded thrilled when we spoke, eager to catch up after such a long time. However, just a few minutes later, my phone rang again. It was her, but her tone had changed. She apologized, explaining that her husband didn't want to receive any guests for fear of attracting the virus. While I wasn't entirely shocked, the rejection was still a bit unexpected. They were the same couple who had welcomed David and me with open arms when we had moved from California. Their fear, though understandable given the uncertainty, stung a little. It was a poignant reminder of how much the pandemic had reshaped people's comfort levels and social interactions.

Not wanting to let the moment dishearten me, I reached out to another friend. She and her husband were devout Christians, and our shared faith had always been a strong bond between us. Recently, though, their lives had been upended in a different way. Her husband had been diagnosed with thyroid cancer shortly after receiving the COVID vaccine. At the time, she had considered it a blessing that the cancer was caught in its early stages. "Had it not been for the vaccine, we wouldn't have found it so soon," she had initially thought. But as time went on and more cases of cancer linked to the vaccine began to emerge in the news, they started to wonder if the vaccine had actually played a role in his illness. It was a lingering question in their minds, yet they didn't dwell on it with anger or frustration.

When I contacted her to arrange a visit, she responded with warmth and enthusiasm, inviting me to stay overnight since their daughter would be away for the weekend. Despite their ongoing challenges, her spirit remained resilient. Their son had grown up with David, and the two had played together when they were young. It was comforting to see how her family had remained grounded in faith, even amidst the uncertainties of life.

That evening, we sat together, reminiscing about our children, laughing over old memories, and exchanging updates on their lives. We also prayed together for her husband, asking for strength and healing in the face of his diagnosis. Their grace and resilience deeply touched me. They were not bitter, nor did they allow fear or doubt to consume them. Instead, they placed their trust in God and remained hopeful in His plan, despite the trials they were facing. It was an enjoyable evening, one filled with peace, even in the midst of personal and societal turmoil.

Reflecting on that visit later, I realized how much these contrasting experiences represented the division in the country at large. Some were overwhelmed with fear and retreating into isolation, while others found solace in their faith and the connections they maintained with loved ones. The pandemic had exposed and widened the gaps between people, not just in political or social views, but in how they coped with the challenges of life.

In contrast to American culture, where people often refer to their class by the year of graduation, in Chinese culture, we use the year of enrollment to mark the class. For example, I enrolled at Peking University in 1985, so we refer to ourselves as the class of 85. On WeChat, there was even a group called *Class85fromPekingUniversityInDC*, which had over 40 members. We all shared the common bond of being in our senior year at Peking University in 1989, the year of the Tiananmen Square protests, and many participated in the hunger strike. It was a defining time in our lives, a fight for freedom and individual liberties. Yet, over the years, I've found myself puzzled by a strange shift among my former classmates — about 90% of them had become liberal after leaving China to pursue freedom. I could never quite understand how, after such a pivotal moment in our youth, their political views evolved in that direction.

Despite our political differences, we used to attend the same parties and gatherings, keeping in touch with the community. One couple, in particular, kept regular contact with me. After we finished the backyard project at our new home, we decided to host a few parties, mostly inviting our conservative friends, many of whom shared similar values and political beliefs. As the event approached, I found myself hesitating over whether I should invite this couple.

I reached out to the husband, wanting to be upfront. "We're hosting a party at our house," I told him, "but I'm not sure if you'd be comfortable attending because some of the guests are GOP candidates." I didn't want to cause any discomfort or create an awkward situation. He appreciated my candor and said, "Maybe another time when you hold a private party just for friends." It was a polite way of declining, and I understood. We haven't yet had a private gathering like that, only with friends.

Interestingly, another member of our WeChat group, Peter, was one of the few classmates who shared conservative views. He had faced criticism from many of our classmates and was eventually kicked out of the group for posting his opinions. However, we remained close, and he attended several of our gatherings at the house. Peter's resilience in standing up for his beliefs, despite the backlash from our peers, was something Paul and I admired. His presence at our gatherings added depth to the discussions, reinforcing the importance of holding onto one's convictions, even when it felt like the world was against you.

It's interesting how relationships can evolve over time, and how political beliefs can create new boundaries even among old friends. It's something that continues to give me pause, especially as I think back to the ideals we all once fought for during those unforgettable days in Tiananmen Square.

Chapter 38: Faith and Cornerstone Chapel

I'll never forget that first service Paul and I watched together during Memorial Day weekend of 2020. We sat in our living room, not knowing what to expect, but as soon as Pastor Gary began to preach, we were both captivated.

Pastor Gary's words were powerful, rooted deeply in biblical truth, yet incredibly relatable to the challenges we were all facing during those uncertain times. His message was filled with hope and conviction, and it was clear that he was unafraid to speak the truth boldly. He addressed the cultural shifts happening around us and the growing divide in society, reminding us that as Christians, we are called to stand firm in our faith, even when the world around us feels like it's falling apart.

But it wasn't just Pastor Gary's preaching that drew us in. There was something different about Cornerstone Chapel, something that made us feel connected even though we were watching from a distance. It was as if the church reached out through the screen and embraced us with open arms, offering hope and encouragement at a time when everything felt so uncertain. Paul and I made the decision that day to attend Cornerstone Chapel regularly, even if it meant watching the services online for the time being. We felt like we had found our spiritual home.

As the weeks turned into months, and the lockdowns gradually eased, Cornerstone Chapel made the bold decision to reopen its doors. While many churches remained closed, offering only online services, Cornerstone Chapel took a stand. They recognized that faith is essential, especially during times of crisis, and they were determined to provide a place where people could come together to worship, pray, and find comfort in their faith.

The decision to reopen wasn't just about returning to normal — it was about standing up for the freedoms that we, as Christians, hold dear. When Paul and I made the trip to Leesburg to attend a service in person for the first time, I remember feeling a mixture of excitement and anticipation. Walking through the doors of the church felt like coming home. The sanctuary was filled with people, shoulder to shoulder, eager to worship together. What struck me most was that not a single person was wearing a mask.

In a time when masks had become a symbol of the pandemic's grip on daily life, here, in this sacred space, people were free — free to breathe, free to sing, free to worship God without fear.

The church building itself exuded a sense of warmth and welcome. Cornerstone Chapel is an impressive structure, modern yet grounded in tradition. From the moment you walk in, you're met with high ceilings and large windows that flood the space with natural light. The sanctuary is grand, with rows of comfortable seating that can hold a large congregation.

The campus surrounding the church is equally beautiful, with green spaces where families gather after services, enjoying the peaceful atmosphere. It's a place where community is built, where conversations flow freely, and where connections are made. After being apart from others for so long, it was refreshing to experience that sense of belonging again.

But the real beauty of Cornerstone Chapel wasn't just in the building or the campus — it was in the atmosphere. There was a palpable sense of freedom, of defiance against the restrictions that had been imposed across the country. People weren't just gathered to worship; they were gathered to celebrate their faith and their freedom. It felt like we were standing together, united not only by our belief in God but also by our shared commitment to the freedom He grants us. Despite the fear that had permeated society outside those doors, inside, we stood close together, confident in our faith and in God's protection.

As we stood there worshiping with the congregation, Paul and I were overwhelmed by the spirit of resilience and faith that filled the room. Pastor Gary, with his clear, unwavering voice, preached about the essential nature of faith in the life of a Christian. He reminded us that faith is not just something we carry with us in times of ease, but something we must hold onto, especially in moments of trial. His words resonated deeply with us. He made it clear that while many things in life had been deemed "essential" during the pandemic, the most essential thing of all was faith. It is faith that grounds us, that keeps us steady when everything around us seems uncertain.

His message wasn't just inspiring — it was a call to action. He urged us to live out our faith boldly, without compromise, and to trust that God was still in control, even in the midst of the chaos. Paul and I left that day with a renewed sense of purpose.

Cornerstone Chapel wasn't just a new church for us; it had become a symbol of the strength and freedom that faith provides.

The sense of community we found at Cornerstone Chapel was profound. In a time when so many were isolated, separated from friends and family, it felt like a gift to be able to worship together in person. It felt as if we were no longer alone in facing the fear and confusion of the pandemic. Instead, we were standing together, united by our shared faith and purpose.

After that first in-person service, Paul and I talked about how transformative the experience had been. We were struck not just by the message but by the sense of belonging we felt.

As the months passed, we continued to attend services at Cornerstone Chapel regularly. Each time we returned, we felt more connected to the church and to the people around us. Pastor Gary's sermons continued to challenge and inspire us, calling us to live out our faith in practical ways.

One of the most significant moments for us came when we decided to start a Bible study group in our home. The idea had been on our hearts for a while, and we felt that God was calling us to use the beautiful home He had blessed us with for His purposes. After talking to the church leaders, we hosted our first group, inviting people from Cornerstone Chapel and other friends who were seeking a deeper relationship with God. It was a humbling experience to see how God used our home to bring people together in His name. The group grew, and with it, so did our faith.

Through Cornerstone Chapel, we not only found a church but also rediscovered the power of prayer, the importance of fellowship, and the joy of serving others. The church didn't just offer us a place to worship; it became a place of transformation for both Paul and me. It reminded us that faith isn't just about what happens within the walls of a church building — it's about living out that faith in every aspect of our lives, whether through our relationships, our work, or even the way we navigate difficult times like the pandemic.

Looking back, I see how God's hand was in every step of our journey to Cornerstone Chapel. It wasn't by chance that we ended up there, and it wasn't just the sermons or the people that kept us coming back. It was the deep sense of belonging, the feeling that we were part of something bigger than ourselves — a community of believers who were committed to following Christ wholeheartedly. Our time at Cornerstone has not only deepened our faith but has given us a renewed sense of purpose, knowing that we are called to be light in the world, especially in times of darkness.

As we continue to walk this journey of faith, I am constantly reminded of how grateful I am for the spiritual home we have found at Cornerstone Chapel. It's a place that has not only strengthened our marriage but has also grounded us in our faith, equipping us to face the challenges ahead with confidence and hope.

Chapter 39: Hosting K-Group Gatherings

The idea of hosting K-group wasn't completely new to us. Paul had always enjoyed having friends and family over for lively discussions, often touching on politics, faith, and the big questions of life. Now, in the context of Cornerstone Chapel and the spiritual growth we had experienced, we wanted to focus these gatherings in a new way — to center them around the Word of God, to view the world through a Christian lens, and to provide a space where people could engage in meaningful conversations about faith, culture, and the challenges we faced as believers in an ever-changing world.

The decision to host a K-Group — short for Koinonia Group — was one we did not take lightly. We knew the responsibility that came with it. Cornerstone Chapel's K-Groups were designed to foster community and spiritual growth, offering small groups a chance to dig deeper into the Bible and support each other in their walks with Christ. It was a big step, and though we were nervous, we knew God had placed this on our hearts for a reason.

Our first K-Group gathering was both exciting and nerve-wracking. We weren't sure how many people would come or how the discussions would unfold, but we trusted that God would lead the evening. We decided to keep the format simple — a time for fellowship, prayer, Bible study, and open discussion about the issues that mattered most to us as Christians living in an increasingly complex and divided world.

That first night, about eight people gathered in our living room. The atmosphere was warm and inviting, with soft lighting and the scent of freshly brewed coffee filling the air. Paul had made sure the backyard was ready in case anyone wanted to take the conversation outside, and I had prepared a spread of snacks and refreshments. We began the evening with prayer, asking for God's guidance and wisdom in our discussions.

As we opened our Bibles and began to read together, it became clear that the Holy Spirit was moving among us. People who had come in feeling uncertain or burdened by the weight of the world started to open up. The discussions that followed were profound. We talked about the challenges we were facing as Christians in a world that seemed increasingly hostile to our values. The conversation naturally shifted to the social and political issues of the day — the pandemic, government mandates, religious freedoms, and the growing divide between those who sought to live by biblical principles and those who followed the secular trends of the culture.

What struck me most that night was the depth of the conversations. These weren't superficial discussions; people were wrestling with real issues, seeking to understand how their faith informed their views on the political and social challenges they were encountering. We talked about the role of government, the importance of personal responsibility, and the need for Christians to be actively engaged in the cultural and political arenas, not just as citizens but as followers of Christ who are called to be the salt and light of the world.

At the beginning, our K-Group was very successful, with an attendance rate of over 90%, far exceeding the average of 50% for most groups. We were thrilled. The steady turnout gave us a sense of purpose, knowing that the people attending were committed to exploring their faith and engaging in deep, meaningful discussions. There was a great energy in the room every time we met. It was as though the group had tapped into something vital — the desire for community, for open dialogue, and for a deeper understanding of how to live out our faith in these challenging times.

However, after hosting the group for several months, we decided to take a break during the summer, as suggested. We thought the break would allow people to rest and recharge, but when we reopened in the fall, to our surprise, nobody returned. Most of the attendees had moved out of the area, and the rest simply stopped coming. It was as if the momentum we had built up had suddenly disappeared, and it left us feeling defeated. We couldn't help but wonder what we had done wrong. Did we fail in some way? Were we not good enough hosts or leaders? These thoughts weighed heavily on us, and we even considered whether we should continue hosting the group at all.

Feeling uncertain, we reached out to the pastor in charge of K-Groups, sharing our concerns. His response was both simple and profound: "It's in God's hands. You only need to do your part." Those words encouraged us to continue, reminding us that success isn't always measured in numbers. We had done our part by opening our home and hearts, and God would take care of the rest. From that point on, we no longer felt defeated, regardless of how many or few people showed up. We had peace in our hearts, knowing that we were being obedient to God's calling. Slowly but surely, our group began to grow again, and we've been blessed with a steady attendance rate ever since. Praise God for the work He is doing, even when we don't fully understand His timing.

Throughout the course of our K-Group, we've had the privilege of hearing many incredible testimonies. One story that deeply touched our hearts was that of Andy, a young man who attended our group for several months before moving out of the area. Andy had a twin brother who lived in another state and had suffered a severe reaction to a misdiagnosed medical treatment. The treatment caused his skin to literally melt away, and doctors didn't expect him to survive. But through prayers and the grace of God, his twin brother made a remarkable recovery. Andy shared with us that his brother had experienced an out-of-body journey during his time in the hospital, where he visited the gates of hell. Despite being left almost blind and with crippled fingers, his brother learned how to play the piano and now sings gospel tunes to everyone's delight. It was a miraculous transformation, and many of us believed that his recovery was a direct result of God's intervention.

Andy had always tried to preach the gospel to his twin brother, but his words never seemed to penetrate his brother's heart. Yet through this tragedy, his brother had experienced new life in Christ. "Maybe that was God's way of saving him from eternal suffering," Andy said, reflecting on the experience. The story brought tears to our eyes, as we marveled at how God works in ways we often don't understand. Though Andy eventually moved out of the area, he kept in touch with Paul. When Andy lost his job later, he called Paul for help, seeking guidance during a difficult time. Paul felt honored by his trust and we welcomed him to stay with us, reminding him of God's faithfulness even in seasons of hardship.

Hosting these K-Group gatherings not only enriched the lives of those who attended but also deepened our own faith. We learned that ministry isn't about numbers or outward success — it's about obedience to God's calling and trusting Him with the results. The connections we made, the stories we heard, and the prayers we lifted up together were a testament to the power of community and faith.

We have come to realize that our role is simply to create a space where people can come together, explore their faith, and support one another in their journeys. Each gathering, whether large or small, is an opportunity for God to move in our midst. Hosting these gatherings has been one of the greatest blessings in our lives, reminding us that when we open our hearts and homes to others, God can use us to make a difference in ways we never imagined.

What truly sustained us during the ups and downs of hosting was the sense of calling. We felt that God had placed this ministry in our hands for a reason, even when it wasn't clear. There were times when we felt discouraged — like when no one returned after the summer break — but we were reminded that faithfulness in the little things is what God asks of us. We were not responsible for the results; we were only responsible for being obedient.

Reflecting on our journey with the K-Group, I realize that God taught us invaluable lessons in perseverance, trust, and the true meaning of Christian fellowship. We didn't always have the answers, but we knew that God was guiding us through every step of the way. He used the gatherings to shape not only the lives of the attendees but also our own spiritual growth, deepening our dependence on Him.

Through the K-Group, we also had the privilege of discussing some of the most pressing social and political issues of our time, always through a Christian lens. From navigating the challenges of living in a post-pandemic world to exploring how our faith should inform our views on government and culture, these conversations were rich and thought-provoking. They pushed us all to think more deeply about what it means to be a follower of Christ in today's world and how we can engage the culture while staying true to biblical values.

Chapter 40: Reflections on Faith and Responsibility

As I sit here, reflecting on the past few years, one thing has become abundantly clear: faith is not just a part of my life — it is the foundation upon which all my decisions are built. It has shaped the way I view the world, guided the paths I've chosen, and helped me navigate the complexities of life. Yet, with faith comes responsibility, not only to ourselves but to others, to our society, and to God. Understanding the weight of that responsibility has been one of the most transformative lessons I've learned on this journey.

When the world was thrust into chaos during the pandemic, many found themselves questioning the role of faith in such unprecedented times. The pandemic brought fear, confusion, and a sense of helplessness, but for me, it was a time of deep reflection on what it means to trust God even when circumstances are beyond my control. Paul and I spent countless hours talking about the role of faith, not just in our personal lives but in how we responded to the challenges of the world around us. We recognized that as Christians, our faith couldn't be compartmentalized — it had to inform every aspect of our lives, especially in times of crisis.

In the early days of the pandemic, the question of societal responsibility became a point of intense debate. With lockdowns, government mandates, and restrictions on personal freedoms, everyone had an opinion on how we should balance public safety with individual liberty. For Paul and me, the answer came back to our faith. As followers of Christ, we knew that we were called to love others and protect the vulnerable, but we also recognized the importance of personal freedom. It was a difficult balance, and one that required careful thought and prayer.

Faith led us to make decisions that were not always easy. While many of our friends and neighbors chose to isolate themselves, we felt compelled to reach out to others — not recklessly, but thoughtfully. We hosted virtual meetings, made phone calls, and sent notes of encouragement to those we knew were struggling. And when it was safe to do so, we opened our home to others. We knew that in a time when so many felt isolated and alone, it was more important than ever to foster community and remind people they were not walking this journey alone.

The pandemic served as a reminder that our faith is not just about our relationship with God; it's about how that relationship affects the way we engage with the world. We are called to be salt and light, to be agents of change and hope in a world that so often seems devoid of both. It is easy to retreat into our own worlds, especially when things feel overwhelming, but our responsibility as Christians is to step out in faith, trusting that God will use us to make a difference, even if we don't always see the fruits of our labor right away.

This sense of responsibility extended into the realm of social and political issues. As the world became increasingly polarized, it was tempting to shy away from difficult conversations, to avoid the discomfort that comes with discussing faith, politics, and the intersection of the two. But Paul and I knew that our faith called us to engage with these issues, not just from a political standpoint, but from a biblical one. We had to ask ourselves: what does God's Word say about justice, about freedom, about government and authority? How should our faith inform our views on these issues, and more importantly, how should it inform our actions?

Faith and responsibility are deeply intertwined. It's not enough to have faith in a vacuum; faith must be lived out in the decisions we make every day. Whether it's the way we interact with our neighbors, the way we vote, or the way we raise our children, our faith should be the guiding force behind it all. We are responsible for living out our faith in tangible ways, for being examples of Christ's love and truth in a world that desperately needs both.

As Paul and I continued to host K-Group gatherings, we saw firsthand how faith could transform lives. We witnessed people wrestling with difficult questions, seeking to understand how their faith should shape their views on the world around them. It was in these moments that we realized the incredible responsibility we had to lead by example. We weren't perfect — far from it — but we knew that God had called us to this role for a reason. Our responsibility wasn't just to host meetings or facilitate discussions; it was to walk alongside people in their faith journeys, to encourage them, challenge them, and point them to Christ.

Looking back, I can see how faith has guided every major decision in my life. From my choice to move to Pittsburgh, to my decision to work for the U.S. government, and even the way Paul and I navigated the challenges of the pandemic, faith has always been the constant. It has given me clarity when the world seemed confusing, strength when I felt weak, and a sense of purpose when I felt lost.

But with that faith has come a deep sense of responsibility — a responsibility to use the gifts God has given me to serve others, to speak truth, and to live a life that reflects His love and grace. It's not always easy, and there have been times when I've failed to live up to that calling. But each time, God has reminded me that His grace is sufficient, and that He is the one who equips me for the responsibilities He has placed before me.

One of the greatest lessons I've learned is that faith isn't just about believing in God; it's about trusting Him enough to take action. It's about stepping out in obedience, even when the path ahead is unclear. And it's about understanding that we are part of something much bigger than ourselves — that our lives have a purpose beyond our own desires and ambitions. We are called to be part of God's redemptive plan for the world, and that is a responsibility I don't take lightly.

As I reflect on the journey Paul and I have been on, I am filled with gratitude for the ways God has led us, challenged us, and shaped us through our faith. I know that the road ahead will not always be easy, but I also know that we are not walking it alone. God is with us, guiding us, giving us strength, and calling us to live out our faith with courage and conviction. And as long as we continue to place our trust in Him, I am confident that we will be able to fulfill the responsibilities He has entrusted to us — both in our personal lives and in the broader world around us.

In the end, faith is not just about what we believe; it's about how we live. It's about allowing our relationship with God to transform every aspect of our lives, and it's about taking responsibility for the role we play in His kingdom. Whether it's in our families, our communities, or the world at large, we are called to be faithful stewards of the gifts and opportunities God has given us. And that, to me, is the greatest responsibility of all.

Scripture is filled with wisdom and guidance that can help us discern right from wrong, justice from injustice, and truth from falsehood. Therefore, when we approach the complex issues we face in the world today — whether political, social, or cultural — we are called to evaluate them through the lens of Scripture.

Historically, pastors and Christian leaders have played a critical role in helping to shape the moral and political landscape of nations by teaching how faith should influence and inform the decisions of their congregations. In the centuries leading up to and following the Revolutionary War in the United States, many pastors understood their duty not only as spiritual leaders but also as moral guides, using the pulpit to speak to the most pressing issues of the day. These pastors didn't shy away from discussing politics, policy, or even the character of political candidates because they believed that God's Word was the ultimate authority on all matters, including those that governed society.

One of the most powerful examples of this is found in the recorded sermons from the American founding era. The *Political Sermons of the American Founding Era, 1730–1805* is a two-volume collection that captures the sermons delivered by pastors during a time when the future of the nation hung in the balance. These sermons reveal the critical role that the church played in shaping the ideals of liberty, justice, and governance that would come to define the United States. Pastors used Scripture to speak boldly about freedom, tyranny, the rights of individuals, and the responsibilities of those in power. They addressed the moral failings of leaders and governments while reminding their congregations that it was their duty as citizens and Christians to stand for truth, justice, and righteousness.

These sermons were not just political in nature; they were deeply theological, grounded in the belief that God's sovereignty extends over all aspects of life, including government and political authority. Many of these pastors drew directly from biblical examples to demonstrate how God's people have historically been called to influence and challenge the systems of power in their day. From the prophets of the Old Testament, who spoke truth to kings and rulers, to the apostles in the New Testament, who proclaimed the gospel in defiance of Roman authorities, Scripture is filled with examples of God using His people to hold governments accountable to His standards of righteousness.

One of the clearest examples of this is the story of the prophet Nathan, who confronted King David after his sin with Bathsheba. Nathan, speaking on behalf of God, held David accountable for his actions, reminding him that even as king, he was subject to

God's law. This biblical example highlights the idea that no leader is above the moral law of God, and that those who are called by God must speak truth to power, even when it is uncomfortable or dangerous.

In modern times, we face different but equally pressing challenges. Issues such as abortion, religious freedom, social justice, economic inequality, and the sanctity of marriage are all areas where faith must inform our political and social engagement. As Christians, we are called to bring biblical truth into these discussions, recognizing that God's Word is not only relevant but also authoritative in addressing these issues.

There is often a misconception that faith and politics should be kept separate, that religion should be a private matter that does not influence public life. However, this idea runs counter to the teachings of Scripture. Jesus Himself told His followers that they are to be "the salt of the earth" and "the light of the world" (Matthew 5:13-16), meaning that we are called to preserve what is good and shine light into the darkness. This includes engaging with the political process and influencing society in ways that reflect God's justice, mercy, and truth.

Throughout Scripture, we see God's people actively involved in shaping the direction of nations and influencing leaders. The prophet Daniel, for example, was placed in a position of authority in Babylon, where he advised the king according to the wisdom of God. Esther, another biblical figure, was called to use her influence as queen to save the Jewish people from destruction. In both cases, these individuals did not shy away from their faith but instead allowed it to guide their decisions, even in the face of great danger. Their stories remind us that no aspect of society is beyond the influence of faith.

This responsibility to speak truth to power and to influence society in accordance with biblical principles is not limited to pastors or political leaders. Every Christian is called to live out their faith in all areas of life, including how they engage with political and social issues. This doesn't mean that we impose our beliefs on others, but rather that we allow our faith to shape how we view the world and how we interact with it. When we vote, when we advocate for policies, when we engage in debates, we must do so with the understanding that we are called to represent the values of the kingdom of God.

The idea that faith should influence our politics is not about partisanship; it's about aligning our actions and decisions with the moral and ethical teachings of Scripture. Christians are called to be people of integrity, justice, and compassion, and these values should be evident in the way we approach societal issues. Whether we are advocating for the protection of the unborn, standing up for religious freedom, or fighting against systemic injustice, our faith should be the foundation from which we act.

As we reflect on the historical role that pastors and churches have played in shaping the moral and political landscape, we are reminded that the church today still has a critical role to play. In a world that is often hostile to biblical values, it can be tempting to retreat into the safety of our church buildings and avoid engaging with the difficult issues of the day. But if we truly believe that God's Word is the standard by which all issues must be evaluated, then we cannot remain silent. We must speak the truth in love, offer a biblical perspective on the challenges we face, and encourage others to do the same.

As we face the challenges of our time, may we be faithful to His calling evaluate every issue through God's Word, knowing that God's Word is sufficient to guide us in all things.

As Pastor Gary said, voting is not just a right; it is a sacred duty for believers. In the United States, where we enjoy the privilege of participating in the democratic process, this duty takes on a special significance, especially for Christians who seek to influence society according to biblical principles. Pastor Gary pointed out that among the 90 million Christians in America, a staggering 40 million do not vote, and 15 million are not even registered to vote. These statistics are a sobering reminder of the missed opportunities for Christians to have a meaningful impact on the direction of the country.

For Christians, voting goes beyond simply choosing between political candidates; it is about using our influence to support policies that align with our values and the teachings of Scripture. It's about standing up for life, justice, freedom, and truth. When we choose to disengage from the voting process, we leave a vacuum that allows policies and leaders to be chosen that may not reflect our beliefs. This is where the danger lies. As Pastor Gary emphasized, "When we choose to exclude ourselves from the voting process, we have no one to blame except ourselves for wicked policies."

While it is easy to become disillusioned with politics, especially when the choices presented may not seem ideal, it is important to remember that disengagement is not a solution. Pastor Gary's challenge is a reminder that government, in and of itself, is not the solution to the moral and spiritual needs of a nation. Only Jesus can transform hearts and restore the soul of a people. But until His return, we are called to be His ambassadors, representing His truth and love in every sphere of life — including the political arena.

The responsibility to vote is not just about making personal preferences known; it is about advancing God's kingdom and working to stem the tide of evil in our land. Pastor Gary's sermon serves as a rallying cry for believers to take their civic duty seriously and to view it as a form of stewardship over the freedom we have been given.

Finally, Pastor Gary calls on the church to pray for revival. He recognizes that while voting is important, it is ultimately the power of God working in the hearts of individuals that will bring lasting change. Government policies can only go so far; true transformation comes through a move of the Holy Spirit. "May God again bring revival to the United States of America," he prayed, reminding the congregation that while we do our part in the public sphere, we must also be diligent in seeking God for spiritual renewal in the land.

This sermon is a powerful reminder of the dual responsibility Christians have — to participate actively in the political process, while also praying fervently for God's intervention in the hearts of people. Voting is a critical way for Christians to influence society, but it is only one part of the larger mission to be salt and light in a world that desperately needs the hope and truth of Jesus Christ.

Chapter 41: The Shift Toward Political Involvement – Chinese Patriots in Action

As the years passed and I grew deeper in my faith, one thing became increasingly clear: being a Christian is not just about living a life of personal piety or attending church on Sundays. It's about bringing the principles of God's kingdom into every aspect of life, including the political arena. This realization didn't come all at once but through a gradual shift — a growing sense of duty that arose from observing the direction in which society was moving and feeling compelled to stand up for what I knew was right according to God's Word.

There was a time when politics didn't seem like my responsibility. Like many, I thought my role as a Christian was to focus on personal spiritual growth, my family, and volunteer work at church or in the community. Politics, with all its division and rancor, seemed best left to politicians and activists. But over time, as the cultural landscape around me began to shift, I found it impossible to ignore the connection between my faith and the policies being enacted in the world.

The pandemic was one of the first major catalysts for this shift. Government decisions — lockdowns, restrictions on personal freedoms, and mandates — directly affected our lives, churches, and communities. Suddenly, it became evident that politics wasn't something "out there" — it had a real impact on our daily lives. I began to realize that if people of faith remained silent, the policies being enacted would continue to reflect values contrary to Christian principles.

The more Paul and I discussed it, the clearer it became: I couldn't sit on the sidelines any longer. I began to understand that politics is, in many ways, an extension of our moral and ethical beliefs. Laws reflect the values a society upholds. One pivotal moment came during a Sunday sermon when Pastor Gary spoke about the responsibility Christians have to vote. How could we, as followers of Christ, not see that voting is not only our right but our duty? Disengaging from the political process wasn't just an abdication of civic responsibility — it was a failure to use the influence we've been given to stand for biblical values in the public sphere. His words were a wake-up call. Government is not the ultimate answer to the soul of a nation—Jesus is. But until He returns, we are called to be His ambassadors. That includes voting, advocating for policies that align with biblical values, and speaking out against injustice and evil in the public square.

From that point on, I felt an undeniable sense of duty to get more politically involved. Not because I believed politics could save us — only Jesus can do that — but because I knew that Christians are called to shape society in ways that reflect God's justice and love.

I began paying more attention to local elections, reading up on candidates and their platforms. Politics is messy, and the choices we had to make were often far from perfect. But we understood that it wasn't about finding the perfect candidate; it was about doing our part to stand for what was right, even if that meant voting for the candidate who was simply the better choice in an imperfect system.

As we became more engaged, we also saw the power of community in political involvement. The K-Group gatherings we hosted at home became a space where we could discuss not only our faith but also the pressing political and social issues of the day. These discussions were rich, thoughtful, and at times challenging, but they were always rooted in the question: How should our faith inform our response to these issues? It was in these conversations that we realized just how deeply our faith could impact the political realm.

One story that stands out is the experience of a young woman, Katie, from our K-Group. After high school, she took a break from college and accepted an internship at a conservative think tank. What started as a learning opportunity turned into a leadership role when she was promoted to director within a year. Soon after, she was recruited to work on Team Trump during the 2024 presidential campaign. She traveled across the country, engaging with young conservatives and helping shape the political conversation on a national level. Her story was a powerful reminder that God can use anyone, at any stage in life, to make a difference in the political landscape.

Our involvement in politics grew steadily over time. We attended rallies, joined community discussions, and hosted Meet & Greet gatherings. The more we engaged, the more we realized that political involvement wasn't just an option for Christians — it was an essential part of our witness in the world. Just as we are called to serve the poor, care for the sick, and share the Gospel, we are also called to influence the direction of society through political engagement.

But with this growing involvement came a realization: political engagement isn't just about voting or attending rallies. It's about being informed, thoughtful, and prayerful in every decision we make. It's about recognizing that our ultimate allegiance is to God's kingdom, not any political party or candidate.

We also learned that political involvement, like all aspects of life, must be grounded in prayer. As much as we wanted to make a difference, we knew that real change could only come through the power of God. So, we prayed. We prayed for wisdom in the choices we made. We prayed for our leaders, even those we disagreed with. We prayed for our country, asking God to bring revival and healing to a nation deeply divided.

As Paul and I continued to deepen our political involvement, one thing became abundantly clear: we were not alone on this journey. Over the past few years, we found ourselves standing shoulder to shoulder with a growing community of Chinese patriots who, like us, recognized the importance of being active participants in the political process. Many of these fellow immigrants had fled oppressive regimes or seen firsthand the dangers of unchecked government power. We shared a unique appreciation for the freedoms we enjoy in America. And with that appreciation came a deep sense of duty to protect those freedoms, especially as we felt increasingly threatened by the rising tide of government overreach.

The 2020 presidential election was a turning point for many of us. Chinese patriots across the country mobilized to show support for President Trump, whose policies on China and his strong stance on religious freedom resonated with us. His leadership seemed a safeguard against the socialist tendencies that had wreaked havoc in our native country, and we were determined to make our voices heard.

One of the most memorable moments for Paul and me during that time was attending two Trump rallies in 2020. The energy was palpable. The atmosphere was electric, with a sense that we were part of something bigger than ourselves — a movement of people who believed in preserving American values of freedom, faith, and opportunity. One rally was particularly special because we volunteered alongside many other Chinese patriots. We handed out flyers, waved flags, and spoke with attendees about the importance of standing up for the values that made this country great. There was a shared sense of pride in being both Chinese and American patriots, working together to protect the freedoms we cherished.

Later that year, our involvement deepened when we participated in a car rally organized by Chinese patriots. This wasn't just any rally — Paul and I led the rally in our RV, which had become a symbol of our political activism. The RV, adorned with Trump flags and signs, was the lead vehicle in a long line of cars, many driven by fellow Chinese immigrants who shared our passion for freedom. The Proud Boys also participated, adding to the diverse group that had united for a common cause. It was a powerful sight — so many different people, bound by a shared love for this country and a determination to protect its future. One of our proudest moments came when the picture of our RV, leading the rally, was featured on the front page of *The Epoch Times*. It was a tangible symbol of our commitment to freedom and our determination to make our voices heard.

In 2021, when Glenn Youngkin ran for governor of Virginia, Chinese patriots organized another car rally to show their support, and once again, Paul and I led the rally in our RV. The enthusiasm was undeniable — Youngkin represented a fresh perspective, someone who could bring needed change to Virginia. We were proud, not only because we supported the candidate but because we did so alongside fellow patriots who shared our values and vision for the future.

In 2022, we found ourselves leading yet another car rally — this time for Dan Cox, the Republican candidate for governor of Maryland. Organized again by Chinese patriots, the rally was a testament to how much our community had grown in political involvement. The RV took its place at the front of the convoy, leading the way through the streets as dozens of cars followed behind. These rallies were more than just political events — they were celebrations of freedom, community, and the belief that together, we could make a difference.

But our involvement didn't stop with rallies. Over the past several years, Paul and I, along with other Chinese patriots, attended countless fundraisers for political candidates. These events gave us opportunities not only to support the candidates we believed in but to meet other like-minded individuals equally committed to preserving the values of freedom, personal responsibility, and limited government. Conversations at these fundraisers were often inspiring, as we exchanged ideas, shared experiences, and encouraged one another to stay engaged in the political process.

In addition to attending fundraisers, Paul and I hosted five Meet and Greet events for GOP candidates in our backyard. These gatherings combined two of our passions — faith and political involvement. Many attendees were Chinese patriots who, like me, had fled regimes that stifled freedom and sought refuge in America. We shared stories of our journeys, discussed the importance of political engagement, and provided a platform for candidates to speak about their vision for the future. The food, prepared and contributed by members of the Chinese patriot community, reflected our shared heritage, adding a warm and familial atmosphere to the events. Xi Van Fleet, the author of *Mao's America*, attended several of the parties, her presence adding yet another layer of significance to our political journey.

Through these experiences, Paul and I realized political involvement wasn't just a duty — it was a calling. It was about using our voices and influence to shape the future of the country we loved. We were inspired by the courage and dedication of our fellow Chinese patriots, who had faced incredible adversity to come to America and who now stood with us in the fight to protect the freedoms we had all worked so hard to attain.

Chapter 42: Vaccine Mandates and the Freedom Convoy in Canada

The year 2021 was a pivotal one for so many reasons. The world was still reeling from the effects of the pandemic, and while vaccines were being rolled out, new challenges emerged — especially regarding personal freedom and government overreach. For Paul and me, the issue of vaccine mandates became deeply personal, and it led us to not only reflect on our beliefs but also to actively support those who were pushing back against what we saw as an infringement on individual rights.

The vaccine mandates came swiftly. Governments worldwide began to require proof of vaccination for various aspects of daily life — whether it was traveling, entering public places, or even keeping a job. Many people, including some of our own friends, were relieved that these measures were being implemented, believing they would help bring the pandemic under control. But for us, and millions of others, the mandates represented something far more troubling: a breach of individual freedom.

Paul and I had no issue with vaccines themselves; we understood that many people chose to get vaccinated for personal or medical reasons, and we respected that choice. What we couldn't accept was the government forcing individuals to take the vaccine or face consequences, especially when it came to employment and access to basic freedoms. To us, this wasn't just about public health — it was about the fundamental right of every person to make decisions about their own body without coercion.

The Freedom Convoy of 2021, which started in Canada but quickly gained international attention, became a symbol of this resistance. Thousands of truck drivers banded together to protest the vaccine mandates, driving their massive rigs across the country in solidarity. They called it the "Freedom Convoy," and it was a powerful display of people standing up against what they saw as unjust government overreach. These truckers were not just fighting for themselves; they were fighting for everyone who believed in the importance of personal freedom.

As we watched the convoy grow, Paul and I felt a deep sense of solidarity with the movement. The protests weren't about being anti-vaccine, but about being pro-freedom. The truck drivers, many of whom had worked tirelessly throughout the pandemic to keep supply chains moving, were now being told that if they didn't comply with the mandates, they would lose their livelihoods. It was a stark reminder that when governments are given too much power, they can overstep their bounds — and that's exactly what we were witnessing.

We saw the news reports of how the convoy was being received by both supporters and detractors. On the one hand, the truckers were hailed as heroes by those who valued freedom and saw the mandates as an assault on personal rights. On the other hand, they were vilified by certain media outlets and government officials who painted them as reckless and selfish, endangering public health. It was heartbreaking to see how divided people had become over the issue.

One evening, while sitting together at the dinner table, Paul turned to me and said, "We need to do something to show our support. This isn't just about the truckers — it's about standing up for freedom before we lose it." I couldn't have agreed more. While we couldn't physically join the convoy, we made the decision to contribute in other ways. We donated to funds that were set up to support the truckers, providing them with food, fuel, and legal assistance. Paul also took to social media, sharing our thoughts on the matter and encouraging others to consider the broader implications of government mandates.

As we engaged more deeply in the issue, we found ourselves having conversations with friends and family who were on both sides of the debate. Some of them saw the mandates as necessary, a means of keeping people safe during an unprecedented global crisis. Others, like us, were deeply concerned about the erosion of personal freedoms. These conversations were often difficult, but they were also important. It was clear that this was about more than just a vaccine; it was about how much control we were willing to allow the government to have over our lives; and the mandates were a challenge to the very freedoms that our country was built on; it was about the principle. If the government could force individuals to take medical treatment under the threat of losing their jobs or their ability to participate in society, what else could they mandate in the future? These were the kinds of questions we wrestled with, not only as citizens but as Christians. We knew that God values both justice and mercy, and part of living out our faith meant standing up for those who couldn't stand up for themselves.

The Freedom Convoy continued to gain momentum. Social media was flooded with images of truckers lining highways, their vehicles covered in signs that read "No Mandates" and "Freedom Over Fear." It was a movement that was impossible to ignore, and it felt like a turning point — a moment when people were finally standing up and saying, "Enough is enough."

Of course, the response from the government was swift. Canadian authorities attempted to shut down the convoy, using everything from legal threats to freezing bank accounts associated with the protestors. It was a sobering reminder of how much power the government could wield when it felt threatened. The situation became a global talking point, with some seeing the crackdown as necessary for maintaining order and others viewing it as an egregious overreach of authority.

Paul and I continued to follow the news, our hearts heavy with the knowledge that these brave men and women were being vilified for standing up for something so fundamental. But despite the hardships they faced, the truckers remained resolute. Their courage inspired us, and it served as a reminder that sometimes the fight for freedom requires sacrifice.

While the specifics of the Freedom Convoy revolved around vaccine mandates and government-imposed restrictions, the larger issue at play was one that transcended this immediate cause. It touched on a fundamental Christian principle: the need to resist unjust overreach by authorities and to safeguard the liberties that God has entrusted to each of us. God has given us freedom — not just spiritual freedom through Christ but also the right to live in societies where justice, fairness, and human dignity are upheld. When governments infringe upon these freedoms, especially in ways that disproportionately affect the most vulnerable, such as those who cannot easily comply with mandates due to their personal, religious, or medical convictions, Christians have a moral responsibility to stand against such actions.

The Freedom Convoy, though centered on the specifics of vaccine mandates, became a symbol of a broader struggle — one that aligns with our call to defend liberty. It underscored the importance of questioning government actions when they appear to overstep their rightful bounds, particularly when these actions threaten personal autonomy, freedom of conscience, and the right to live out one's faith without coercion.

In supporting movements like the Freedom Convoy, Christians are not merely aligning with a political cause; we are fulfilling a biblical mandate to seek justice and uphold the God-given freedoms that allow human flourishing. It is about ensuring that individuals are free to make decisions that honor both their personal convictions and their responsibilities to society without undue pressure from authorities. As we stand up for these freedoms, we are also standing up for the belief that all authority is ultimately under God's rule, and that no human government has the right to infringe upon the liberties He has ordained for us.

In doing so, we not only defend our own rights but also bear witness to a higher truth — that true justice and freedom are found in aligning our societies with God's will, where love, respect, and the protection of the vulnerable are at the forefront of our actions.

Looking back, I realize that this moment was a defining one in my journey toward greater political involvement. It wasn't about aligning with a political party or ideology — it was about standing up for what was right, for what aligned with my faith and values. Supporting the Freedom Convoy wasn't just an act of defiance against the mandates; it was an affirmation of our belief in the God-given rights that every person possesses.

The truckers who drove across Canada, and those around the world who supported them, weren't just fighting for their own freedom — they were fighting for all of us. And while the outcome of the protests may not have been exactly what we hoped for, the movement itself was a powerful reminder that there are still people willing to stand up for freedom, even in the face of great adversity.

As Paul and I reflect on this experience, we are reminded that the fight for freedom is ongoing. Governments will always seek to expand their power, and it is up to the people — guided by faith, wisdom, and courage — to push back when necessary. Our involvement in supporting the Freedom Convoy was just one small part of that larger battle, but it reaffirmed our commitment to standing up for the values we hold dear.

And so, as the world continues to navigate these uncertain times, we hold fast to the belief that true freedom comes not from governments, but from God. And it is our responsibility, as His people, to protect and defend that freedom whenever it is threatened.

Chapter 43: Supporting the American Trucker Convoy

In February 2022, American truckers launched a powerful cross-country drive known as *The People's Convoy*. Inspired by the Canadian Freedom Convoy that had captured the world's attention before being forcibly broken up by the Canadian government, these American truckers set out to petition governments at all levels — local, state, and federal — to end all COVID-19 mandates. For Paul and me, having followed the Canadian convoy so closely, we felt an immediate connection to this new movement that had now arrived in our own backyard.

The People's Convoy wasn't just another protest; it became a symbol of resistance against government overreach, and it resonated with countless people across the country. The COVID-19 pandemic had brought many unforeseen challenges, but the mandates — especially those requiring vaccines — felt to us like an infringement on individual freedoms. We had seen how governments worldwide had taken extreme measures during the pandemic, often without the consent or consideration of the people they served. For us, The People's Convoy was more than just a protest — it was a stand for freedom.

The conservative Chinese community in the Washington, D.C. area, including many of our friends, closely followed the convoy's journey through social media and news outlets. We kept track of the truckers' schedule, eagerly awaiting their arrival in our region. As the convoy made its way to Hagerstown, Maryland, where they planned to set up camp, we knew we had to get involved. We discussed among our group how best we could support them and show solidarity. The convoy represented more than just truckers — it stood for everyone who valued personal liberty and was tired of government mandates that, in our view, overstepped their bounds.

When the truckers finally arrived in Hagerstown, a group of Chinese supporters went out to meet them during the weekdays. They brought supplies, expressed their appreciation, and spent time with the truckers who had sacrificed so much to be a part of this movement. Unfortunately, due to work commitments, I couldn't join them during the week, but I made sure to go out on weekends. I remember one Saturday when we brought all the ingredients needed to cook a large meal in the convoy's kitchen. The truckers were so grateful to have hot, homemade food. They appreciated the warmth and camaraderie we shared with them, knowing that the support extended beyond cultural and language barriers.

In addition to the food we prepared ourselves, we also ordered boxes of food from a local Chinese restaurant to feed the truckers and their supporters. The truckers, who had been driving for days and living on the road, were touched by the outpouring of support from our community. Many of them shared stories of the hardships they had endured along the way, and the atmosphere was one of unity, as people from all walks of life came together to stand up for freedom.

At one point, the convoy organizers mentioned that they needed a large, sturdy tent for worship services. Without hesitation, our group stepped in to help. We not only bought them a large tent for their worship gatherings, but we also bought several more tents for other purposes within the convoy. The truckers had a need, and we were more than happy to fill it. This was about more than just providing material support — it was about standing in solidarity with those who were risking everything to defend the freedoms we hold dear.

Some members of our community also donated gas gift cards to help the truckers continue their journey. With fuel prices skyrocketing, these cards were a lifeline for the convoy, ensuring they could keep their rigs moving. We organized ourselves in such a way that, no matter when the truckers circled around the city, there were always supporters on the overpasses. We held up signs, waved flags, and cheered as they drove by. The sound of truck horns blaring in response to our cheers was electrifying. We knew we were part of something bigger — a movement that was gaining momentum across the country.

One of the highlights of this experience was when we gathered at a friend's spacious apartment to make large banners for the truckers. We spent hours working together, cutting out letters, painting signs, and assembling banners that would be displayed along the convoy's route. The host of our banner-making party had prepared delicious food for us, and we spent the day eating, chatting, and working. There was a sense of camaraderie and joy in knowing that we were doing something meaningful to support the truckers. By making the banners ourselves, we saved a lot of money, but more importantly, it allowed us to put our personal touch on the messages of freedom and resistance we wanted to share.

Throughout the convoy's time in our area, a few white supporters joined us on the overpasses. While most people driving by honked in support or gave us thumbs up, a few — mostly younger individuals — flipped us off or shouted insults. It was clear that not everyone supported the convoy or understood what it stood for, but we weren't discouraged. The overwhelming amount of support, including from people who had never met us or the truckers, made it clear that the movement resonated with far more people than it alienated.

As the convoy's lease at their Hagerstown location neared its end, the truckers were in desperate need of a new place to set up camp. Once again, our group stepped in to help. We helped them find a new location, and even paid for the rent.

Supporting The People's Convoy was one of the most rewarding and meaningful experiences of my life. It wasn't just about opposing mandates — it was about standing up for the rights and freedoms that form the foundation of our society. As I reflect on our involvement in the convoy, I am reminded that the fight for freedom is ongoing, and it is up to each of us to remain vigilant and defend the principles we hold dear.

The American Trucker Convoy, much like its Canadian counterpart, became a powerful symbol of resistance against government overreach. The truckers, along with their supporters, showed that when people come together to stand up for what is right, they can make a real difference. For Paul, me, and the rest of the conservative Chinese community who supported the convoy, it was about more than just a protest — it was about being part of a movement that sought to protect the freedoms we had come to America to enjoy.

Chapter 44: Meet & Greet Gatherings at Home

Throughout 2022, our home became a hub of political engagement and activism. After becoming more involved in political causes, Paul and I felt the natural next step was to open our home to host *Meet & Greet* gatherings for GOP candidates, trucker representatives, and other activists. These events allowed us to connect with like-minded individuals who shared our passion for freedom, personal responsibility, and limited government. They also became an avenue for us to strengthen the bond between the Chinese American community and the broader conservative movement.

The gatherings were a unique mix of people — political candidates, community leaders, grassroots activists, and everyday citizens who had been deeply affected by government overreach during the pandemic. We organized these events in our spacious backyard, setting up chairs and tables under the shade of the trees, creating a welcoming atmosphere where attendees could have meaningful conversations. These events were not just political rallies; they were opportunities for dialogue, reflection, and strategizing about the future of our nation.

One gathering stands out in my memory. In addition to local GOP candidates, we invited representatives from *The People's Convoy* — the truckers who had captured the nation's attention with their fight against the vaccine mandates. The truckers were eager to share their experiences with our guests, and we were thrilled to have the opportunity to host them. This wasn't just an ordinary event; it was an opportunity to bridge two powerful movements — conservative political activism and the grassroots resistance to government mandates.

Paul and I wanted to show our unwavering support for the truckers, and we made sure our attire reflected that. We wore specially made t-shirts that boldly stated, *Chinese Americans Support Truckers*. Our guests, many of whom were part of the Chinese American community, also wore the shirts, showing solidarity with the truckers who had fought so hard for the same freedoms we cherished.

As the event unfolded, the atmosphere was lively yet focused. Conversations buzzed about everything from the truckers' harrowing journeys across the country to the political candidates' plans to protect freedom and ensure government accountability. The trucker representatives shared powerful stories about their experiences on the road — stories of resilience, unity, and determination in the face of government overreach. These stories resonated deeply with us, as many in our community had fled regimes that suppressed personal freedoms. The parallels were not lost on anyone present.

A special highlight of the event came when we took a group photo with the trucker representatives, all of us proudly wearing our *Chinese American Support Truckers* t-shirts. The photo was more than just a keepsake — it was a symbol of the growing alliance between Chinese Americans and other freedom-loving individuals in the fight against tyranny.

To our surprise and excitement, a Chinese freelance journalist who had been attending the event decided to stream the entire gathering on YouTube. His livestream brought the event to a much wider audience than we had anticipated. As the camera panned over the group, capturing the energy and enthusiasm of the gathering, we realized that our efforts to bring people together were reaching far beyond our backyard. Comments flooded the livestream, with viewers expressing their support for both the truckers and the Chinese American community's involvement in the movement. It was heartening to see how many people were watching and engaging in our event, and it reaffirmed our belief that we were part of something much bigger than ourselves.

The *Meet & Greet* gatherings we hosted weren't just about networking or political activism. They were about fostering a sense of community among people who valued freedom and personal responsibility. They were about standing in solidarity with those who had risked everything to fight for their rights. And they were about building bridges between different communities — showing that Chinese Americans, like many others, were committed to the cause of freedom in America.

As we gathered for that group photo, wearing our T-shirts and standing shoulder to shoulder with the trucker representatives, I felt a profound sense of pride. We were making a difference, not only in our local community but on a broader scale. These gatherings were a testament to the power of grassroots activism and the importance of standing up for what you believe in, no matter the obstacles.

Chapter 45: Conversations with the Trucker Representatives

The day we hosted the trucker representatives at our *Meet & Greet* was filled with energy, but it wasn't just about speeches or slogans. What made the gathering truly memorable were the intimate conversations we had with the truckers themselves — the stories they shared of resistance, freedom, and unity. These men and women weren't just symbols of the movement; they were individuals with powerful personal experiences that shaped their decision to join *The People's Convoy*. Sitting down with them, listening to their stories, was both humbling and inspiring.

As the event began to wind down and many of the guests left, Paul and I found ourselves seated around a small table with a few of the truckers who had come to represent *The People's Convoy*. Their weathered faces told a story of long hours on the road, but their eyes gleamed with passion and determination. These were people who had spent countless days in their trucks, crisscrossing the country, not just to make a living, but to stand up for what they believed was right. They had seen firsthand how government mandates were affecting not just their own lives, but the lives of countless others, and they had decided enough was enough.

One of the truckers, a tall man with a booming voice, shared how he had felt the need to act when the vaccine mandates started to threaten his livelihood. He spoke about how, for years, truckers like him had been the unsung heroes of the pandemic, ensuring that supplies reached every corner of the country while the rest of the world stayed home. "We did our job," he said, his voice cracking with emotion. "We kept this country moving when everything else was shut down. And then they turned around and told us we weren't good enough to keep our jobs unless we took the shot. That's not freedom. That's coercion."

His words hit home for everyone sitting at the table. We all nodded in agreement, understanding that this fight wasn't just about vaccines; it was about the principles of personal freedom and government overreach. The truckers had become unlikely heroes in the battle for individual rights, and their courage to stand up against such powerful forces was both admirable and inspiring.

Another trucker, a woman with short, graying hair and a firm, unwavering gaze, shared her story of joining the convoy. "I'm a grandmother," she said, "and I'm not doing this just for me. I'm doing this for my grandkids. They deserve to grow up in a country where they have the freedom to make their own choices. If we don't push back now, what kind of world are we leaving for them?" Her resolve was palpable, and as she spoke, I couldn't help but think about my own children and the future we were shaping for them.

The stories of resistance weren't just about the mandates themselves; they were also about the solidarity that had grown out of the movement. The truckers spoke of the deep sense of unity they had found with their fellow drivers, even those they had never met before the convoy. One man described how the convoy had started with just a few trucks but had quickly grown into a massive force, with people joining from all over the country. "We were driving down the highway," he said, "passing overpass, when we saw you waving flags, holding signs, cheering us on, it gave us strength. It reminded us that we weren't alone in this fight."

That sense of unity extended far beyond the truckers themselves. They talked about the support they had received from people all across the country — from individuals who donated money to keep them fueled, to families who brought them meals, to communities that opened up their homes and churches so they could rest. It was a reminder that the fight for freedom isn't fought by individuals alone; it's fought by communities who come together in times of need.

They spoke passionately about how the government was using fear to strip people of their liberties, and how important it was to stand firm, even in the face of adversity. One of them said something that stuck with me: "We're not doing this because we hate the government. We're doing this because we love our country. And if we don't fight to keep it free, who will?"

By the end of the evening, these conversations had deepened my respect for the truckers and solidified my belief in the importance of their cause. Their stories were a powerful reminder of how ordinary people could rise to defend the freedoms that so many of us take for granted. Paul and I had always believed in the value of personal liberty, but hearing these stories firsthand — from people who had risked so much to protect it — made us even more committed to doing our part in this fight.

Before the truckers left, we gathered around to pray for them. It was a fitting end to a day filled with conversations about freedom, faith, and unity. As we bowed our heads, I felt an overwhelming sense of gratitude for these men and women who had the courage to stand up for what was right, even when the world seemed against them.

Our conversations with the trucker representatives were more than just an exchange of ideas — they were a call to action. They reminded us that the fight for freedom requires sacrifice, courage, and above all, unity. The stories they shared were not just their stories; they were the stories of every person who believes in the importance of personal liberty and the right to make decisions free from government coercion.

Chapter 46: Meeting the Author of *Mao's America*

Through our involvement with the Chinese conservative community, Paul and I had the privilege of befriending Xi Van Fleet, a fellow Chinese patriot with a deep understanding of the dangers of authoritarian regimes. Xi had fled Mao's China and had become a strong voice against the rising tide of government overreach in the United States. It was through mutual friends in the conservative community that we met, and our shared experiences of fleeing oppression and fighting for freedom bonded us immediately.

While Xi was working on her now-famous book, *Mao's America*, she often discussed the content with us, seeking feedback and engaging in long conversations about the parallels between the political shifts happening in America and those she had witnessed in China. The discussions were enlightening and at times sobering, as we explored how the values of freedom, personal responsibility, and limited government were under threat. Xi even asked Paul for suggestions for the book's title, although she ultimately chose another option.

When the book was finally published, the entire Chinese conservative community rallied behind her, attending and helping organize her book signing events, buying copies of her book to give as gifts to friends and family. Xi's journey, much like our own, had been one of awakening and action. Her book became a powerful tool to educate others about the dangers of government overreach and the importance of standing up for freedom before it's too late.

The discussions we had with Xi during the writing process left a deep impact on us. Her insights were invaluable in helping us connect the dots between our personal experiences in China and the political shifts we were witnessing in America. It was clear that the lessons of Mao's China were more relevant than ever, and Xi's book provided a powerful warning of what could happen if we did not remain vigilant in defending our freedoms.

Chapter 47: Reflections on the Chinese American Political Awakening

Over the past several years, I have witnessed a remarkable transformation within the Chinese American community. For a long time, many of us had been politically disengaged, content to focus on our families, careers, and personal lives. Politics, with its divisive rhetoric and seemingly distant impact, felt like something best left to the professionals. But as the political and social landscape of the United States began to shift, a slow but steady political awakening began to take hold within the Chinese American community.

For many of us, this awakening was deeply personal. It wasn't just about aligning with a political party or ideology — it was about recognizing the very real and present dangers of government overreach, social control, and the erosion of freedoms we had come to value so much. Many Chinese Americans had fled countries where oppressive regimes dictated nearly every aspect of life. We knew firsthand what could happen when governments are given too much power, and we began to see alarming similarities between the rhetoric and policies being implemented in America and the systems we had escaped.

The pandemic played a significant role in accelerating this awakening. As government mandates grew stricter, many within the Chinese American community began to question the balance between public safety and personal freedom. Vaccine mandates, mask mandates, lockdowns — these measures reminded us of the type of control we had once fought to leave behind. For many, the realization that the freedoms we cherished were under threat became a catalyst for deeper political engagement.

We saw Chinese Americans begin to speak out at school board meetings, attend political rallies, and organize grassroots efforts to support candidates who aligned with their values. It was no longer enough to sit on the sidelines and hope for the best. We had seen the consequences of apathy in our own countries, and we knew that in order to protect the freedoms we had gained, we had to be willing to fight for them.

In many ways, this political awakening felt like a reclaiming of the American Dream. The Chinese American community had worked hard to build successful lives in the United States, but now we understood that success wasn't just about financial stability or social standing — it was about ensuring that future generations would have the same opportunities we had. This meant engaging with the political process, standing up for conservative values, and advocating for policies that protected freedom, personal responsibility, and limited government.

I had the opportunity to witness this awakening firsthand, not just through our own involvement but through the growing activism of our friends and fellow Chinese patriots. We attended rallies, hosted Meet & Greet events, and organized support for movements like the Freedom Convoy. At each of these events, we saw more and more Chinese Americans coming together, united by a shared belief in the importance of defending freedom.

One of the most inspiring aspects of this awakening was the sense of solidarity that emerged within our community. For so long, many of us had felt disconnected from the political process, unsure of how to engage or if our voices would even be heard. But as more of us began to step forward, we found strength in our shared experiences and values. We realized that, together, we could make a difference — not just for ourselves but for the future of our children and for the country we had come to love.

This awakening wasn't without its challenges. Many within the Chinese American community had spent years trying to assimilate, to blend into the fabric of American society without making waves. But now, we understood that our voices mattered. We could no longer afford to be silent. The political awakening of Chinese Americans was about more than just voting or attending rallies — it was about recognizing our power as citizens and using that power to shape the direction of the country.

One of the most emotional moments in this political awakening was the sudden passing of a dear sister in Christ, Grace. Grace had been a fighter — someone who stood beside us, shoulder to shoulder, through countless struggles. Together, we had attended rallies, supported our community, and raised our voices for the values we cherished. Her passion and dedication were unwavering, and her faith in God and country was the foundation of everything she did.

When we received the news of Grace's passing, it was like a light had been extinguished too soon. Her absence left a void in our hearts and in the Chinese American community she had fought so hard for. But what struck us most was the letter her husband received, written personally by President Trump. We couldn't believe it. President Trump, who had likely never met Grace personally, had somehow taken note of her efforts and acknowledged her in a way that gave her a voice on a larger stage. It made us realize that any one of us could be seen, could matter. Grace wasn't a high-profile leader or someone in the spotlight, but her contributions had still made an impact that reached all the way to the President. His words were a tribute to the life she had lived:

"Grace will always be remembered for her dedication to the Chinese American community, her love for our country, and her steadfast devotion to your family. Her unwavering support meant a tremendous amount to me, and I am grateful that she was a proud member of Team Trump!"

It was a moment of profound realization. Grace's commitment to the cause had reached farther than we had ever known. She had made an impact not just within our small circle but at the highest levels of leadership. Her voice, which had once felt small and distant, had resonated all the way to the President of the United States.

Grace's story is a testament to how one person, even when seemingly unnoticed, can make a difference. She reminds us that every effort, no matter how small, contributes to a larger movement. Her legacy continues to inspire us, and her memory fuels our determination to keep fighting for the values we hold dear.

Looking back, I am filled with a sense of pride for the way the Chinese American community has risen to the occasion. We have come together, not just as individuals, but as a collective force for change. We have found our voices, and we are using them to stand up for the values that matter most: freedom, family, faith, and responsibility.

As this awakening continues to grow, I am hopeful for the future. The Chinese American community, once politically passive, is now becoming a driving force in the fight to preserve the very freedoms that brought us to this country in the first place.

It is a powerful reminder that no matter where we come from, we all have a role to play in shaping the future of America.

Chapter 48: Reflections on Freedom Corner

As 2024 unfolded, I found myself reflecting deeply on the events of the past few years — the political shifts, the protests, and the ongoing debates surrounding freedom and justice in America. One place that held particular significance in this reflection was Freedom Corner in Washington, D.C. This humble street corner became a powerful symbol of dedication and solidarity for many who sought to support those affected by the events of January 6th.

Freedom Corner was initiated by a small Chinese church, a close-knit community that understood the value of standing up for one's beliefs. Two individuals from this church stood out in their unwavering commitment: Dwight, an elder, and Rebbeca, the wife of another elder. Every single day for over three years, Dwight and Rebbeca were present at Freedom Corner, holding vigil for those who had been imprisoned following January 6th. Their dedication was nothing short of extraordinary.

Another constant presence at Freedom Corner was the mother of Ashley, a woman who tragically lost her life on that fateful day. Ashley's mother stood alongside Dwight and Rebbeca, her grief fueling her determination to seek justice and remembrance for her daughter. The three of them formed the heart of Freedom Corner, their diverse backgrounds united by a common purpose.

Though I only attended Freedom Corner in person occasionally, I felt a deep connection to their cause. During the Christmas seasons, I wrote cards to the prisoners, hoping to offer them a measure of comfort and letting them know they were not forgotten. It was a small gesture, but one that I hoped would make a difference in their lives.

Dwight and Rebbeca's commitment extended beyond the corner itself. They forged friendships with other supporters, including Ashley's mother. Their compassion and openness created a community bound by empathy and shared convictions. On one occasion, they invited Ashley's mother and other supporters to attend a service at their church. By chance, I was there that day. Although Cornerstone Chapel is my home church, I sometimes attend this small church to stay connected with friends like Dwight and Rebbeca.

Meeting Ashley's mother was a profound experience. Her strength in the face of unimaginable loss was both humbling and inspiring. She spoke not with bitterness, but with a steadfast resolve to honor her daughter's memory by advocating for fairness and accountability. Her presence at Freedom Corner was a testament to a mother's love and the lengths to which one will go to seek justice.

The small church that nurtured Freedom Corner embodied the spirit of community activism. Many members, including other Chinese Americans, occasionally joined the daily vigils. Their collective action served as a poignant reminder that ordinary people can make an extraordinary impact when united by a common cause.

Reflecting on Freedom Corner, I was struck by the quiet power of consistent, peaceful protest. Dwight, Rebbeca, and Ashley's mother didn't seek the spotlight or engage in grand gestures. Instead, they demonstrated their commitment through daily presence and personal connections. Their actions spoke volumes about the importance of standing up for one's beliefs, even when the path is challenging and the outcomes uncertain.

The dedication of my friends at Freedom Corner also highlighted the broader political awakening within the Chinese American community. The events of January 6th and their aftermath stirred something within us — a reminder of the fragility of freedom and the necessity of vigilance in its defense.

While opinions about January 6th vary widely, for those at Freedom Corner, the focus was on compassion, justice, and the protection of constitutional rights. Their unwavering commitment served as a beacon for others who might feel powerless or uncertain about how to make a difference.

As I continue to navigate my own journey of faith and political involvement, the example set by Dwight, Rebbeca, and Ashley's mother remains a guiding light. Their dedication teaches me that meaningful change often begins with small, consistent actions rooted in love and conviction. It reinforces my belief that, even in the face of adversity, we each have the capacity to contribute to the betterment of our community and our nation.

Freedom Corner may not be widely known or covered extensively in the media, but its impact on those who participate and those who observe is profound. It stands as a testament to the power of grassroots movements and the enduring human spirit that seeks justice and reconciliation. In a world often divided by ideology and misunderstanding, the simple act of showing up — day after day — can bridge gaps and foster a sense of shared humanity.

Through my reflections on Freedom Corner, I am reminded that the pursuit of justice and the defense of freedom are ongoing responsibilities. They require courage, compassion, and, above all, a steadfast commitment to our principles. I am grateful to be part of a community that understands this and strives to embody it each day.

Chapter 49: The Husband's Campaign

When Paul was first approached about running for city council in spring 2023, neither of us could have imagined the journey that would follow. It began unexpectedly when Maryanne, the vice chairwoman of the GOP committee for the county, called Paul one afternoon. She asked him to consider being a candidate for the upcoming election. Paul, caught off guard, chuckled and said, "I'd rather be the kingmaker than be a candidate myself." He was accustomed to being behind the scenes, offering advice and support, not standing in the spotlight. But when Maryanne explained the situation further, Paul's attitude shifted slightly. "There is no GOP candidate," she told him. "If you don't run, the incumbent will be reelected unopposed again." The weight of her words hung in the air.

Paul didn't dismiss the idea outright. Instead, he said, "Let me talk about it with my wife."

At that time, Paul was dealing with a severe bone spur in his left ankle, which caused him a great deal of pain and made walking difficult. He had to rely on a cane to get around. When he told me about the idea, my immediate reaction was grounded in concern for his health. "No," I said firmly. "How could you think of running for anything when you can't even walk?" It seemed clear to me that this campaign would be too much for him to take on.

The next day, Paul drove our RV to a scheduled service appointment, preparing for a cross-country trip we had planned. It was a normal day, filled with errands and the usual tasks. While waiting for the RV to be serviced, Paul dozed off in his chair at the service center. Hours later, the technician jingled the keys to wake him up, calling his name. Paul stood up, fully expecting to feel the familiar pain in his ankle. But something was different — the pain was gone. He realized, with a sense of awe, that he was standing without his cane and without pain.

When Paul returned home, he called me downstairs with a burst of energy I hadn't seen in a long time. "Look!" he said, before jumping in place. I was stunned. "You'll have to run," I said, still trying to process the sudden change. "This is a miracle."

It seemed that fate, or perhaps divine intervention, was pushing Paul toward this path. With that newfound determination, we committed ourselves to the campaign. We embarked on our long-awaited cross-country trip, using the time away to reflect and plan for the race ahead. By the time we returned, we were ready to throw ourselves into the campaign wholeheartedly.

However, this wasn't Paul's first foray into community leadership. When we had first moved into our house, Paul was frustrated with the outdated restrictions in the HOA handbook. Many of the rules no longer reflected the needs of the neighborhood, and Paul felt they needed updating. After settling in, he decided to run for the HOA board of directors. At that time, Paul was healthy and energetic, walking around the neighborhood and talking to residents. His personable approach and his passion for improving the community impressed many, although he didn't win because too many surrogated votes gave the chairman enough power to pick any candidate. However, Paul's dedication to addressing local issues left a lasting impact on the neighborhood, and many of those same neighbors would go on to support him during his city council run.

The support from our community, particularly the Chinese community, was overwhelming. The small Chinese church I attended sometimes provided the strongest backing, both in donations and action. A close friend of ours, Daniel, from the church, became Paul's campaign controller. He was an organized and resourceful leader, helping to rally volunteers and coordinate efforts. Paul's campaign quickly grew to have more volunteers than any other candidate running for office that year, and many of those volunteers were Chinese.

Daniel even organized a car parade to show support for Paul's campaign, and it was an incredible sight. Dozens of cars lined the streets, honking and waving signs as they drove through neighborhoods, spreading the word about Paul's candidacy. It felt as though the whole community had come together, united by the desire to see positive change in local leadership.

Before the campaign began, I had started a personal project — a YouTube fitness channel called *Age Gracefully with Hope*, where I posted exercise videos. I had taught myself to create and edit videos using Wondershare Filmora, and it became an unexpected skill that proved essential for Paul's campaign. As the campaign intensified, we paused my fitness videos and shifted focus to producing campaign content. It felt as though everything I had learned up until that point had prepared me for this. We created numerous campaign videos, each addressing critical issues in the community, from infrastructure concerns to the future of the Rosehill Shopping Center.

One of the most significant issues Paul addressed was the controversial proposal to tear down Rosehill Shopping Center and replace it with a high-rise apartment building. Residents in the surrounding area were strongly opposed to the development, and they formed a group called *Save Rosehill Shopping Center* to fight against it. Paul promised that, if elected, he would stand with the residents and keep the shopping center intact. His commitment to the cause earned him support from people across the political spectrum, including many Democrats who lived nearby. They told him that, because of his stance, they would be voting for him.

Paul didn't stop there. He identified key issues in different precincts, offering solutions that resonated with voters. His pragmatic approach appealed to people from all walks of life, and it was clear that many Democrats, frustrated with the current state of leadership, were ready to cast their votes for Paul. We heard it time and again as we canvassed neighborhoods: "I'm a Democrat, but I'm voting for Paul."

Despite the growing support and all our efforts, Paul ultimately lost the election. It wasn't just him, though. All the GOP candidates, except one incumbent, lost — and they all lost by the exact same percentage. The results were eerily consistent across the board, raising questions about the fairness of the process. Some candidates had barely campaigned at all, yet their losses mirrored Paul's exactly.

Throughout the campaign, I had played an active role in organizing our outreach efforts. I compiled a list of local restaurants where we could distribute flyers, making sure we covered every corner of the city. I also designed the routes for our door-knocking efforts, mapping out the most efficient paths for our volunteers. One of our volunteers even came up to me and said, "These are the easiest and most efficient routes I've ever used!" It was a small victory, but it meant that we were maximizing our efforts and reaching as many voters as possible.

By the end of the campaign, I had become so familiar with the city that it was remarkable. Streets and neighborhoods that had once felt foreign to me were now part of my everyday experience. Campaigning may not have led to a win, but it certainly gave me a newfound appreciation for the city and its people.

Another key part of Paul's campaign was the *Great American Walk-of-Fame* — a visionary project he proposed that captured the imaginations of many. For decades, the county had been searching for ways to attract more of the estimated $8.1 billion tourist dollars spent annually in Washington, D.C.. Despite various attempts, they hadn't been able to create something that would lure visitors a little further south. That is, until Paul came up with his idea.

The concept was simple yet grand: a pedestrian attraction akin to the iconic Hollywood Walk of Fame, but with a patriotic twist. The *Great American Walk-of-Fame* would be a tribute to the war heroes, first responders, politicians, activists, and historic figures who shaped the United States. Leveraging the ongoing rebuild of US-1 (Richmond Highway), which was the nation's first highway, Paul envisioned the Walk-of-Fame as a monumental project that would align perfectly with the upcoming 250th anniversary of the United States.

This project had the potential to attract thousands of tourists to the county, bringing much-needed revenue without the use of tax dollars. Visitors would be drawn to explore the Walk-of-Fame, learning about the individuals who made America great, while also visiting nearby historical landmarks like Mount Vernon and Gunston Manor. The idea met with enthusiasm, especially among local business owners who saw the economic benefit it could bring to the area.

Paul's proposal for the *Great American Walk-of-Fame* was more than just an election promise — it was a visionary idea that could have reshaped the region. He also had detailed plans to fund the project without any taxpayer's money. Unfortunately, with his loss in the election, this bold concept may never be realized. It was a shame, as the project could have been a lasting tribute to American values and a boon to the local economy.

Paul's journey into the campaign also sparked a significant idea that would become central to his platform: the rebranding of Franconia District as *Washington's Backyard*. The district, formerly known as *Lee District*, had undergone a name change but lacked a strong identity to unite its residents. Paul believed that in the face of increasing violent crime, zoning changes, and the cultural and socio-economic challenges affecting Franconia, the district needed a fresh sense of pride. It was this belief that gave birth to his concept of a new brand image that would emphasize Franconia's rich history and natural beauty, while fostering community engagement.

Paul saw the district's unique proximity to Mount Vernon, George Washington's historic estate, as an opportunity to reframe its identity and solidify a connection to the nation's founding father. He proposed adopting the brand *Washington's Backyard* to evoke a sense of legacy and pride. The rebranding would also tie into a new slogan for the district: *Live, Work & Play Here!*, emphasizing that Franconia was not only a place to build a life but also a district full of historical and recreational value.

"Franconia has always been more than just a name on a map," Paul would tell voters, *"It's part of George Washington's story, and that story is ours to celebrate."* He envisioned annual celebrations to reflect this pride, with district-wide events such as *The Big Backyard Sale, Family Reunion Weekend, Backyard Cookouts,* and other activities that could build a sense of community and belonging.

To strengthen the district's brand, Paul suggested a subtle yet impactful change to its name — from *Franconia District* to *The District of Franconia*. This play on words would evoke familiarity with *The District of Columbia*, further establishing the connection to Washington, D.C., and grounding Franconia's identity as part of the historical narrative of the United States.

Paul's campaign worked tirelessly to promote this idea. He spoke with local business owners, community leaders, and even members of the Mount Vernon Ladies' Association, the caretakers of George Washington's estate, who confirmed the historical accuracy of referring to Franconia as *Washington's Backyard*. The idea caught the attention of residents, many of whom loved the thought of turning Franconia's proximity to Mount Vernon into a source of pride and tourism.

Paul's vision wasn't just about tapping into history, though — it was about revitalizing the district's present and future. He hoped that by embracing this new identity, the district could attract new businesses, increase home ownership, and cultivate a thriving community that residents would be proud to call home. The introduction of a new website, *WashingtonsBackyard.com*, would allow residents and potential newcomers to engage with Franconia's offerings, further encouraging a sense of connection and belonging.

Central to this branding effort was the area's natural gem, *Huntley Meadows Park*. The park, once a favorite hunting ground for George Washington, held a special place in Paul's campaign. He often spoke about how George Washington loved the park's beauty and how it could serve as a symbol of the district's potential for growth while maintaining its natural roots.

In addition to pushing for this rebranding, Paul continued to engage with voters on issues like zoning and economic development. But the idea of *Washington's Backyard* became the heart of his campaign, rallying the community around a shared sense of identity. While Paul ultimately lost the election, his vision for *The District of Franconia* left a lasting impression. Many in the community still spoke of the rebranding idea with excitement, recognizing that it could have reshaped their district for years to come.

As Paul and I reflected on the campaign, we realized that this branding proposal — while not realized — was an opportunity to unite people around something bigger than themselves. Franconia's future lay in embracing its past while forging a path toward economic growth and community pride. For us, the campaign had been about much more than winning votes; it had been about offering a vision that could bring lasting positive change to a district we loved.

The campaign was exhausting — physically, emotionally, and financially. The days were long, and the pressure was relentless. I remember the day the voting finally ended, I was simply grateful for the people who had supported us and relieved that it was finished. It was an experience of a lifetime, even though the results didn't go our way.

Chapter 50: The Aftermath of the Campaign

When Paul decided to run for city council, we both knew it would be an intense journey, but we couldn't have foreseen the full impact the campaign would have on our lives. Throughout the campaign, Paul nearly halted his business, dedicating all his time and energy to creating campaign websites, literature, and videos, as well as speaking directly to business owners and voters. He logged most of these efforts as in-kind donations to his campaign, and in some cases, as a personal loan to the campaign, hoping for reimbursement if more donations came in. However, donations were never enough to cover all the expenses, and the debt piled up. By the end of the race, Paul had amassed significant personal credit card debt. When he lost the election, we were left with no choice but to take a second mortgage on our home just to avoid the continuous usurious interest on the credit cards.

One particularly memorable incident occurred when Paul parked our RV at the Rosehill Shopping Center parking lot to set up a mobile campaign station. He opened the awning to attract attention from shoppers, hoping to strike up conversations and win votes. Suddenly, a strong gust of wind came out of nowhere, ripping the awning off its hinges along with part of its holder. Paul tried to act quickly, but the damage was already done. It cost about $3,000 to have it repaired, a blow to an already stretched campaign budget. That incident became a painful reminder of the risks involved in such a high-stakes effort.

As if the financial toll wasn't enough, the shift from traditional voting day to an extended voting season brought new challenges. Every day after work, I would visit different polling sites to check in with voters until the booths closed for the day. At night, I worked tirelessly on campaign videos, adding English and Chinese (simplified and traditional) subtitles, cover pages, keywords, and descriptions. I even promoted the videos through Google Ads, carefully targeting specific postal codes to reach potential voters. Designing canvassing routes for distributing door hangers became my daily routine. Each day felt impossibly long, filled with endless tasks that demanded both mental and physical endurance.

During door-knocking, although many people thanked me for my efforts, some were not friendly at all. One afternoon, after I had just hung a doorhanger on a townhouse door and was walking back to my car in the parking lot, a man stepped out of his car with his two young daughters. He yelled at me, demanding that I remove the door hanger from his door. His tone was harsh, and his expression was filled with disdain, as if he viewed me as a beggar — and all this in front of his daughters. He was clearly the homeowner. In Chinese, the word for canvassing literally translates to "begging for votes," and in that moment, it felt like I was seen that way.

Although most people were kind and supportive, not everyone treated us with respect. We even faced malicious rumors within the broader Chinese community, and though we didn't hear about them right away, our most loyal supporters shielded us from the gossip. They defended us fiercely, often without us even knowing. But one rumor eventually reached us through a white supporter, and it was deeply hurtful. The rumor accused me of being a spy who had once worked for Speaker Pelosi. The absurdity of the claim was beyond belief. I have been working at the Office of the Clerk, which serves the Speaker, regardless of which party holds power. To suggest that I was aligned with Pelosi in any personal capacity was not only ignorant but malicious. It was clear that whoever started this rumor didn't misunderstand — they were intentionally spreading lies to discredit us.

This infighting within the Chinese community broke my heart. The old saying echoed in my mind: "One great Chinese fighter can defeat five Japanese soldiers, but five Chinese fighters would lose to five Japanese soldiers." The community's tendency to turn against each other instead of uniting was both frustrating and painful. I told myself that after the election was over, I would reach out to those who opposed us, not to gain support, but in an effort to mend divisions and foster unity. However, when I expressed this idea to our supporters, they were furious. They had defended us so fiercely during the campaign that any suggestion of reconciliation felt like a betrayal to them. Their reactions made me realize just how much they had sacrificed to protect us. Wanting to honor their loyalty, I abandoned my plans for reconciliation. Paul had lost the election anyway, so there seemed to be no point in pursuing it further. Yet, the bitterness from the infighting still weighs on me whenever I see divisions within our community.

The campaign had drained us — physically, mentally, and emotionally. I vividly remember the day voting finally ended. As I drove home, an overwhelming sense of relief washed over me. The months of tireless work, the long hours spent canvassing, and the relentless pressure were finally behind us. For the first time in weeks, I didn't care about the outcome. I just wanted it all to be over. That night, I went straight to bed, too exhausted to even watch the vote tally. The outcome, when it came, didn't disappoint me. We had done everything we could, and I took comfort in knowing that we had given our best effort.

After the campaign, Paul found himself reflecting on why God had allowed him to run for office, knowing he would lose. At first, he was confused, but over time, he came to believe that God had a purpose for him beyond winning the election. Paul realized that God had wanted him to witness firsthand the issues surrounding election integrity. He had seen troubling inconsistencies during the campaign, and this experience ignited a new determination in him: to ensure the integrity of future elections. With 2024 on the horizon, Paul was resolute in his commitment to protecting the democratic process.

Even though Paul lost the election, the experience was unlike anything we had ever gone through. We met incredible people, built strong connections within the community, and stood up for the values we believed in. The campaign had been a journey of discovery — about our community, about politics, and about ourselves. The lessons we learned were invaluable, and the friendships we forged would last long beyond the election. For Paul and me, the campaign wasn't just about winning votes; it was about standing up for what we believed in, fighting for our community, and offering a vision of positive change.

Looking back, the campaign was a test of endurance, faith, and commitment. We faced adversity in many forms — financial strain, rumors, and infighting — but we never wavered in our dedication to the cause. While the loss was hard to accept, we walked away with no regrets. We gave it everything we had, and that was enough.

In the end, Paul's run for office was about much more than a political race — it was about the belief that ordinary citizens can stand up and make a difference. It was about seeing what could be improved and having the courage to pursue it. And though Paul didn't win the seat, his resolve to fight for election integrity in the future remained stronger than ever. The campaign may have ended, but the lessons and the mission it inspired were far from over.

Chapter 51: Taking a Vacation to Visit My Family in China

After Paul's campaign ended, I found myself reflecting not only on the political challenges we had faced but also on the need for a break. It had been an intense period, and I felt it was the right time to reconnect with my roots and visit my family in China. The last time I had been to Hangzhou in Zhejiang Province was over 11 years ago, and much had changed since then. My sister and her husband, who used to live in Xinjiang, had moved to Hangzhou after they retired a few years ago, and this visit gave me the perfect opportunity to stay with them in one of China's most beautiful cities.

Hangzhou has long been celebrated as a place of unparalleled beauty. The famous Chinese saying, *"There is heaven above, while there are Hangzhou and Suzhou on Earth,"* always comes to mind when thinking of the city. Known for its serene West Lake, lush greenery, and vibrant culture, Hangzhou did not disappoint. What struck me most, though, was how much more modern and efficient everything had become since my last visit.

Shortly after arriving, I learned something new about China's regulations. Foreigners who don't stay in hotels are required to report to the local government for a temporary stay permit within 24 hours of arrival. I hadn't realized this until a week before I was supposed to leave. Nervously, I approached the local office, fully expecting a fine or some kind of bureaucratic headache. I had heard enough stories about the Chinese government to know they could be strict when it came to rules. But to my surprise, when I explained that I hadn't seen the requirement until now, the clerk simply issued me the permit without a second thought. There was no penalty, no problem. It was a small gesture, but it stood in contrast to many of the things I had heard and even experienced in the past.

During my stay, I also had a small medical situation that I had been struggling to resolve in the U.S. After dealing with frustrating delays and inefficiencies at my doctor's office back home, my sister suggested that I take care of it while I was in China. I was skeptical at first, but after visiting a nearby hospital on a Friday morning, I was amazed at how quickly and efficiently the system worked. The doctor suggested a small surgery and told me I could have it done the very next day. I was given the choice of checking in on Friday afternoon to get ready or coming back early Saturday morning. My sister thought it would be more comfortable for me to stay overnight, so I decided to check in on Friday.

By the time I arrived at the hospital that afternoon, everything had been arranged. Within hours, I had undergone all the necessary tests — blood draw, x-rays, everything. It was all done seamlessly. The experience left a lasting impression on me: today's China is no longer Mao's China.

What impressed me even more was the fact that the hospital receipts I received met the standards of my health insurance, Blue Cross Blue Shield (BCBS). I was able to submit the receipts after returning to the U.S. and got reimbursed without any trouble at all. The level of service and the compatibility with international health insurance amazed me, further reinforcing the idea that China has truly modernized its systems to align with global standards.

There were many other things I marveled at during my stay. Social security and medical insurance in Hangzhou were comprehensive, particularly the care policies for the elderly. Public transportation was incredibly reliable, and the cities, even down to the areas under bridges, were clean and beautifully maintained — better than many places in the U.S. Even the types and quality of vegetables, fruits, and seafood available in the markets were beyond what I could easily access back home.

I also experienced a level of safety and honesty that surprised me. I heard stories of lost wallets and mobile phones being returned to their owners almost immediately, a scenario we often believe only happens in North America. While not all cities in China are governed as well as Hangzhou, it was striking to see that Hangzhou isn't even considered a first-tier city! It made me reflect on how much China has changed in such a short time.

As I spent more time with my family, we often talked about the differences between life in China and life in America. When my cousins asked about the retirement system in the U.S., I told them about social security, Roth IRAs, 401(k)s, and pensions. To my surprise, they shared that Hangzhou had adopted many of the same ideas, copying the best aspects of Western retirement systems. The growth of China's economy, they explained, was largely due to their embrace of free market principles and their departure from the planned economy of the past. What remained unchanged, however, was the one-party rule — something the government refused to relinquish.

This conversation made me realize how little many Americans understand about China's evolution. The rapid modernization and the efficiency of their systems are often overlooked, as the fact that these advancements are largely due to China's embrace of capitalism in many areas. Many Americans assume that China's growth is due to its government's control, but in reality, much of it comes from abandoning the planned economy and adopting Western systems and ideas. This is why, when Americans advocate for socialism without fully understanding it, they don't see the dangers. China's rise happened *because* they moved away from socialism and toward market-driven solutions — something we risk forgetting if we don't carefully consider our own political path.

In the end, my trip to China was more than just a family visit. It was an eye-opening experience that gave me new perspectives on the country's rapid development and how much it has learned from the West. But it also reminded me of the importance of understanding the delicate balance between economic freedom and political control. The China I saw was prosperous, modern, and forward-thinking — yet, behind it all, the one-party system remained firmly in place.

Chapter 52: Supporting Election Integrity Efforts for 2024

After the campaign ended, Paul found himself contemplating what he had learned through the entire process. The loss had been disappointing, but it had opened his eyes to the deeper issues within the electoral system. He realized that his journey wasn't meant to end with the campaign — God had shown him the challenges of election integrity and sparked a new mission. This mission would become *Operation Eyeball*, a nationwide effort to protect the fairness and transparency of the 2024 presidential election.

Paul's vision for *Operation Eyeball* was ambitious, but it came from a place of deep conviction. "See Something, Say Something!" became the rallying cry of the operation. The initiative aimed to unite Election Integrity Groups across the United States under one banner, empowering ordinary citizens to be vigilant and report any suspicious activities they saw. Paul believed that restoring trust in elections required every voter's involvement, and he was determined to be a part of the solution. As he often said, "Do nothing, and you're part of the problem."

His plan included educating voters about the different methods that could be used to tamper with elections — from ballot harvesting to equipment tampering, to the malicious use of media and legal systems to defame and attack political opponents. *Operation Eyeball* also went beyond simply observing elections; it was about creating a united front to deter potential bad actors, ensuring they knew they were being watched by a vast network of concerned citizens.

Paul's commitment to this cause became all-consuming. He poured his energy into developing websites, literature, and video content that would spread the message far and wide. He organized events, participated in conferences, and reached out to Election Integrity Groups across the country to bring them into *Operation Eyeball*. Once he was even invited to Virginia Beach conservative gathering to talk about Operation Eyeball. In his mind, this was more than just a political effort — it was a call to protect the fundamental democratic right of free and fair elections.

In September, Paul had the opportunity to present his idea at a donor's black-tie gala at Trump National in Jupiter, Florida. Surrounded by influential figures, he seized the moment to mention *Operation Eyeball* to President Trump himself. To Paul's surprise and delight, President Trump was immediately receptive to the idea. Standing before the crowd, Trump said over the microphone, "I love the idea. I've never heard of that, and I think it's a great idea to help restore fair and honest elections in America." The public endorsement from a former president gave Paul's efforts a significant boost, filling him with renewed motivation.

While Paul's *Operation Eyeball* gained momentum and national attention, the Chinese community was also busy with election activities, though their efforts were not directly tied to his operation. Many Chinese Americans had become deeply involved in supporting election integrity through various means, including poll watching, canvassing, door knocking, and fundraising. Their work was a testament to the growing political awareness within the Chinese community, as more and more individuals recognized the importance of participating in the democratic process.

However, despite the overlapping goals, there was little direct involvement between Paul's initiative and the broader Chinese community. Most of the election integrity efforts by Chinese Americans were localized, focusing on specific districts or regions, whereas *Operation Eyeball* sought to unite groups across the entire country. Still, the passion and dedication to ensuring fair elections were present on both sides.

One of the few Chinese who connected with Paul directly on the issue of election integrity was Xi Van Fleet, a Chinese-American activist and our friend. Xi was a steadfast supporter for defending election integrity. Having lived through the Cultural Revolution in China, she had firsthand experience with government control and the suppression of democratic rights. Xi's personal story, combined with her activism in America, made her a natural ally to Paul's cause. Together, they discussed how election integrity was not just a political issue but a moral imperative, especially for immigrant communities.

Xi shared her insights with Paul during a podcast interview, explaining how the Chinese community's increasing involvement in election-related activities was a sign of growing political maturity. Many Chinese Americans, she noted, had historically been hesitant to engage in American politics, wary of drawing attention to themselves or unsure of how the system worked. But in recent years, that hesitation had given way to a more active and engaged approach. The Chinese community had realized that their voices mattered, and they had begun to take part in protecting the electoral process, even if it wasn't directly linked to Paul's initiative.

Across the country, Chinese American groups organized to watch over polling stations, ensuring that the process remained transparent and fair. Some worked with local candidates, fundraising to support campaigns that aligned with their values. Others knocked on doors to encourage voter turnout, educating their neighbors about the importance of voting and how their ballots could impact the future of their communities. It was inspiring to see so many people — many of whom had once been indifferent to politics — now playing such an active role.

While the efforts of *Operation Eyeball* and the broader Chinese community were not aligned, they shared a common goal: ensuring the integrity of the 2024 election. Whether through Paul's nationwide initiative or through localized poll watching and door knocking, there was a sense of shared responsibility. Both Paul and the Chinese American community understood that democracy thrived when its citizens were engaged, vigilant, and dedicated to protecting the process.

As Paul continued his work with *Operation Eyeball*, Chinese Americans across the country also stayed busy with their election-related activities. Together, even if not working hand in hand, they formed part of a larger movement aimed at preserving the sanctity of the vote.

In the months leading up to the 2024 election, Paul and I reflected on the journey we had taken since the campaign. While it had been exhausting, both physically and emotionally, the work was far from over. We knew that restoring trust in the electoral system required ongoing effort, and we were both committed to seeing it through. For Paul, *Operation Eyeball* represented the next step in that mission, and for me, seeing the Chinese community step up in various capacities was a source of pride.

Together, we believed in the power of citizen involvement, whether it was through national efforts like *Operation Eyeball* or local initiatives led by dedicated volunteers. The future of democracy, we knew, depended on the collective will of its people to protect and uphold the integrity of the vote. And as we moved forward, we were grateful for the support and dedication of those around us, knowing that we were all working toward a common goal: fair and honest elections in 2024 and beyond.

Infighting and Operation Eyeball: A Clash of Personal and Political Agendas

While the GOP is often united in its broader goals, particularly in moments of national importance like the 2024 election, internal divisions can still run deep. Operation Eyeball, a grassroots election integrity initiative, was meant to rally supporters and ensure fair voting practices. However, its success became entangled in the internal politics of the county GOP, where personal grievances and rivalries overshadowed the shared mission.

Paul's involvement in the county GOP had always been rooted in his commitment to election integrity and his unwavering support for the Republican Party. He had developed strong relationships with many in the local leadership, including the previous GOP chairman, who chose not to run for another term. During the county GOP election to select a new chairman, Paul supported a candidate who ultimately lost the race. Unfortunately, the winning candidate interpreted Paul's support for her opponent as a personal slight rather than a simple difference in political strategy.

This perceived betrayal by Paul set the stage for ongoing tension. The new chairman's approach to leadership seemed to reflect a desire to assert her authority, and Paul's continued efforts to promote Operation Eyeball began to face resistance. Despite his long-standing dedication, Paul found himself increasingly at odds with the party's leadership. He was eventually removed from key volunteer roles and banned from representing the county GOP at early voting sites.

The personal nature of the conflict was evident in the communications that followed. While the official reasons for Paul's removal revolved around minor rule violations, such as the use of sound amplification or the promotion of Operation Eyeball at GOP tables, it was clear that the real issue stemmed from the earlier election and the new chairman's resentment. What should have been a united effort to ensure election integrity instead became a battleground for internal disputes.

In contrast, the Democratic Party has historically demonstrated a much stronger internal cohesion. A quick look at voting records in Congress shows that almost all Democrat congresspeople vote in sync with party leadership on major issues. This unity is striking compared to the Republican Party, where factions often emerge, leading to inconsistent voting patterns and internal conflict. This difference in party dynamics became painfully clear as Operation Eyeball struggled to gain full support within the GOP, even though it aligned with the party's broader goals of election integrity.

While Democrats are known for rallying around their leadership to push through legislation or political initiatives, Republicans, particularly in local settings like the county GOP, often find themselves in internal battles over strategy, tactics, or personal loyalties. This lack of unity can be a significant disadvantage, especially when the stakes were as high as they were in the 2024 election.

Paul's efforts to escalate the issue to the RNC highlighted the seriousness of the division. The fact that a high-ranking RNC official agreed to intervene spoke volumes about the depth of the infighting. What started as a local power struggle had drawn the attention of national party leadership, exposing how personal rivalries within a party can escalate and disrupt broader efforts.

The incident with Operation Eyeball is emblematic of a larger problem within political organizations: when personal grievances take precedence over shared goals, it is the cause that ultimately suffers. While Paul remained committed to the mission of election integrity, the internal struggles of the county GOP served as a reminder that unity within a party is not always guaranteed — even when the stakes couldn't be higher. The contrast with the disciplined unity often seen in the Democratic Party underscores the challenges the GOP faces from within, as ideological and personal differences threaten to undermine their collective efforts.

Chapter 53: Political Conversations in the Church

As the 2024 election season approached, political discussions began to dominate more and more conversations, even within the walls of Cornerstone Chapel. While the church had always been a place of worship and spiritual guidance, it had also become a forum for broader discussions about the state of the nation and the role that Christians should play in shaping its future. For Paul and me, the intersection of faith and politics was nothing new, but as we engaged in more frequent conversations with fellow church members, it became clear just how central these topics were to many in our congregation.

The growing political divide in the country had naturally sparked differing opinions among Christians, even within our church. Some members felt that faith should be kept separate from politics, focusing solely on spiritual matters. Others, like Paul and me, believed that preserving Christian values was essential to the health of the nation and required active participation in the political process. This belief wasn't just about aligning with a political party but about defending the principles of freedom, morality, and justice that we believed were foundational to both our faith and our country.

One Sunday after service, a group of us gathered in the fellowship hall for coffee and casual conversation. It didn't take long for the topic of politics to surface. Steve, one of the church elders, expressed his concerns about the increasing hostility towards Christian beliefs in the public square. "It's not just about policy anymore," he said. "It's about whether we, as Christians, can even express our faith without being vilified." His words struck a chord with many in the group, myself included. We had all witnessed the growing tension between maintaining religious freedoms and navigating the secular policies that often seemed at odds with our beliefs.

Paul, ever the conversationalist, chimed in. "That's exactly why we can't sit on the sidelines," he said. "If we don't engage politically, we're leaving the future of our faith — and the values that built this country — up to others who may not share our convictions. We have a responsibility, not just as citizens but as Christians, to ensure that our voices are heard."

The discussion that followed was lively but respectful, as we all shared our thoughts on what it meant to live out our faith in the political arena. Some felt called to focus on community service and outreach, believing that changing hearts was more important than changing laws. Others, like Paul, emphasized the importance of advocating for policies that aligned with Christian values, particularly in areas such as religious freedom, the sanctity of life, and family rights.

At the heart of these conversations was a shared concern for the future of the country. We all saw the erosion of traditional values and the challenges facing religious communities. We recognized that, while the church should be a refuge from the divisive nature of politics, it could not be entirely separate from the issues affecting the nation. After all, our faith called us to be "salt and light" in the world, to influence society for the better.

Cornerstone Chapel had always been a place where faith and politics intersected, but these conversations were becoming more urgent as the 2024 election loomed. Many in our congregation were worried about the direction the country was heading and felt a growing sense of duty to protect the values that were under threat. While some preferred a quieter, more private expression of their faith, others, like Paul, felt compelled to engage more directly with the political system.

Another Sunday, Pastor Gary gave a sermon that perfectly captured the essence of these conversations. He spoke about the importance of discernment and the role of Christians in influencing culture. "We are called to be obedient to God above all else," Pastor Gary said, "but that doesn't mean we are to disengage from the world around us. In fact, it's the opposite. We are called to stand up for truth, to protect the freedoms we have been blessed with, and to ensure that future generations can live in a country where they can worship freely."

Pastor Gary's words resonated deeply with the congregation, particularly with those of us who had already been wrestling with these issues. His message reinforced what Paul and I had been feeling for some time: that political engagement was not just a civic duty but a spiritual one as well. It was about standing up for what was right, even when it wasn't easy, and ensuring that the principles of our faith remained a guiding light in the public sphere.

After the service, Paul and I stayed behind to talk with some of the other church members. Several of them expressed their concerns about the upcoming election and asked Paul for his thoughts on how Christians could make a difference. Paul, always eager to share his insights, reminded them that voting was only the beginning. "It's about more than just casting a ballot," he said. "It's about staying informed, getting involved in your community, and supporting candidates who share our values. And if there aren't any, maybe it's time to step up and run yourself."

These words hit home for many of us. Paul's own experience running for city council had shown us just how much work went into a campaign, but it also demonstrated the impact that one person could have when they chose to engage. As Christians, we couldn't afford to be passive observers. We had to be active participants, working to preserve the freedoms and values that were so critical to our way of life.

In the months that followed, political discussions continued to be a central part of our interactions at Cornerstone Chapel. Whether it was over coffee after service or during smaller Bible study groups, the topic of how to engage in the upcoming election was never far from our minds. Paul became a source of guidance for many in the congregation, helping them navigate the complexities of local and national politics. He often encouraged them to get involved in whatever way they could — whether it was volunteering for a campaign, attending city council meetings, or simply educating their friends and family about the importance of voting.

For Paul and me, these conversations were not just about politics — they were about living out our faith in every aspect of our lives. We believed that preserving Christian and conservative values required more than just prayer; it required action. And while not everyone in the church shared our level of political engagement, there was a growing sense among many that the time had come to stand up for what we believed in.

As the 2024 election drew nearer, the discussions at Cornerstone Chapel became more focused and urgent. The church had always been a place of refuge and spiritual growth, but now it was also a place where we could come together as a community to talk about the future — not just of our nation, but of our faith. We knew that the challenges ahead would be great, but we were ready to face them, united by a shared belief in the power of prayer, action, and the responsibility we had to preserve the values that made our country — and our church — strong.

Chapter 54: The Role of Chinese Americans in Politics

A close friend of ours, John, played a pivotal role in awakening political awareness within the Chinese American community. While he was an actuary and director at an anti-neoplasm pharmaceutical company by profession, he was also a passionate evangelist who dedicated much of his time to the church and the political awakening of Christians. John's multifaceted approach to both his faith and politics influenced many of us in profound ways, encouraging us to rethink our roles as Christian citizens. Through his leadership, we learned the importance of aligning our faith with our actions in the political sphere.

John preached at the small Chinese church twice a month, and sometimes, he would stay overnight at our house since he lived further south. His sermons were always filled with energy and conviction, and you could feel the Holy Spirit moving when he spoke. He didn't limit his work to just the church; John was also an avid street evangelist. He often went to public places like shopping malls and college campuses to preach the gospel, and I had the privilege of accompanying him with others on several occasions. His boldness and unwavering faith were awe-inspiring. His ability to seamlessly integrate his religious convictions with his political views created a powerful message for anyone who listened.

One of John's greatest strengths was his ability to articulate the importance of the First Amendment and the role of religious freedom in American society. He often shared an essay he had written about the First Amendment's protection of religious freedom, using it as both a teaching tool and a rallying cry for action. The essay was clear, direct, and focused on educating people, especially young students, about the real meaning behind the First Amendment.

In one instance, John talked with a group of high school students and posed a question to them: "From whom was the First Amendment set to protect your freedom from being intruded upon?" Out of the entire group, only a few students could answer correctly. Most of them were unaware that the First Amendment was designed to protect people's rights from government intrusion. John's heart sank at the lack of understanding but was not surprised. When he followed up by asking, "Why is the freedom of religion the very first right listed?" the students fell silent, no one having an answer.

John then explained, "Our Founding Fathers understood that the government could evolve into a powerful entity that might want to control every aspect of life, including what people believe. The first freedom the government would want to suppress is the exercise of religion because religion shapes people's beliefs, their worldview, and their actions. If the government controls what you believe, it controls what you say. Without freedom of religion, freedom of speech becomes meaningless."

He went on to emphasize that religious freedom is not simply about the right to believe in private but to practice those beliefs publicly. "If we are restricted from expressing our religious beliefs in public spaces," John argued, "then our religion is effectively being locked in a cage. And if Christianity is removed from public schools and only secular or atheistic views are taught, it creates a culture that is hostile to Christianity." He warned that this kind of culture would ultimately lead to an authoritarian government, similar to what we saw in China and the former Soviet Union.

John's insights resonated with many of us, particularly those who had come from countries where religious and political freedoms were restricted. His essays circulated among our church members, and we often discussed them during our gatherings. It was clear to us that, just like in China, the erosion of religious freedom in America would have far-reaching consequences, not just for Christians but for everyone.

One of John's most impactful essays was titled "To All American Churches – Get Involved in Politics Now to Save America!" In this essay, he urged churches to take an active role in the political process. He drew from examples in the Bible where prophets were sent to rebuke kings and leaders when they strayed from God's will. "In ancient Israel," John wrote, "whenever kings or priests went astray, God called prophets to correct them." He cited the story of Nathan rebuking King David for his sins and the many prophets who openly testified about God in public.

John wasn't just calling for passive political participation; he was calling for bold, unapologetic involvement. He explained that Christians, as citizens of heaven, have a duty to be involved in earthly matters, including politics. "You are the salt and the light on earth," he often reminded us, quoting Jesus' words from the Bible. For John, this wasn't just a spiritual calling; it was a practical one. He saw the growing influence of secularism and atheism in America and believed that Christians needed to counter it by reclaiming their place in the public sphere.

In his essay, John lamented how churches had given up their right to practice Christianity in public spaces, particularly in public schools. He pointed out that even a football coach could be fired for praying on the field, while other movements, like LGBTQ pride, were openly celebrated. He argued that Christians needed to be bold in expressing their faith, not just inside the church but in every aspect of life, including politics.

John often expressed frustration with some well-known Bible teachers who, in his view, had failed to teach Christians how to discern political issues through a biblical lens. He was particularly critical of those who focused more on criticizing President Trump than on acknowledging the good he had done for religious freedom. They wrote articles (exp. John Piper's "Policies, Persons, and Paths to Ruin") firing relentlessly on President Trump, being totally blind to what Trump did in his four years presidency. On the very first day, Trump boldly removed all LGBTQ trash from Whitehouse website. Trump immediately reversed Obama's ridiculous "bathroom executive order". Trump strongly supported Pro-life supplication; the first president ever presented in Pro-life rally. Many times, Trump publicly declared: "In our country, we trust in God, not the government! We knee to no one else but Almighty God only", much bolder than all religious leaders. Those teachers, from their Pharisees' perspective, saw Trump as the tax collector (Luke 18), they grabbed and despised Trump's past failures while forgetting their own cowardness and unfaithfulness. In their eyes, Trump always bragged. John argued, did any president humbly blame himself in their presidency? Didn't Obama boast about his presidency all the time? John firmly believed, in that day, those coward teachers would either face their Lord shamefully, or face the "fury of fire that will consume the adversaries" (Hebrew 10:27)! "These teachers are like the Pharisees," John would say, "blind to the truth and focused on superficial issues." He saw Trump's actions, such as supporting pro-life causes and reversing harmful executive orders, as examples of someone fighting for Christian values, even if he wasn't perfect.

John's political engagement was not limited to essays and sermons. He was deeply involved in efforts to bring his message to a wider audience. He encouraged all of us in the Chinese Christian community to reach out to churches and spread the message of political engagement. I personally helped him email his letter to a list of large churches in Pennsylvania, urging them to take a stand and get involved.

One of John's most memorable stories came from an experience he had while preaching at a shopping mall parking lot. A policeman approached him and told him to leave. John, never one to back down, calmly told the officer that he was exercising his First Amendment rights and would sue if the officer interfered with his religious expression. Surprised by John's assertiveness, the policeman walked away without further confrontation. John's courage in that moment served as an example for all of us of the importance of standing firm in the face of opposition.

John's political activism extended beyond the Chinese American community. While he had a heart for Chinese Christians, he often said that his burden was for all Americans. He believed that America could only be saved if the American people woke up to the realities of what was happening in our country. John saw the growing secularism and the erosion of Christian values as the greatest threats to America's future, and he dedicated his life to waking people up to those threats.

Over time, John's message began to resonate with a broader audience. His online Bible studies and essays gained attention, and more people began to see the connection between their faith and their political responsibilities. John's influence within the Chinese American community was undeniable, but his vision extended far beyond it. He believed that Chinese Americans, with their unique experiences of living under authoritarian regimes, had a special role to play in the fight for religious and political freedom in America. He saw our community as a bridge between the past struggles of our homelands and the present challenges facing America.

Through John's influence, many of us in the Chinese American community became more politically active. We began to see that our faith was not something to be kept private, but something that should inform our political decisions and actions. We saw that if we didn't take a stand now, the freedoms we enjoyed in America could be lost, just as they had been lost in the countries many of us had come from.

John's call for action was not just about political involvement for its own sake. It was about preserving the values that made America a beacon of freedom and hope for so many. His passion and conviction continue to inspire us to this day, and his legacy lives on in the countless lives he touched through his sermons, his essays, and his bold stand for truth.

John often spoke about the heavy burden he felt for the American people as a whole, not just the Chinese American community. He believed that America's spiritual and political health were deeply intertwined and that without a revival of Christian values, America was at risk of following the same path as authoritarian regimes like those in China or the former Soviet Union. He urged us all to take action before it was too late, to engage in politics, to speak out against injustices, and to make sure our voices were heard in every aspect of public life.

In addition to his essays and sermons, John also organized several political events where Chinese Americans were encouraged to participate in election-related activities, such as door knocking to support candidates with same values in swing states. These events became a crucial part of the growing political involvement of the Chinese American community, as many of us began to see the importance of taking a stand not only for our own rights but for the future of the entire nation.

At these events, John would often say, "If we do nothing, we are part of the problem. It is not enough to complain about the state of the world or the direction the country is heading. We must act, and we must act now. God has given us the responsibility to be stewards of this great nation, and we cannot shirk that duty."

John's leadership galvanized many of us to take action in ways we had never imagined. Through his example, we learned that political involvement was not just a duty but a calling — one that could not be ignored if we hoped to preserve the freedoms we cherished.

Chapter 55: Reflections on Faith, Freedom, and Responsibility

Throughout my journey in America, I have come to realize that the involvement of Chinese Americans in politics has not only grown, but it has also produced significant results. A key example of this is the lawsuit against Harvard University regarding its admissions process. For years, Harvard and other elite institutions have faced accusations of discriminating against Asian American students, particularly Chinese Americans, by holding them to higher standards than other applicants. This legal battle, led by groups of Asian American families, many of whom are Chinese, has brought the issue of race-based admissions into the national spotlight.

The lawsuit represents more than just a fight for fair admissions — it's a reflection of the deep values that many Chinese Americans hold, especially the emphasis on education. For centuries, education has been the cornerstone of Chinese culture, a path to betterment and success. Seeing their children face discrimination in the very institutions meant to provide opportunities for the brightest minds struck at the heart of the community. The Harvard case has mobilized Chinese Americans to engage more in political and legal battles, proving that when a community stands up, it can make its voice heard on a national level.

Interestingly, this battle mirrors a similar struggle that took place over a century ago. In the early 1900s, Jewish students faced similar forms of discrimination in the admissions processes of Ivy League universities. Jewish students, like Chinese students today, were often excluded or held to unfairly high standards. It took years of advocacy, lawsuits, and a persistent demand for fairness before these discriminatory practices began to change.

History, it seems, has a way of repeating itself. Just as Jewish students fought for their right to be judged on their merits rather than their backgrounds, Chinese Americans are now standing at the forefront of a similar battle. The outcome of the Harvard case will not only affect Asian Americans but will have implications for fairness and equality across all racial and ethnic groups. It is a reminder that political engagement is essential to protecting the rights we value most.

In recent years, the political landscape has made it clear that Chinese Americans are no longer on the sidelines. The Harvard case is just one example of how our community is becoming more politically active, fighting for fairness in education, workplace discrimination, and social policies. The increasing number of Chinese American candidates for local and national offices also reflects this change. This growth in political engagement is a sign that we understand the importance of standing up not just for ourselves, but for future generations.

In China, we have always valued education as one of the highest virtues. It is deeply ingrained in our culture that academic excellence opens doors to opportunity and success. Our respect for teachers, our commitment to hard work, and our relentless pursuit of knowledge have been key tenets passed down from generation to generation. These values were what many Chinese immigrants, including my family, brought with us to America. We believed that in this land of opportunity, our children would thrive if they studied hard and adhered to the same principles.

However, in recent years, changes in the American educational system have jolted our community out of complacency. Issues such as the lowering of academic standards, the shift towards equal outcomes instead of equal opportunities, and the introduction of gender and LGBTQ+ ideologies in schools have raised alarms for many Chinese parents. These changes not only threatened our core belief in merit-based success but also clashed with the traditional values we hold dear regarding family structure, gender, and personal responsibility.

The push for "equal results" rather than rewarding hard work and excellence was particularly disturbing. In a system where students are no longer rewarded based on their achievements but are instead pushed toward a homogenized outcome, the fundamental value of effort seemed to be eroding. For many Chinese families, this felt like an attack on our deepest cultural belief — that through diligence, one can achieve greatness. The lowering of academic expectations wasn't just an educational issue for us; it felt like a rejection of our way of life.

Among the most disturbing developments was the promotion of gender transformation for children. It is a lie — pure and simple. A boy can never become a girl, and a girl can never become a boy. A boy undergoing "gender transformation" would only be castrated, and a girl would lose the opportunity to ever become a mother. Influencing young children to pursue gender transformations is nothing short of evil, especially when these children are not even mature enough to decide whether they want pizza or a hot dog for lunch. How can we expect them to make such life-altering decisions about their bodies? For parents who had fled authoritarian regimes and come to America for its freedom and promise of a bright future for their children, the idea of schools pushing ideologies that conflicted with traditional family values felt like a betrayal. The discussion around parent rights and the limitations placed on them when trying to intervene in their children's education only intensified the frustration. Many felt that they were being shut out of decisions regarding their own children, decisions that would shape the course of their development.

Parents began to mobilize, attending school board meetings, voicing their concerns, and even running for local education offices. The traditionally quiet and non-confrontational Chinese community was finding its voice. Our sense of duty to our children's future was too strong to allow these changes to go unquestioned. Many of us realized that staying silent or uninvolved was no longer an option.

The confluence of issues like the Harvard admissions case and radical gender ideology in schools has shown that Chinese Americans, historically focused on family and education, now see the importance of political involvement. Just as the Jewish community before us took up the mantle of activism to fight discrimination, we, too, must rise to the challenge of ensuring that the values we hold dear — meritocracy, family, and freedom — are preserved for future generations.

As I reflected on these events, I couldn't help but think about how the political and civic responsibilities of Chinese Americans had shifted in response to these issues. For decades, the focus had been on personal and family success, but the realities we were now facing forced us to engage in broader societal issues. For me, it became a matter of faith, freedom, and responsibility. How could we stand by when the very foundations of the education system and the future of our children were at risk?

Faith, of course, played a crucial role in this awakening. Many in the Chinese American community, including myself, found ourselves turning to our faith for guidance. It was no longer just about protecting academic values; it was about preserving the moral fabric of society. Christian values taught us the importance of protecting the family, defending truth, and standing up for what is right. These values were what had guided us through centuries of struggle and adversity, and they were what gave us strength as we faced new challenges in a foreign land.

I often thought back to John's teachings during this time. His insistence that Christians be actively involved in the political and civic processes had resonated with me. He had been right all along — remaining passive was not an option. Faith was not just a private matter; it had to be lived out in the public square, especially when the moral and ethical underpinnings of society were at stake. This sense of duty, of being called to defend not only our children but also our country's future, became a rallying cry for many Chinese families.

As more Chinese Americans found themselves engaging in political issues — whether through school boards, community meetings, or simply raising awareness — our role in American society began to change. We were no longer just immigrants focused on survival and success; we were becoming active participants in shaping the future of this nation.

This new era of engagement reminded me of why we had come to America in the first place. We had come for the promise of freedom — the freedom to build a better life, the freedom to raise our children with values we believed in, and the freedom to practice our faith. But with freedom comes responsibility. And now, more than ever, that responsibility extended beyond our individual families and into the fabric of society.

The political engagement that was born out of concern for our children's education and future is part of a larger journey — one that many Chinese immigrants are beginning to walk. It's about reclaiming the freedoms that brought us to this country and ensuring they are preserved for future generations. It's about using our voices, our votes, and our collective power to protect the values we hold dear.

As I reflect on this journey, I realize that it's not just about political activism — it's about understanding the role that faith, freedom, and responsibility play in the shaping of a society. The Chinese American community, once quietly focused on academic and personal achievement, is now finding its place in the broader American narrative. We are waking up to the fact that we have a responsibility not just to ourselves but to this nation as well.

And so, our story continues. From the classrooms to the voting booths, from school board meetings to community gatherings, Chinese Americans are stepping forward, driven by faith, emboldened by freedom, and guided by the responsibility we feel toward our children and this nation. It's a path we walk not just for ourselves, but for all those who will come after us, ensuring that the freedoms we cherish today will still be here tomorrow.

Chapter 56: The Importance of Preserving Christian Values

The most important reason it is of utmost importance to preserve Christian values in order to defend freedom lies in a fundamental principle that is central to both faith and liberty: Christian values assert that freedom and rights are given by God, not by man. This concept forms the bedrock of true freedom, for if rights are understood to be God-given, they are inherent to every individual and cannot be taken away by any earthly authority, including the government. This is a powerful notion that has shaped the foundation of modern democracy and Western civilization, and it remains critical in the ongoing defense of freedom.

Christianity teaches that all human beings are created in the image of God, which means that each person carries intrinsic dignity, value, and worth. The rights that belong to us as human beings — such as the right to life, liberty, and the pursuit of happiness — are not privileges granted by governments or rulers. They are natural rights endowed by our Creator, a truth emphasized in the Declaration of Independence, which states, "We hold these truths to be self-evident, that all men are created equal, that they are endowed by their Creator with certain unalienable Rights, that among these are Life, Liberty, and the pursuit of Happiness."

When we affirm that these rights are given by God, we affirm that no human institution, no matter how powerful or influential, has the authority to take them away. Preserving Christian values is essential to defending freedom: it anchors the concept of rights in something transcendent, beyond the reach of governments and political systems. It ensures that freedom is not contingent on the whims of those in power, nor can it be redefined or diminished according to political agendas.

In contrast, when society turns away from Christian values or from the belief in a higher moral authority, the nature of freedom becomes precarious. If rights are viewed as merely social constructs or privileges bestowed by governments, then they can just as easily be taken away. In such a worldview, rights and freedoms are no longer inviolable but become subject to negotiation and erosion. Governments, especially those with authoritarian tendencies, may begin to see themselves as the ultimate source of power, believing they can determine who is deserving of rights and who is not.

This has been seen throughout history in regimes that have rejected the notion of God-given rights. In places where atheistic ideologies or secular humanism have taken hold, governments have frequently assumed the role of granting and restricting freedoms. Without the moral framework provided by Christian values, the state itself becomes the arbiter of morality, deciding what is right or wrong, permissible or forbidden. And because the state's power is not anchored in a belief in an objective, transcendent truth, it can become tyrannical, suppressing dissent, limiting freedom of speech, curtailing religious liberties, and violating individual rights in the name of collective or governmental interests. In China, it's common to say that the constitution has granted us the right to .... The danger of this is if the constitution is the entity that has granted people the rights, the constitution could be modified to take the rights away from certain people in certain conditions.

Christian values, on the other hand, serve as a safeguard against such tyranny. By affirming that all human beings possess inherent rights that flow from their relationship with God, Christian values establish a moral boundary that the state cannot cross. Governments are reminded that their role is not to grant rights but to protect the rights that have been bestowed upon individuals by a higher authority. This recognition restrains the state's power and promotes a culture of respect for individual liberty and human dignity.

Moreover, Christian values promote the idea of responsibility alongside rights. The concept of God-given rights is deeply intertwined with the call to live a life of virtue, compassion, and justice. Christian teachings emphasize love for one's neighbor, the pursuit of justice, and the duty to care for the most vulnerable members of society. This creates a moral framework where freedom is not simply about doing whatever one pleases but about using one's freedom responsibly in the service of others and for the common good.

Without this moral foundation, freedom can devolve into license or selfishness, where individuals or groups prioritize their own desires over the well-being of others. Christian values encourage a balance between individual liberty and communal responsibility, promoting a society where freedom is protected but also where justice, charity, and virtue are cultivated.

In today's world, where cultural relativism and secular ideologies are gaining prominence, the importance of preserving Christian values has never been more urgent. As these ideologies seek to redefine morality and human rights based on subjective preferences or social trends, there is a growing risk that fundamental freedoms will be eroded. By rejecting the idea of God-given rights, these worldviews open the door to a society where rights are fluid and can be altered or revoked by those in power.

Preserving Christian values, therefore, is not just about defending a particular religious tradition — it is about defending the very principles that make freedom possible. It is about ensuring that the rights we hold dear are grounded in something unchanging and eternal, not subject to the shifting sands of political opinion or cultural trends. It is about standing firm in the belief that our freedoms come from God, and that no government or institution has the authority to take them away.

Ultimately, the preservation of Christian values is essential to the defense of freedom because it affirms that freedom is not a gift from the government, but a gift from God. This truth not only protects our rights, but it also serves as a powerful check on government overreach and tyranny. As long as we hold fast to this belief, we can ensure that the freedoms we enjoy today will continue to be safeguarded for future generations.

As I look back on my journey in America and reflect on the challenges we face today, I am increasingly convinced that faith — specifically, the Christian values that have guided so many throughout history — is essential to the preservation of our freedoms. In many ways, the freedoms we enjoy in this country are rooted in Christian principles, and as those principles come under attack, so too does the foundation upon which our society is built.

For centuries, the Christian faith has been intertwined with the concepts of liberty, justice, and personal responsibility. The founding fathers of the United States, though not all devout Christians, were heavily influenced by Christian teachings. They understood that without a moral and ethical foundation, freedom could quickly descend into chaos or tyranny. The rights and liberties enshrined in the Constitution — freedom of religion, freedom of speech, and the right to pursue happiness — were framed with the understanding that these rights must be exercised responsibly, with respect for the dignity and worth of every individual. Christian teachings, with their emphasis on love, service, and moral integrity, provided a framework for ensuring that this balance was maintained.

Today, however, we find ourselves at a crossroads. The cultural shifts toward secularism and the growing rejection of traditional values threaten to erode the moral fabric of our society. The rising acceptance of ideologies that undermine the sanctity of life, the institution of marriage, and the inherent value of each person, as created in the image of God, are symptoms of a larger problem — a turning away from the faith that has long anchored this nation.

One of the most troubling developments is the growing pressure to exclude Christian values from public life. We see it in the removal of prayer from schools, the banning of religious symbols in public spaces, and the increasing hostility toward those who express their faith openly. The push to keep faith "private" and out of the public sphere is not just an attack on religious expression; it is an attack on the very principles that make freedom possible.

Faith, particularly the Christian faith, plays a vital role in guiding individuals to live in a way that respects the rights and freedoms of others. Without a moral compass grounded in something greater than ourselves, it becomes all too easy to justify actions that harm others or violate their freedoms. When society no longer values the teachings of Christ — teachings that call us to love our neighbor, seek justice, and show mercy — it opens the door to self-centeredness, corruption, and, ultimately, oppression.

As Christians, we are called to be the "salt of the earth" and the "light of the world." This means we have a responsibility to preserve the goodness and truth that sustains freedom. We cannot afford to be passive in the face of cultural shifts that seek to dismantle the values we hold dear. If we do not stand up for Christian principles, who will? If we allow our voices to be silenced, we risk losing the very freedoms that generations before us fought to preserve.

I often think about the stories of those who came before us, particularly in the Chinese Christian community. Many of us fled authoritarian regimes where freedom of religion was non-existent, where expressing one's faith could lead to imprisonment or worse. We came to America because we believed in the promise of freedom — the freedom to worship, to raise our children with our values, and to live out our faith without fear. But as I look around today, I fear that we are losing sight of what makes this nation great.

One of the most important battles we face today is the preservation of religious freedom. It is no coincidence that the First Amendment to the Constitution protects the free exercise of religion. The founding fathers understood that without religious freedom, all other freedoms would eventually crumble. Religion is not merely a private matter; it shapes our worldview, our actions, and our understanding of what it means to live in a free society. When religious freedom is curtailed, so too is freedom of speech, freedom of assembly, and freedom of conscience.

This is why it is so crucial that Christians remain engaged in the political and cultural battles of our time. We cannot allow ourselves to be sidelined or silenced. Our faith compels us to speak out against injustice, to stand up for the vulnerable, and to protect the freedoms that make life in this country possible. Whether it is advocating for the unborn, defending traditional marriage, or protecting the rights of parents to raise their children according to their faith, we must be unwavering in our commitment to preserving Christian values in the public square.

At the heart of this effort is the understanding that freedom is a gift from God, not from the government. The government's role is to protect that freedom, not to grant or restrict it based on shifting cultural norms. When we, as Christians, stand up for our values, we are not only defending our faith — we are defending the rights and freedoms of all people to live according to their conscience.

I am reminded of the words of the Apostle Paul in Galatians 5:1: "It is for freedom that Christ has set us free. Stand firm, then, and do not let yourselves be burdened again by a yoke of slavery." As Christians, we are called to stand firm in the freedom that Christ has given us — not just spiritual freedom, but the freedom to live according to His truth in every area of our lives. This is a responsibility we cannot take lightly.

As I reflect on my own journey, I am deeply grateful for the opportunities this country has provided — for myself, my family, and my community. But I also recognize that with those opportunities comes the responsibility to preserve what is good, true, and just. We cannot afford to be complacent. The preservation of Christian values is not just about protecting our way of life; it is about ensuring that future generations will continue to enjoy the freedoms we so often take for granted.

In the end, the fight to preserve Christian values is about more than politics — it is about protecting the soul of this nation. It is about ensuring that America remains a place where faith is not just tolerated, but celebrated as a vital part of human experience. It is about recognizing that without a strong moral foundation, freedom cannot endure. And it is about remembering that as Christians, we have a unique role to play in shaping the future of this country.

As I continue to walk this path of faith and freedom, I am reminded of the words of Proverbs 14:34: "Righteousness exalts a nation, but sin is a reproach to any people." May we, as Christians, strive to live lives of righteousness, both in our private and public lives, and may we work tirelessly to ensure that the values we hold dear are preserved for generations to come. Only then can we truly say that we have fulfilled our responsibility to God, to our fellow citizens, and to the future of this great nation.

Chapter 57: Looking to the Future

As I reflect on the outcome of the 2024 election, I find myself filled with both hope and renewed resolve. The challenges we face as a nation remain significant, but the direction we have chosen speaks volumes about the values and priorities of many Americans. The results have ushered in a new era with Donald Trump returning to the presidency, and this moment calls for reflection on what it means for our collective future.

This election was more than a political contest; it was a pivotal moment for America to reaffirm the principles that have guided us — freedom, justice, and individual rights. For some, this outcome offers hope that these values will be protected and strengthened. For others, it presents an opportunity to reexamine what kind of nation we want to become as we navigate both the familiar and new challenges ahead.

One of the key issues that dominated the 2024 election was the preservation of our freedoms — religious liberty, freedom of speech, and the protection of individual rights. The challenges we faced leading up to this point were emblematic of broader societal shifts, from government overreach to the erosion of parental and individual rights, to the growing divide over cultural and religious norms. The result of the election demonstrates that these concerns resonated with a significant portion of the American people.

The role of the Christian community in shaping this outcome was evident, as many voters sought to protect values rooted in faith, family, and individual liberties. We are reminded of the importance of standing strong in our convictions, even as we seek to bridge divides and foster understanding in a nation that is more diverse than ever before.

For Chinese Americans and other immigrant communities, this election highlighted both our influence and our responsibility in shaping the country's future. Our voices were heard, and our values were represented in the broader debate over parental rights, education, and family preservation. As we continue to engage politically, our collective strength will play a pivotal role in shaping the America we want for our children.

The fight for election integrity remains critical. As efforts like Operation Eyeball, led by figures like Paul, demonstrated, ensuring fair, transparent, and trustworthy elections is essential to maintaining faith in our democratic system. We must continue to work toward this goal, building on the foundations laid during this past election season.

Looking ahead, I am reminded of the power of vigilance and engagement. While the path may be complex and fraught with challenges, we must hold firmly to the values that have sustained this nation. Our faith, our commitment to freedom, and our belief in the inherent worth of every individual remain the pillars that uphold our republic.

This election was not just a test of political will; it was a test of our character and our resolve. Moving forward, we must rise above division, seek common ground, and protect the rights and dignity of all individuals while remaining true to our principles.

As I look to the future, I am filled with hope. Hope that we will rise together to meet whatever challenges come our way. Hope that we will safeguard the freedoms we cherish. And hope that, no matter the divisions that may exist, we can come together to create a future defined by faith, freedom, and justice.

The journey continues. While the road ahead may still be uncertain, we walk it together, guided by the values that unite us and the faith that sustains us.

Chapter 58: The Role of the Church in Modern Politics

As I look back on the many influences that have shaped my political journey, I cannot ignore the critical role the church has played in my personal awakening and that of my community. The church, once seen primarily as a place for spiritual guidance, has now become a hub of political discourse and action. This transformation did not happen overnight, but over the past few years, I've noticed a significant shift in how we, as believers, engage with the world around us.

For many, the church was always a place of sanctuary, a retreat from the troubles of the outside world. But as the political landscape in America has grown more turbulent, the separation between faith and politics has become increasingly blurred. The church, far from being immune to these changes, has become a place where political ideas are shared, debated, and often acted upon. This is particularly true for churches like Cornerstone Chapel and the small Chinese church, where faith is not just a private belief system, but a force that compels us to engage with the broader world.

The realization that the churches could and should be involved in shaping the political landscape began to grow within me, and I could see the same stirring among others in our congregations. The issues we faced — whether it was religious freedom, the protection of family values, or the defense of life — were not just political issues; they were deeply moral and spiritual matters. It was becoming increasingly clear that our faith had a place in the public square and that we had a duty to engage.

One of the most important lessons I learned from this transformation is that churches are not just buildings where we come to worship on Sundays. They are communities, bodies of believers who are called to be the salt and light in the world, as the Bible teaches. This means that we are not only responsible for nurturing our faith within the walls of the churches but also for bringing that faith into the world, particularly into areas that impact society's moral compass.

This sense of duty became even more pronounced as I saw the growing encroachment of secular ideologies on Christian values.

Issues like gender identity, the sanctity of life, and the erosion of parental rights began to take center stage in political debates, and these were not abstract concepts for us — they were attacks on the very principles our faith was built upon. The church communities, once content to stay out of such matters, could no longer afford to be silent. Silence, after all, was often seen as tacit approval of these changes.

In recent years, I've witnessed an incredible shift within my own and other churches across the country. Pastors who once avoided discussing politics now feel compelled to address these issues from the pulpit. They are reminding us that our faith has always been political in nature, not in the partisan sense, but in the sense that it challenges the status quo, demands justice, and calls out unrighteousness in high places. The Bible itself is filled with stories of prophets, judges, and kings who were called to stand up for God's truth in the face of political and societal pressure.

It's not just the clergy who have taken on this responsibility. Lay members of the church, too, have become more engaged. Bible studies, once focused solely on personal spiritual growth, now frequently include discussions about how our faith should inform our voting decisions, our involvement in local government, and our activism on issues that matter to us. For many of us, this political awakening has been tied to a deeper understanding of what it means to live out our faith in every aspect of life.

One of the most significant issues that catalyzed political engagement within the church communities was the growing concern over religious freedom. With increasing pressure on Christian organizations to conform to secular policies, many in the churches began to realize that if we didn't stand up now, we could lose the freedom to practice our faith openly. We saw it happening in small ways at first — the banning of prayer in schools, the removal of Christian symbols from public spaces, and the legal challenges faced by Christian businesses. But these small steps pointed to a larger trend that threatened the very fabric of religious liberty in America.

As these challenges mounted, the church communities became places where we could come together not only to pray for our nation but also to strategize on how we could make a difference. We organized voter registration drives, held discussions about the importance of voting for candidates who shared our values, and encouraged each other to get involved in local government. Some members even decided to run for school boards and city councils, recognizing that these smaller platforms were often the first battlegrounds in the fight to protect Christian values.

Our church's involvement in politics wasn't limited to elections, though. We also found ways to advocate for issues that aligned with our beliefs, such as pro-life causes, religious freedom legislation, and the protection of traditional family values. We organized protests, wrote letters to our representatives, and partnered with other churches to amplify our voices on issues that mattered. The church had truly become a place of political activism, but it was activism grounded in faith and a desire to see God's will done in our society.

I also noticed that this political awakening within the churches was not confined to a single demographic. Both the older generation, who had lived through times when faith played a more prominent role in public life, and the younger generation, who were coming of age in a more secular society, were equally passionate about preserving Christian values in the public sphere. This cross-generational engagement was one of the most encouraging aspects of the movement. It reminded me that the fight for faith and freedom is not just for today — it is for future generations as well.

At the heart of this political awakening was a recognition that the church has always had a role to play in shaping society. From the early days of Christianity, believers have been called to be agents of change, advocating for justice, mercy, and truth in the face of a world that often opposes these values. In the modern world, this calling has taken on new urgency. The church's role in politics is not about aligning with a particular party or candidate; it is about standing for principles that transcend political divides.

As I reflect on the journey that led our church communities to this place of political engagement, I see it as part of a larger trend within the body of Christ. More and more believers are waking up to the reality that faith cannot be separated from the issues of the day. Whether it's the sanctity of life, the definition of marriage, or the protection of religious freedom, these are issues that require us to speak out and take action.

I also believe that this awakening is not just about preserving our rights as Christians. It is about ensuring that the values we hold dear — values of love, justice, and compassion — are reflected in the laws and policies of our nation. We are called to be salt and light, and that means we must influence the culture around us, not be shaped by it. The church's role in modern politics is to be a moral voice in a society that increasingly lacks one.

Looking forward, I see great challenges ahead. The political and cultural battles we face are far from over, and in many ways, they are intensifying. But I am also filled with hope. I have seen what can happen when believers come together, not just to worship, but to work for change. The church has always been a force for good in the world, and I believe it will continue to be so in the years to come.

As we approach the future, particularly with the outcome of 2024 election, I am more convinced than ever that the churches have a vital role to play. Our involvement in the political process is not just a matter of civic duty — it is a matter of faith. And as long as we remain faithful to our calling, I believe we can make a difference. The churches, with their deep-rooted commitment to truth and justice, will continue to be a beacon of hope and a guiding light in the midst of an increasingly dark and divided world.

Chapter 59: Leaving a Legacy of Faith and Freedom

As I reflect on my journey from China to America, from a life marked by political timidity to one shaped by activism, I am struck by the profound transformation I have undergone. It has been a long road, one filled with challenges and moments of uncertainty, but also moments of clarity, faith, and a growing sense of purpose. Now, as I look toward the future, I contemplate the legacy I hope to leave behind for my family, my community, and perhaps even for those who will follow in my footsteps.

When I first arrived in America, my concerns were focused on the basics: finding stability, providing for my family, and ensuring that my son had access to the best opportunities. Like many immigrants, I was grateful for the chance to build a life here, but I was also hesitant to engage too deeply with the political landscape. The trauma of living under an authoritarian regime in China had left its mark on me, and I carried with me a reluctance to get involved in politics, a fear of drawing too much attention or challenging the status quo.

But as the years passed, I began to realize that staying on the sidelines was no longer an option. The freedoms I had sought for myself and my family were not guaranteed, and the values I held dear — values rooted in faith, hard work, and the belief in individual rights — were increasingly under threat. The more I witnessed the cultural and political shifts happening in America, the more I understood that my voice, and the voices of those in my community, needed to be heard.

The journey from political timidity to activism was not an easy one. It required me to confront my fears and step into unfamiliar territory. But along the way, I found strength in my faith. My belief in a higher power, in the God who created us all and endowed us with inalienable rights, became the foundation for my activism. I could no longer stand by and watch as the values I cherished were eroded. I had to act, not just for myself, but for my family, for future generations.

One of the most important lessons I have learned is that freedom is not something we can take for granted. It must be protected, nurtured, and passed down from one generation to the next. This is the legacy I hope to leave behind — a legacy of faith and freedom, one that will inspire others in the Chinese American community to stand up for what is right, to defend our values, and to participate fully in the life of this nation.

For me, leaving a legacy of faith means living out my beliefs in every aspect of life, both private and public. It means ensuring that my family understand the importance of faith and how it can guide us, not just in our personal lives, but in our role as citizens. I want my family to know that our Christian faith is not something to be hidden or kept within the walls of the churches, but something that should inform our actions, our decisions, and our engagement with the world.

Leaving a legacy of freedom means standing up for the principles that have made America a beacon of hope for so many. It means defending the rights of individuals to live, work, and worship according to our conscience. It means ensuring that the freedoms we enjoy today are preserved for future generations. I want my family to understand that freedom is a gift, but it is also a responsibility. It requires vigilance, courage, and a willingness to speak out when those freedoms are under attack.

As I reflect on my own journey, I am reminded of the countless others who have walked this path before me. My story is just one among many, but it is part of a larger narrative — the story of Chinese immigrants who came to America seeking freedom and opportunity, and who found themselves becoming part of the fabric of this nation. Many of us started with little more than the clothes on our backs, but we worked hard, built lives for our families, and in doing so, contributed to the strength and diversity of America.

We brought with us values deeply rooted in our cultural and spiritual traditions — values like respect for education, hard work, and family. And now, as we become more engaged in the political and civic life of this country, we are bringing those values to bear on the issues that matter most to us. The fight for fair admission, the defense of religious liberty, the protection of family values — these are battles we are waging not just for ourselves, but for the future of this nation.

Looking forward, I see both challenges and opportunities. The political and cultural landscape is rapidly changing, and with it, the issues we face. But I am hopeful. I believe that as long as we remain committed to our faith and our values, we will be able to navigate whatever challenges come our way. We have a responsibility to ensure that America remains a place where freedom and opportunity are available to all, and where the principles of justice and righteousness are upheld.

One of the most meaningful aspects of this journey has been seeing the growing political engagement of the Chinese American community. For so long, we remained quiet, focused on our personal and family successes, hesitant to involve ourselves in the broader political discourse. But now, we are finding our voice. We are stepping into leadership roles, advocating for policies that reflect our values, and standing up for the rights and freedoms that brought us here in the first place.

I hope that my own journey will serve as an example to others in my community. I want them to see that it is possible to go from political timidity to activism, that it is possible to make a difference, even if you start with nothing. I want them to know that our voice matters, that our values matter, and that we have a role to play in shaping the future of this country.

As I look to the future, I am filled with gratitude — for the opportunities I have been given, for the community that has supported me, and for the faith that has sustained me. But I am also filled with determination. The challenges we face are great, but so is the potential for change. I believe that as long as we remain true to our values, as long as we continue to fight for what is right, we can leave a lasting legacy of faith and freedom for future generations.

This is the legacy I hope to leave behind — a legacy rooted in faith, shaped by freedom, and driven by the belief that each of us has a role to play in the story of America. It is a legacy I hope next generations will carry forward, one that will inspire them to live lives of purpose, to stand up for what is right, and to work for a future where freedom, justice, and faith continue to flourish.

In addition to my passion for advocating freedom and political involvement, I've also written several books on topics that reflect my diverse interests and expertise. *Unified Field Theory*, which I've self-published in three editions (first edition, Academic edition, and popular science edition), represents my interests in science. It explores the relationship between fundamental forces in the universe, framed through a unique perspective that challenges traditional thinking. Writing these books allowed me to combine my intellectual curiosity with my desire to contribute to the ongoing dialogue in scientific and philosophical communities.

I've also explored creative storytelling in *Horizon Shift* and *Adventure Throughout Planet Guoke*, where I pushed the boundaries of imagination and intertwined elements of discovery and exploration with deeper moral and ethical themes. These works reflect my belief that no matter where we turn — whether in the realms of science, fiction, or faith — there is always a greater truth waiting to be uncovered.

Afterwords

The idea of writing a biographical fiction began to take shape when I started working for The U.S. House of Representatives in 2019. However, it wasn't until early 2023 that I decided to begin the process. Just as I was getting started, my husband was nominated as the GOP candidate for a city council position, and with the campaign in full swing, I had to put everything on hold.

After the election in November, *Mao's America* by Xi Van Fleet was published and quickly became a bestseller on Amazon. I hesitated to continue my book, plagued by the fear that no one would read it. Yet, over time, my perspective shifted. I realized that my desire to tell my story and inspire others to engage in political activities — to shape the future of our nation — would never become a reality if I didn't write.

The concept of a "one-way relationship" applies here: I would write my story to fulfill my desire to make a difference, even if no one reads it. That would be okay too. Once I began writing, the words flowed easily, as if they had been waiting for this moment. Now that the book is finished, I feel at peace. I have done my part, and the rest is in God's hands.

About the Author

Hope Grace, the pen name of a senior IT security analyst, brings a diverse background to her work. She holds CISSP and CCSP certifications and has worked for notable institutions, including the National Family Planning Committee in China and the U.S. House of Representatives. Her academic journey includes a Bachelor of Philosophy from Peking University, a Bachelor of Divinity, a board certification in Nuclear Medicine Technology, and a Master's in Information Science.

Hope's path from China to America has been shaped by a deep commitment to faith, freedom, and political activism. Her experience of life under authoritarian rule in China ignited her passion for protecting the values of freedom and individual rights, which she continues to defend through both her professional and personal endeavors.

While her career has primarily been in IT security, Hope's intellectual curiosity extends beyond her field, having authored Zhang XiangQian's *Unified Field Theory* (word-for-word translation edition, Academic edition, and popular science edition), *Horizon Shift,* and *Adventure Throughout Planet Guoke.* These works reflect her wide-ranging interests in philosophy, science, and creative storytelling.

Hope's journey from political timidity to activism, inspired by her Christian faith and her desire to protect the next generation, has led her to become a voice for change within the Chinese American community and beyond. Her unique blend of professional expertise and life experience continues to guide her efforts to defend the principles of liberty and justice for all.

www.ingramcontent.com/pod-product-compliance
Lightning Source LLC
Chambersburg PA
CBHW020433130626
46549CB00001B/119